Cities, like people,
are alike in some respects
and different in others.

Asa Briggs,
Victorian Cities

D I S T A

A Comparative History of Seattle & Vancouver

University of Nebraska Press   Lincoln and London

N T

NEIGHBORS

Norbert MacDonald

Acknowledgments for the use of previously published
material appear on pages xvi–xvii.
The paper in this book meets the minimum require-
ments of American National Standard for Information
Sciences–Permanence of Paper for Printed Library
Materials, ANSI Z39,48-1984.

Library of Congress Cataloging-in-Publication Data
MacDonald, Norbert, 1925–
Distant neighbors.

Bibliography: p.
Includes index.
   1. Seattle (Wash.)—History.   2. Vancouver (B.C.)—History. I. Title.
F899.S457M33   1987   971.1′34   86-30892
ISBN 0-8032-3111-3 (alk. paper)

To Carolyn
who helped me in so many ways

Contents

Illustrations

Figures and Tables

Preface

I have attempted a comparative history of Seattle and Vancouver for a variety of reasons. Having lived and worked in both I was aware of the similarities in their superb coastal settings, rainy climate, lush vegetation, and comfortable, prosperous residential neighborhoods. I was also aware of differences, especially the lack of interest of Americans in things Canadian, and the condescending attitude of Canadians toward the United States. As a Canadian I have often wondered if there was anything truly distinctive about my society and nation. I saw a comparative history of Seattle and Vancouver as a means for understanding city development in the two nations, as well as an avenue for seeing how comparable institutions had differed over time.

Several pairs of cities in the United States and Canada—Boston and Halifax, Buffalo and Toronto, Detroit and Windsor, Minneapolis and Winnipeg—would all be worthy of comparison. Yet Seattle and Vancouver seemed an especially pertinent choice. First of all, they were of comparable size and importance, and throughout much of their history had followed parallel paths in their growth and development. Both were settled in the mid-nineteenth century, depended on lumber industry for their early existence, and became firmly established only with the completion of transcontinental railroads in the 1880s. Both experienced similar boom-bust cycles. Not until the first decade of the twentieth century did they achieve the size and diversity that established each as the unquestioned leader of its region. Their parallel development continued through the 1930s and only with the massive changes instituted by World War II did they proceed along more divergent paths. Throughout their history they have been removed from the center of national power and population. And though both have been settled for well over a century, they are still seen by their residents as young and vital communities, with a style and tone quite unlike that of eastern cities.

When I began this study I considered focusing on a single topic, from the early years through to the late twentieth century. A comparative analysis of social mobility in Seattle and Vancouver was one such possibility. I also considered an exclusive emphasis on urban elites, municipal politics, or the impact of federal programs. All such topics seemed feasible and potentially rewarding, but I thought each one a somewhat artificial slice of the city's total experience. In addition, many of these topics required a specific theoretical structure and a detailed quantitative analysis. I had no desire to follow such a model. I had read enough of the new urban history to know that although such techniques often provided valuable new insights, they did not automatically guarantee significant findings. Indeed in many cases such elaborate analysis did little more than restate long-accepted historical themes.

Ultimately I decided I would attempt a comprehensive survey of the history of both cities, with a focus on those processes and events which I considered significant for their development. I also wanted to capture the character and nature of Seattle and Vancouver at a series of stages, for whether one considers the frontier towns of the 1870s, the depressed cities of the 1930s, or the prosperous communities of the 1970s, each had a character and identity in its own right. Only by understanding these earlier stages can one understand the contemporary city. Such an approach implies, of course, that the city of the 1980s is a transitory one, and that it too will evolve and change in the succeeding decades.

Earlier versions of parts of this book have already been published. A section of Chapter 3 appeared as "The Canadian Pacific Railway and Vancouver's Development to 1900," *B.C. Studies* 35 (Autumn 1977). A slightly different version of Chapter 2 was published as "Seattle, Vancouver and the Klondike," *Canadian Historical Review* 44, no. 3 (September 1968). The Vancouver portion of Chapter 4 is substantially the same as published in "A Critical Growth Cycle for Vancouver 1900–14," *B.C. Studies* 17 (Spring 1973). The basic statistical data on population over the years appeared originally as "Population Growth and Change in Seattle and Vancouver 1880–1960," *Pacific Historical Review* 39, no. 3 (August 1970). Modifications have been made and the data brought up to date. An early version of part of Chapter 5 appeared as "The Business Leaders of Seattle 1880–1910," *Pacific Northwest Quarterly* 50, no. 1 (January 1959). I wish to thank the editors of those journals for permission to reprint that material.

I am greatly indebted to a host of colleagues and friends, as well as to library staffs and custodians of special collections for their assistance in the research for this book. First and foremost I am indebted to the late W. Stull Holt, my mentor and friend. He gave me the original idea and always maintained his enthusiasm and support for the project. The staffs of the Vancouver City Archives, University of British Columbia Library, Provincial Archives of British Columbia, Probate Office–Supreme Court of British Columbia, Vancouver Public Library, Northwest Collection–University of Washington Library, Seattle Museum of History and Industry, Seattle Public Library, Seattle Municipal Reference Library, City Clerk's Office of Seattle, and Probate Section–Washington State Court House were all helpful in my search for material. Among the many friends and colleagues who have contributed are Peter Ward, Murray and Beverley Greenwood, Keith Ralston, Gilbert Stelter, Thomas Pressly, Randolph Hennes, Gerald Geisert, Alan Artibise, Lillian Mitchell, Gerald Smith, and Barbara Heldt, Jorgen Dahlie, Donald Wilson, Lorna Gibbs, Werner Cohn, William Cunningham. Some read the entire manuscript, others commented on specific chapters or sections only. Others have assisted, encouraged, or cajoled. But each in his or her own way has helped me. I thank them all.

Introduction

Because modern cities touch upon so many aspects of human experience, an immense range of primary sources is available to anyone studying them. These include newspapers, city council minutes, census material, municipal records, government publications, judicial decisions, and autobiographies. All of this material reflects official and public aspects of a city's development. A variety of more specialized materials enables the scholar to study the career patterns, class structure, and social mobility of a city's average men and women. Such sources include marriage records, birth and death statistics, city directories, recorded interviews, assessment rolls, building records, tax sales, wills, and probates. The extensive holdings of the Vancouver City Archives have been especially valuable. Besides the public records of the mayor, city council, and city clerk, and diverse departments, committees, and boards, the archives also have a great variety of privately donated material on businesses, unions, clubs, and associations. No comparable collection of official documents is available for Seattle. The Fire of 1889 destroyed the city hall and with it most of the official records of Seattle's first thirty-five years. Consequently, the rich, precise details on Vancouver's early years cannot be duplicated; for Seattle's early story one must rely on newspaper accounts and pioneer reminiscences.

I faced a scarcity of good sources for Seattle's early years, but the amount of valuable material on both cities for the years after 1900 is much greater. By the time one focuses on the post–World War II era, the abundance of information is overwhelming; journalists, politicians, social workers, marketing experts, police chiefs, transportation planners, property developers, civic bureaucrats, and federal agencies have poured out a host of articles, reports, position papers, and data on an immense range of public and private issues. Though keenly aware of the potential value of this mountain of evidence, the historian can barely scratch its surface.

As is the case with virtually every other North American city, a considerable body of secondary literature exists on Vancouver and Seattle. The two most known and most widely read histories of the Canadian city are by journalists. Alan Morley, *Vancouver: From Milltown to Metropolis* (1961), and Eric Nicol, *Vancouver* (1970) are breezy, popular accounts that cover the city's entire history. Both are informative, but they focus primarily on the dramatic highlights of Vancouver's history, and the activities of a small number of local characters. The interpretation of Seattle's history was long dominated by Murray Morgan, *Skid Road: An Informal Portrait of Seattle* (1951). It is a sprightly, readable account, organized around the activities of six prominent individuals who personified Seattle's earthy, swashbuckling character. Though captivating, it is undocumented and each reader has to decide just where history ends and fiction begins. By all odds the best single book on Seattle appeared in 1976 with the publication of Roger Sale's *Seattle: Past to Present*. Written by a professor of English at the University of Washington, it is perceptive, imaginative, and a positive delight to read.

Beyond these four main works, a great variety of newspaper accounts, pictorial essays, promotional literature, biographies, and brief histories continue to appear year after year. With the exception of a number of journal articles, dissertations, and valuable studies such as Donald Gutstein, *Vancouver Ltd.* (1975), and Patricia E. Roy, *Vancouver: An Illustrated History* (1980), most are based on existing secondary literature. Such accounts contribute information and many fascinating photographs but they are largely descriptive in nature and make little attempt to explain long-term growth and change. Virtually all such work ignores the research techniques and sources used by contemporary urban historians, and focuses almost exclusively on either Seattle or Vancouver.

In the course of my research I became convinced that a comparative history could offer distinctive insights. I also became convinced that to treat the entire history of the two cities would require a broad-gage, general treatment, with an emphasis on citywide characteristics and developments rather than on the distinctive nature of ethnic groups, labor unions, or the internal dynamics of individual neighborhoods. I believed I could discuss local events and appeal to the average reader without being antiquarian or provincial. At the very least, I could show that numerous developments considered unique to one or the other city were in reality shared by both. I also hoped to provide something for the scholar and student interested in the history of cities.

The first half of this book treats the growth and development of the two cities from their original settlement in the mid-nineteenth century up to the eve of World War I. Throughout these chapters I emphasize that both cities were shaped primarily by the decisions of private landowners and business leaders. But whereas private enterprise was virtually unrestricted in the American setting, in Canada a variety of public officials and public agencies played a major role in shaping Vancouver's evolution. Chapter 1 discusses the arrival and activity of the original townsite promoters, with attention centered on the economic activities that sustained these isolated frontier communities. The arrival of transcontinental railroads in the mid-1880s occasioned dramatic growth and change for both cities. Yet the impact of the Canadian Pacific on Vancouver drastically exceeded the effect of the Northern Pacific on Seattle. In Chapter 2 I develop these differences at length. Chapter 3 treats the Klondike Gold Rush of the late 1890s and provides one of the few examples in the entire history of Seattle and Vancouver where the two cities were intensely aware of each other and in direct competition. During the first dozen years of the twentieth century both cities experienced unparalleled growth and prosperity which utterly transformed the small, locally oriented communities of the 1890s. Chapter 4, "Critical Growth Cycles," treats the many significant changes of that transition era; Chapter 5 takes an extended look at the generation of business leaders who were active at that time.

By the eve of World War I, both Seattle and Vancouver had achieved the population size, ethnic diversity, economic function, and general tone and quality that indisputably gave them metropolitan stature, and made each an integral component of a nationwide system of cities. The war itself had a sharply different impact on the two cities. These dissimilarities, and the consequences of diverse technological change in the 1920s, are treated in Chapter 6. Chapter 7, on the Great Depression, studies the impact of these grim years on the local populace, and shows that the massive role of federal programs, agencies, and funds in the American city had no direct counterpart in Canada. In Chapter 8, "World War II and the Postwar Decades," the main focus is on the war itself and the way that conflict contributed to divergent tendencies which would become more and more evident in the two cities as the 1950s and 1960s unfolded. The massive expansion of the aircraft industry in Seattle, the suburbanization during the postwar era, and the impact of new ethnic groups are all treated at length. In Chapter 9, "Thirty Years of Municipal Politics," I have focused on the period from the mid-1940s to the mid-1970s for an in-depth look at an era of non-partisan politics. It is the one extended examination of municipal politics in the entire book, and no attempt is made to do a comparable analysis of politics in earlier or later periods. Like the analysis of business leadership done earlier, the study of municipal politics could be extended to cover the entire political history of the two cities and would make a book-length study in itself. Chapter 10, "The 1970s, 1980s, and a Look Backward," treats the recent past and the contemporary image of these cities. A concluding portion summarizes the main themes of the study, with a focus on those special factors that account for the distinctive character of each city.

Like most historians I am aware of what remains to be done. It is possible of course that a truly comprehensive comparative history of two cities cannot be done by a single scholar, and that only a collective effort can achieve the range and depth required. My hope is that this study, whether by the sins of commission or omission, will provide some guidelines for those who follow.

1

Frontier Villages

It rains a lot in Seattle and Vancouver, especially during the fall and winter months. Occasionally it is a drenching rain, but a steady drizzle, interrupted by heavy downpours and brief clearings, is much more typical. Newcomers often find the rain depressing, but long-time residents find it peculiarly comforting and take a certain pleasure in pointing out that the annual 40-inch rainfall is exceeded by that in many cities in the western United States and Canada. Winters are mild with temperatures in the 34–44° F range. On a year-round basis Seattle is about two degrees warmer than Vancouver. The American city averages 350 frost-free days per year to the Canadian city's 308. When snow does fall it usually amounts to only a few inches. Slippery streets wreak havoc on car fenders and drivers' nerves, and kids love throwing soggy snowballs, but within a day or so the snow disappears in another rain. By February definite signs of spring are evident. The rain slackens, gardens and lawns begin to dry out, and crocuses make their appearance. The changes are very gradual, but as the days warm up and the drying continues, hyacinths, daffodils, and tulips arrive. Summers are delightful—dry, sunny, warm, and comfortable. It is considered "very hot" when the temperature reaches 80° F. Swimmers, bikers, golfers, and picnickers are all active and the rainy months quickly forgotten. Sometime during September a heavy, no-nonsense downpour signals the end of summer. Fine days may continue for a month or more, but by mid-October there is no doubt that another rainy season is well under way.

The basic similarity in their year-round weather pattern is but one of a host of ways in which Seattle and Vancouver are alike. Both are major West Coast cities well removed from the center of power and population in their respective nations. Both enjoy superb coastal settings with nearby mountain ranges, massive evergreens, and lush vegetation. Both started as logging and lumbering communities, developed slowly in their early years, and spurted in the 1880s after transcontinental railroads reached the West Coast. Both grew dramatically in the decade before World War I, and became firmly established as transportation, trading, and financial centers. Only with World War II and the sudden expansion of aircraft manufacture at Boeing did the economy of the American city differ significantly from its Canadian counterpart. But well into the 1960s both prospered with heavy in-migration, high employment, and rapid suburbanization. In both Seattle and Vancouver suicides, divorces, and drug addiction far exceed national averages. Yet both are seen as places where the pace is slower, where one can escape the tensions of eastern cities and enjoy "the good life" of the Pacific Coast.

Such similarities could be elaborated, but it is only on closer examination that one uncovers the significant differences. This first chapter will sketch and compare their development in the years before the arrival of transcontinental railroads. It will show that the motivation of the founding fathers, the land granting process, and the economy of Seattle and Vancouver shared much in common. Yet sharp variations in the scale of development in the two regions, as well as differences in the activities of private, semipublic, and public authorities had significant implications for later development.

From the time that American settlers first pushed across the Allegheny Mountains in the early eighteenth century the promotion of privately owned townsites was a recurring phenomenon.[1] Whether in Kentucky in the 1790s, Michigan in the 1820s, or Oregon in the 1840s, the pattern was essentially the same. The town promoter had to find an unsettled, desirable site, establish a land claim, design a town plat, and then do his utmost to promote his town in the hope that others would see the wisdom of buying and settling there. The great majority of these ventures amounted to little and soon disappeared. A few achieved modest growth, and an even smaller number actually attained the kind of prominence their promoters dreamed about. Among the successes was Seattle, Washington.

The original steps in its development were taken by John Low and Lee Terry when they investigated the unsettled Puget Sound region in September 1851.[2] They represented a larger party in Portland, Oregon, which just that summer had made the long overland journey from Illinois. After a brief exploration Low and Terry chose Alki Point, in what is now West Seattle, as a likely spot for a townsite.[3] On November 13, 1851, the rest of

the party arrived by schooner from Portland. The winter was a very difficult one for the little party of twelve adults and twelve children, and in the
following spring a significant division occurred. A small group lead by Low
and Terry preferred to stay in Alki, convinced that it was a choice site for a
future city. They surveyed the land, registered a town plat, and for a while
it appeared that their little settlement might develop. Yet Alki never prospered; by 1855, after a sawmill venture failed, it was virtually abandoned.

The larger group under the leadership of Arthur A. Denny, Charles D.
Boren, and William Bell had much greater success. After an investigation
of the entire area, they decided to relocate about 4 miles away on the east
side of Elliott Bay. Although the new site had a very hilly terrain, it was
well sheltered, had deep water close to the shore, and was far superior to
the windswept, shallow landing place at Alki. In February 1852, Denny,
Boren, and Bell each located and marked claims. The entire region was
still part of Oregon Territory, and under the provisions of the Oregon Donation Land Act each qualified for 320 acres.

They were soon joined by others. In March, Dr. David S. Maynard arrived. According to Denny's account, "Maynard at first declined to make a
claim . . . but on further consideration he concluded to accept our offer."[4]
Shortly afterward, Henry L. Yesler, a lumberman from Portland, Oregon,
appeared. He wanted to establish a steam sawmill in the region, and those
already on the scene, aware that a mill would give the area a decided boost,
were quick to accommodate him. After Yesler had chosen an appropriate
site Boren and Maynard rearranged their boundaries to give Yesler the
necessary waterfront land for his mill as well as provide access to his main
land claim about a mile to the east.

By 1853 the land claims of Denny, Boren, Bell, Maynard, and Yesler
extended some 2 miles along the east side of Elliott Bay in what would be
the heart of the future city. As Yesler's mill expanded, the population of the
community gradually inched ahead and additional land claims were established north, east, and south of the original nucleus. But although more
and more persons shared in the life of this tiny logging and lumbering
community, it was the decisions of the early landowners that largely determined the shape and layout of the future city.

Within a few months of establishing their claims Denny, Boren, and
Maynard decided to call their town "Seattle" after Chief Sealth of the local
Duwamp Indians. They also agreed on "the policy of laying off a town" and
Denny's former experience as "official surveyor" of Knox County, Illinois,
proved helpful. Whereas the boundary lines of the original land claims ran
due north-south, east-west, the town plat filed by Denny and Boren on

May 23, 1853, had the major streets running approximately north-west to south-east so as to follow the contours of the shoreline and terrain. The plat covered only 30 acres and was just a small fraction of the Denny-Boren holdings, but it was at the heart of early development and would be of fundamental importance in determining Seattle's street pattern and future layout. Like promoters throughout the American West, Denny and Boren followed the long-established and familiar gridiron street plan, with standard-sized blocks and lots, and streets running at right angles to each other regardless of the terrain.[5] Front Street (later First Avenue) ran along the water, with Second and Third streets running parallel and further back from the water. At right angles to these were Spring, Madison, Marion, Columbia, Cherry, and James streets. At the southern limits of Boren's original claim was Mill Street. It led directly to Yesler's mill on the waterfront, and would later be named after that lumberman.

On the very day that Denny and Boren filed, Dr. Maynard too filed a town plat, which covered some 125 acres.[6] The three men had originally planned to work together, but ultimately Maynard acted independently. His survey base point was about a half-block west of that chosen by Denny and Boren.[7] Streets, alleys, blocks, and lots in both plats were of uniform size, but the two plats did not mesh at the common boundary on Mill Street (Yesler Way). Rather, a half-block jog was necessary to link up the Denny-Boren "Second Street," for example, with the Maynard "Second Street."

During the 1850s and 1860s these original plats were followed by others as William Bell and Charles Terry platted portions of their claims; Arthur Denny and Charles Boren also platted additional land. The big burst of activity came between 1869 and 1876 when some sixty separate plats were registered—caused in part by the incorporation of the City of Seattle on December 2, 1869.

This pattern of land acquisition and town platting would continue for years. When times were good and expectations high, land purchases and town plats proliferated. When growth slowed down and real estate activity declined, town platting too fell off. But whether these plats covered 20, 40, or 100 acres, they stayed well in advance of settlement. By 1876 sixty-nine different plats had been registered by individual owners, partners, and groups. They stretched from Lake Union north of the city to Duwamish Valley in the south, over 4 miles in all. Yet most of Seattle's 1,800 residents still lived within a half-mile of Yesler's mill and dock. By the mid-1880s most of the eastern shore of Lake Washington and all of the Lake Union area had been platted—but only a sprinkling of settlement had reached these outlying areas. (See Figures 1 and 2.)

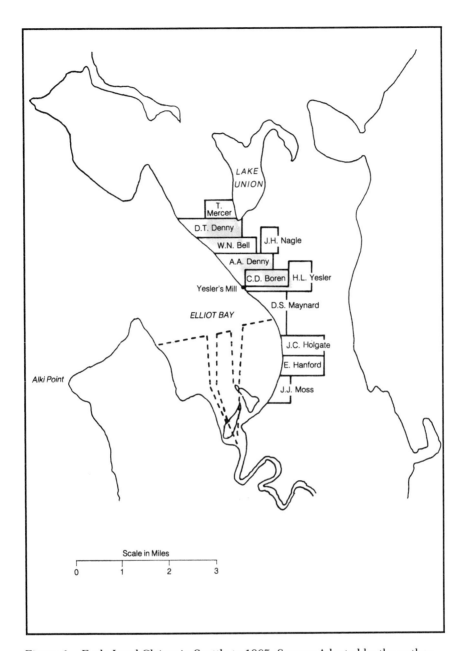

Figure 1—Early Land Claims in Seattle to 1865. *Source:* Adapted by the author from Reconnaissance of Duwamish Bay and Seattle Harbor, Surveyor Generals' Office, Olympia W.T. 1863; A. McIntosh, Map of Seattle, 1879; Whiteworth and Thompson, Map of Seattle, 1887. There are many ambiguities and inconsistencies in these maps, and the boundaries shown above are approximate only.

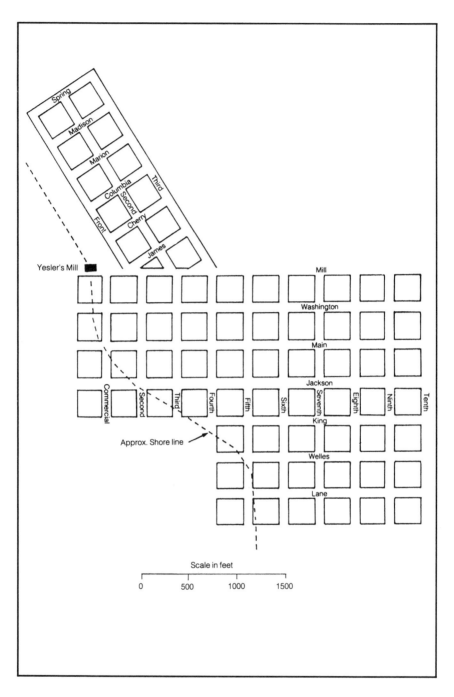

Figure 2—Denny-Boren and Maynard Plats of Seattle, May 23, 1853. *Source: King County Plats,* Vol. 1. (available in University of Washington Library).

The great majority of these plats were developed with little interest or awareness in what had gone before. Owners and promoters were usually indifferent about making their streets link up with earlier streets and seldom made provision for parks, schools, or other public facilities. As was true throughout the United States, land was looked upon as a commodity to be bought and sold for personal gain and not as a public resource to be utilized for the benefit of all. The main idea was to identify lots and facilitate their sale—not to design a city for future generations. Except for the system of streets, blocks, and lots established by the Denny-Boren and Maynard plats of 1853, which would be followed and extended by later builders and city officials, most of these plats had little long-range significance. Like the original land claims of Seattle's founders they remained intact for only a limited period.

Landownership dispersed rapidly and these early claims and plats soon disappeared in a bewildering series of transactions as owners, business firms, real estate agents, and speculators bought, sold, divided, and subdivided the land into smaller and smaller units.[8]

It was Yesler's mill, and the area's topography, that subsequently shaped the character of nearby districts. In the earliest years the mill was the focal point of all activities, with the town's boarding houses, homes, and stores all within easy walking distance. As activity expanded and population crept up, topographical features of the area came more and more into play. The east side of Elliott Bay had a series of hills that began at the water's edge. The southern side was dominated by the extensive tideflats of the Duwamish River. The area near the mill would remain the heart of Seattle's commercial and industrial district, with laborers locating nearby or to the south. Over the years the filled-in tidelands, and low-lying area of the Duwamish Valley would also evolve into an industrial district, with some modest housing. The city's more prosperous elements, on the other hand, gradually moved to the higher ground north and east of the mill. The early identification of a cluster of blocks just south of the mill as Chinatown, and the donation of land for a university site about a half-mile north of the mill, clearly indicated the direction of future development.

While more and more lumber schooners and supply vessels from San Francisco and Portland arrived in Puget Sound in the 1850s and 1860s, settlement remained widely diffused and Seattle's growth was modest. By 1860 Yesler's mill employed some two dozen men, and smaller mills had been established nearby, none of which differed significantly from dozens of similar mills and camps scattered throughout the region. Seattle had a population of about 200, a sprinkling of houses, ships, and stores as well as a schoolhouse, a church, and a hotel. But with men outnumbering women five or ten to one, every marriage, birth, or death in the community was a major event. And though we know something about those settlers who took over a land claim, opened a business, or established a professional practice, we know little about the Whiskey Jim, White Pine Joe, Lame Duck Bill, or Humbolt Jack who felled the trees, sawed the logs, and loaded the lumber before moving on to another temporary job.[9]

When we turn to Canada to examine the early development of Vancouver there is much that is familiar and that corresponds with the Seattle pattern. Yet the differences are even more intriguing. The setting, terrain, and resources were similar, but the land north of the forty-ninth parallel was a British colony and not part of the United States. This fact bears emphasis, for if one single theme is central to the early history of British Columbia it is that the entire region was British and not American. The conviction that the United States was a threat, and that ever-present vigilance was necessary to preserve that separate British identity, helps explain much about Vancouver's early years.

In 1843 the Hudson's Bay Company transferred their main center of operations from the Columbia River in Oregon to Fort Victoria on Vancouver Island. This small British outpost grew slowly, and it was not until the Fraser River gold rush of 1858–59 that significant attention was drawn to the mainland. The rush to the goldfields and the demand for various goods and services gave Victoria a surge of prosperity. New Westminster on the Fraser River also sprang into prominence and was made capital of the newly established mainland colony of British Columbia. As part of the defense network against possible American attack a detachment of Royal Engineers constructed some rough roads to Burrard Inlet about 10 miles away. At the same time the Royal Navy surveyed the entire Burrard Inlet– English Bay region, setting aside a number of military reserves, as well as Indian and townsite reserves.[10]

These reserved lands, amounting to some 9 square miles, would play an important role in Vancouver's later development. Established before any settlement took place, they automatically removed substantial areas from private purchase and control. Such reserves provide an early example of the role of public authorities in the Canadian city which was quite unlike the pattern in Seattle where settlers and potential buyers were free to operate as they saw fit. Although the townsite reserves at Coal Harbour and Hastings soon moved into private hands, the other government and Indian reserves at First Narrows, False Creek, Jericho, Point Grey, and Musqueam remained substantially in the public domain. They not only provided extensive lands for the future University of British Columbia, but over a century later still made up the heart of the city's extensive park system. The map in Figure 3 shows the basic pattern.

Except for the reserved lands, the entire Burrard Inlet area was open for preemption.[11] Settlers could claim 160 acres, have it surveyed, and with the payment of one dollar per acre gain official title. In theory, preemption privileges were for genuine farm settlement only. But as in Seattle the entire area was heavily forested, and most early land acquisition was carried out in full awareness that the site was a favorable one for a future city.[12] And if such a city developed, the rise in land values would dwarf any possible returns from lumbering, let alone farming.

The first permanent settlement in what is now Vancouver began in 1862. John Morton of New Westminster had visited Burrard Inlet to investigate coal and clay resources in the area and the possibility of developing a pottery concern there.[13] He found little coal or clay but was impressed by the natural beauty of the region, the well-protected natural harbor, and the potential for future development. He returned to New Westminster and encouraged a cousin, Sam Brighouse, and a friend, William Hailstone, to join him in obtaining land in that area. All three were immigrants from Great Britain who had worked in the Cariboo goldfields, and now that the rush was over, lived in New Westminster. Dubbed "Three Greenhorn Englishmen" by cynical locals who saw little merit in acquiring land in the Burrard Inlet area, the three men filed a claim for the land between the First Narrows reserve and the townsite reserve on Coal Harbour. In 1862, on the payment of $555.73 they received a Crown grant for 540 acres in what is now Vancouver's West End.[14] All three took turns occupying a cabin on their claim to meet residence requirements, but over the years it was primarily John Morton who remained in the area.

The basic land acquisition process in Vancouver during the 1860s was much like that in Seattle a decade earlier. Grants averaged 160 acres, but on occasion were much larger. Original buyers chose convenient waterfront locations on Burrard Inlet, English Bay, and in the False Creek region. For whether they considered the accessibility of the land, the exploitable timber resources, or the possibility of a quick resale, such waterfront land was a sensible choice. As in Seattle the land was quickly divided and subdivided. Where buyers of the 1860s dealt in units of 100 acres or more, many of the 1880s were concerned with single building lots.

In one characteristic, however, land acquisition in Vancouver was distinctive. Original buyers in Seattle were private citizens; those in Vancouver were often public officials and "insiders." Evidence from British

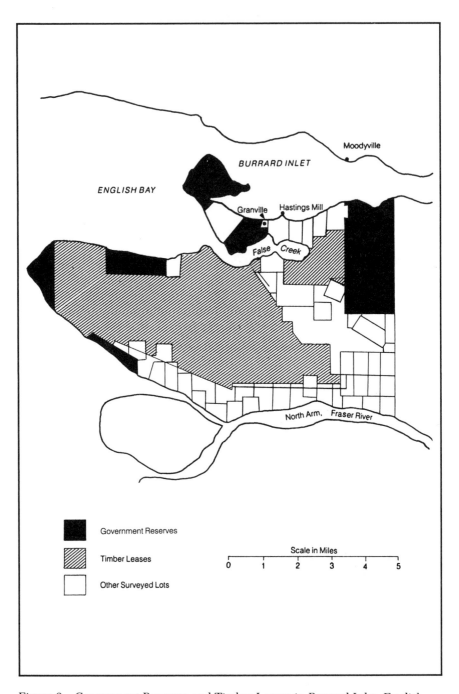

Figure 3—Government Reserves and Timber Leases in Burrard Inlet, English Bay Region, 1876. *Source:* "Surveyed Lands in New Westminster District 1876," Archives of British Columbia, and adapted by author.

Columbia's Land Registry Office is revealing: District Lot 181 was granted to Robert Burnaby, former secretary to Colonel Richard Moody of the Royal Engineers; District Lot 182 went to H. P. P. Crease, attorney-general of British Columbia, the price—$310.42; Thomas Randle, a clerk in the Land Office, was granted District Lot 183; John Graham, a clerk in the Government Treasury, was granted District Lot 184; Crease later purchased lot 183 from Randle, and in 1877, when he was a judge of the Supreme Court of British Columbia, Crease sold the entire parcel for $3,500.[15] It is now known that virtually every public figure in British Columbia from the 1860s to 1910 acquired large holdings of Crown land, and as such the early involvement in Burrard Inlet lands was hardly unique.[16] But when we compare the major role of officialdom in the Canadian setting with the unrestricted opportunities enjoyed by the Denny-Boren-Terry party in the American setting, the contrast is clear. Some idea of the extent of purchases by public officials in British Columbia can be gained from Figure 4.

While landowners were ever conscious of the value of their holdings, the focus of activity on Burrard Inlet was a series of lumber mills established in the 1860s. The original mill started in 1863. It was situated on the

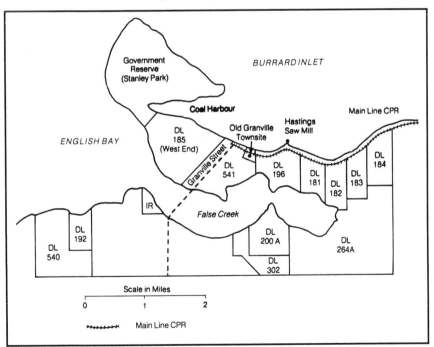

Figure 4—Vancouver as Incorporated in 1886 Showing Earlier District Lots. *Source:* "Surveyed Lands in New Westminster District 1876," Archives of British Columbia, and adapted by author.

north shore of the inlet and served a local market in New Westminster, Nanaimo, and Victoria.[17] By 1865 it was taken over by Sewell Moody, who expanded operations and began exporting to foreign markets. In the same year, after acquiring extensive timber leases in the area, Captain Edward Stamp established a mill on the south side of the inlet. These lumber operations expanded, and in 1869 some forty-five vessels left the inlet carrying lumber to Australia, San Francisco, and South America, with the occasional vessel going to Mexico, China, England, or Hawaii.[18]

Moody's mill on the north shore was clearly the largest, but as the years unfolded the settlement on the south shore gradually inched ahead. Both Moody's and Stamp's mill (renamed Hastings) had similar facilities, but with its San Francisco owners a market was assured for the Hastings' output. In addition Moodyville was located at the base of the inhospitable north shore mountains, whereas the south shore mill was on gently sloping, easily developed land. Finally, Moody himself was a taciturn, hard-driving, authoritarian who kept close control over his employees and his community and did not look kindly on the rowdy behavior and crude living conditions that Captain Ed Stamp allowed.[19]

In any case it was the south shore settlement that took the lead. After "Gassy Jack" Deighton opened a small hotel and saloon about half a mile west of the mill, a new focal point evolved, and more and more people gravitated to the boarding houses, hotels, and stores that accumulated in that area. Locally known as "Gastown," the tiny settlement became "Granville" in 1870, after a survey of the townsite in that year.[20] At that time it covered some 28 acres and had 50 residents at most. The first sale of town lots had only three buyers who gained title to the land on which they had been illegally squatting.[21]

By the early 1870s a pattern of activity and settlement was established on Burrard Inlet that would not change significantly in the next dozen years. The entire region was geared to the production and export of lumber and with the low demand for that commodity, growth was slow. In 1884 Granville remained an undiversified lumbering town. Its heart consisted of a single street that extended about 400 yards along the water's edge. On it were clustered a few houses, stores, and hotels, with a few additional houses and sheds scattered in the rough clearing that extended back into the bush. It had steam ferry connections with other points on the inlet, and stage road connections with New Westminster.[22] Granville had some married couples with children, but the great majority of its 300 residents were unmarried men who worked in the mill.[23] The town was not substantially larger than the farming municipalities of Delta, Richmond, Surrey, or Langley, all of which had some 250 to 300 residents. It was positively tiny compared with New Westminster's 3,000, let alone Victoria's 8,000.[24]

The situation changed abruptly after 1885. In that year the Canadian Pacific Railway (CPR) announced that its terminus would be "in the immediate vicinity of Coal Harbour and English Bay." This set in motion a whole series of developments that would transform Granville from an isolated lumbering town into a substantial city linked with the rest of the nation. But before developing the nature and consequences of this move by the CPR, let us first return to Seattle. For while the Canadian community had shown very modest growth in the previous decades, the story in Seattle was a vastly different one.

In the late 1850s a forthright visitor to Seattle described the community this way: "Cut out a clearing from a dense forest on a side hill, one mile long and a quarter of a mile wide; put about fifty houses in this clearing; divide the settlement into two streets filled with sawdust; give the place three hotels, five boarding houses, and seventeen grog shops and you have a clear idea of Seattle."[25] With only minor variations such a description applied to every lumbering community in the Puget Sound region. For whether it was Bellingham to the north, Steilacoom, Puyallup Bay, or Olympia to the south, or Port Gamble, Port Orchard, Port Blakely, or Port Madison to the west, all looked essentially alike, all were geared to the production of lumber, and all exported to the steadily expanding California market.[26]

Except for such lumbering communities, settlement in the Puget Sound region was modest and growth slow. The entire area was heavily forested and good farming land limited to the valleys of the Duwamish, Puyallup, and Nisqually rivers. Given this pattern of activity and the virtual absence of settlers east of the Cascades, it is meaningless to speak of an advancing "line of settlement," or to think of these communities as a response to the needs of an established agrarian population.[27] Rather than following extensive settlement they preceded it. And rather than meeting the needs of a local population they were geared to the demands of a San Francisco market some 750 nautical miles away. Over time some of these communities developed a concentration of population and specialization of activities typical of an urban society. Merchants, schoolteachers, bankers, and prostitutes appeared, as well as churches, boarding houses, transportation networks, and local government.

Seattle underwent such an evolution in the 1860s and 1870s as it drew steadily ahead of its rivals and established itself as the largest and most significant community in the region. The town was distinctive in having coal resources nearby, and it was the development of these coal-fields in the Issaquah, Newcastle, area 15 miles southeast, that helped it succeed. This coal had been discovered in the early 1860s. With the construction of loading facilities, shipping barges, and narrow-gauge rail lines, about 100 tons of coal a day were delivered to Seattle's wharves by 1871, where it was shipped to San Francisco.[28] Such operations made Seattle unique among Puget Sound communities, for no longer was it solely a lumbertown. Many of the ships arriving at its wharves still sought only lumber, but they were joined by a progressively larger number of coal ships. Because the mining camps were quite isolated, Seattle was the logical center for the food, supplies, and equipment needed by the miners and their families. This role as service center and supply depot was expanded with the opening of the Renton coal mines in 1873 and the Talbot and Cedar River mines in 1874.[29]

During the 1860s Seattle also became the supply center for many of the logging camps, lumber mills, and farms scattered throughout the region. Its central location on Puget Sound was beneficial, as the skippers of the "mosquito" fleet of sloops, schooners, and steamers that crisscrossed the sound found it a logical and convenient place to pick up supplies. By 1870 Seattle was also well on its way to becoming the largest community in the region. By that time it was still slightly smaller than Olympia, 1,107 residents to 1,203, but the next largest towns all fell far behind. Port Townsend had 593 residents, Port Gamble 326, Steilacoom 314, and Tacoma 73.[30]

The combination of lumber, coal, and an active supply trade enabled Seattle to continue its growth, and by 1875 with 1,500 residents it had clearly displaced Olympia as the largest community north of Portland, Oregon. This gave Seattle a certain preeminence on Puget Sound, although it was still only one-tenth the size of Portland and remained a relatively isolated community with a rather meager agricultural hinterland.

Throughout the late 1860s and 70s local businessmen, politicians, and writers offered a host of suggestions as to how to overcome these difficulties. A recurring theme was the need to expand the supply trade by building a series of roads to adjacent farming areas. The editors of the Seattle *Weekly Intelligencer* repeatedly urged that a wagon road be built across the Cascades at Snoqualmie Pass. Only with such a connection, the argument ran, could Seattle hope to become the depot and supply center for the agricultural region east of the mountains. That region traded almost exclusively with Portland, and proponents of the wagon road program insisted that if the citizens of the Puget Sound area cooperated in the effort, the trade of the region could be diverted from Portland to Seattle. Others argued that the wagon road should be pushed all the way to Walla Walla's rich grain fields a further 100 miles to the east. Still others pointed out that Seattle should consider the possibilities of supplying Alaska with a variety of the sound's coal, lumber, and agricultural produce.

All of these suggestions gained attention, but were eclipsed by the effort to obtain railroad connections with the East. Wagon roads, narrow-gauge coal lines, and improved coastal shipping facilities might reduce Seattle's isolation and increase its local supply trade, but most Seattleites agreed that only a transcontinental rail link and a terminal status would guarantee the city's growth and prosperity. Seattle was not alone in this conviction: virtually every town in the Pacific Northwest from Bellingham to Portland shared the same belief and saw itself as an appropriate terminal point.

From the time that Denny, Boren, and Bell first chose the east side of Elliott Bay as the site for a city, local residents were convinced that Seattle was the logical terminus for any northern transcontinental railroad. It had a good harbor, was centrally located in the Puget Sound country, and was also central to the three main mountain passes that linked the coastal region to the agricultural region east of the Cascades. This local conviction in turn was supported by more expert judgment. In 1853 when the federal government first sent out survey parties to investigate various possible routes for a transcontinental railroad, the report on the northern route pointed out "the unfavourable character" of the Columbia River ports, and "the great superiority" of the ports on Puget Sound as possible terminal points. Doubt existed about whether the route to Puget Sound should follow the longer but easier route via the Columbia and Cowlitz rivers, or the shorter, more difficult course across the Cascades. Yet once the sound had been reached it was generally agreed that Seattle was "the most favourable on the eastern shore."[31]

During the Civil War, Congress passed legislation that chartered the Union Pacific and the Central Pacific railroads in 1862, and the Northern Pacific in 1864. But actual construction was still well in the future. By this time Seattle was still only a small lumbering town of some 300 people, while Portland had mushroomed to a city of over 5,000. The officers of the Northern Pacific did not want to ignore such a thriving city, and promptly announced that besides building the main line of their railroad across the Cascades to Puget Sound, they would also build a branch line along the Columbia River to Portland.[32]

In the following years this original plan underwent many, many modifications. The residents of Portland and Seattle, as well as those of Olympia, Tacoma, Port Townsend, and Bellingham were periodically elated or depressed, depending on how the current investigation, plan or rumor affected their particular community. The issue was partly clarified in 1870 when the Northern Pacific announced that the main line of the railroad would follow the Columbia River to Portland. From that point track would be laid north to Puget Sound, with the terminal city on the sound to be determined later.

Actual construction began in 1870 when an eastern section started at Minneapolis, Minnesota. In the west, work also began on the section that would link Portland to Puget Sound. Progress in the west was very slow, but as construction inched its way northward, excitement in the various Puget Sound communities heightened steadily; although it was public knowledge that tracks would be laid all the way to the sound, it was not known precisely which community would be favored with the prized terminus.

As the largest town in the region Seattle was optimistic about its chances, but far from complacent. With a population still under 2,000, it made an impressive offer to Northern Pacific agents. This included 7,500 town lots, 3,000 acres of land, $50,000 in cash, $200,000 in bonds, plus the use of much of the city's waterfront for the big prize.[33] Shortly before the final decision was due the Seattle *Weekly Intelligencer* carried an editorial that speaks for itself.

> Before our next issue, the fate of Seattle will probably be fixed as having won or lost the terminus. That fate depends upon the prompt action of our citizens. If they all contribute generously, we shall be sure to win. If those who are able, fail to do so, we shall be almost sure to lose. If we win our property will be quadrupled in value. If we lose, it will be depreciated one half to two-thirds. Our destiny must now be settled for years to come. Most urgently, more earnestly, then, do we entreat all who can to make donations to the full extent of their means. It is now or never.[34]

The appeal proved of no avail. On July 14, 1873, Arthur A. Denny received a brief telegram from Commissioners R. D. Rice and J. C. Ainsworth of the Northern Pacific Railroad. It read, "We have located the terminus on Commencement Bay."[35]

This was a stunning disappointment for Seattle. It seemed to destroy all hope for the future and doom the city to permanent second-class status behind Tacoma—then a mere village of 200. Seattle's shocked disbelief was understandable; as the largest and most significant community on the sound it seemed the logical place for the terminus. Yet Tacoma's very insignificance in 1873 made its choice a shrewd one, at least for Northern Pacific officials. They apparently reasoned that Seattle was not intrinsically superior to Tacoma as a terminal point. And as a real estate boom was inevitable for the community that got the terminus, they much preferred to reap such profits themselves, rather than let them go to local speculators in Seattle. Prior to the announcement of their terminus decision, Northern Pacific officials purchased extensive lands in Tacoma and were automatically in a very favorable position once the public announcement was made.

The Northern Pacific's rejection of Seattle in 1873 marked a significant division in the city's early history. Up to that time Seattleites were convinced that the city's location, growth, and early prominence guaranteed success. After 1873 no such illusions remained. Although its geographic advantages and thriving local trade could not be ignored, its future expectations were sharply diminished after the Northern Pacific opted for Tacoma. The condemnations of the railroad's action were almost endless, but over and over again Seattle's journalists, businessmen, and citizens asserted that though the setback had been painful, it was not critical. If the entire community worked hard and pulled together it could develop the kind of railroad facilities it needed and do without the Northern Pacific Railroad.

The first overt result of these appeals came on May Day 1874.[36] It marked the official beginning of the locally sponsored Seattle and Walla Walla Railroad, with the avowed purpose of building a 300-mile railroad across the Cascades all the way to the rich farmlands of eastern Washington. Stores were closed and to the firing of a cannon, ringing of bells, and the blare of a brass band virtually everyone in town traveled to the mouth of the Duwamish River to help grade a stretch of the future roadbed. Except for a boatload of people who got stuck on the mudflats, everyone had a fine time. The men put in a vigorous day with picks, shovels, and wheelbarrows, and the women had a good meal ready when dinnertime arrived. Even the speeches were enjoyable as they reinforced the conviction that Seattle could prosper through its own efforts, regardless of what any transcontinental railroad did.

Such a display of civic enthusiasm and cooperative effort, even if orchestrated by a few leaders, seemed to assure success. But 1874 was an inauspicious time to begin a railroad. The entire nation suffered through an economic slump in the mid-1870s, investment capital was hard to come by, and even the Northern Pacific would not finish its Portland to Tacoma section for another nine years. As a result, progress on the Seattle and

Walla Walla Railroad was very slow, and it was only through the energetic efforts of Superintendent J. M. Coleman that it did not stop entirely. Two years after its gala beginnings, the railroad had only reached the coal mines in Renton, about 14 miles from Seattle.[37] In 1877 an additional 6 miles were built to the mines in Newcastle, but there the railroad stopped.[38] These modest achievements were representative of Seattle's development throughout the 1870s. Like its railroad, Seattle faced difficulties and enjoyed only modest growth. Its population rose slightly, coal and lumber exports to San Francisco continued, and its water-borne trade with the Puget Sound region expanded. But there was no dramatic growth or significant new development.

These achievements were modest in themselves, but there is no doubt that the crisis of 1873 and the response to it became one of the pivotal events in Seattle's early history and helped create an entire image of the city and its character. The Northern Pacific Railroad became firmly identified as the city's enemy, and the community was united in its conviction that the railroad was out to destroy it. For not only had Northern Pacific ignored Seattle's obvious superiority, but in a petty, shortsighted way had opted for Tacoma and would do everything possible to develop that city at Seattle's expense. The basic factor that had prevented such an outcome was the "Seattle Spirit"—a complex amalgam of youthful independence, courageous self-help, and plain hard work. Local residents never tired of telling and retelling how they had fought back in the grim days after 1873, how they had built their own railroad, and how they had sustained the community through their own private efforts. For the next forty years the "Seattle Spirit" would be called on time and again to exhort local residents to greater efforts, or to explain some achievement. The city would continue to see itself as the kind of community that could surmount any adversity in its march to greatness.

Though the conviction was upheld, the road proved long and difficult. In 1880 help came from an unexpected quarter when Henry Villard, a well-known railroad magnate, purchased both the Newcastle mine of the Seattle Coal Company, and the little railroad that connected that mine to the city. Villard had originally become active in the Pacific Northwest as the agent for a number of German investors and in an endeavor to bring some order out of a chaotic situation had purchased a number of rail lines and coal properties, with the goal of gaining control both of the railroads and the coal industry in the entire Pacific Northwest. When he gained control of the Northern Pacific Railroad in 1881, Seattle was delighted. Not only did he plan to complete the main transcontinental line and link Minneapolis, Portland, Tacoma, and Seattle, but he also planned to build a Cascade branch directly to the sound.[39] This meant that Seattle-bound traffic could go direct without the long detour through Portland.

As the construction of the main line progressed, the entire Pacific Northwest felt the stimulus. With the steady arrival of migrants Seattle reached a population of some 7,000 by 1883.[40] A buoyant real estate market and extensive house construction kept local mills busy and merchants happy. Yet simultaneously a number of local leaders became disenchanted with Villard. They saw his failure to do any work on the Cascade Branch as "broad discrimination against Seattle" and feared that he might resume the traditional Northern Pacific friendship for Tacoma.[41] In 1882 they chartered the Seattle, Walla Walla and Baker City Railroad, with the old idea of building across the Cascades to eastern Washington. But unlike its predecessor of 1874, this new railroad was little more than a paper organization and within two years was defunct.

The main line of the Northern Pacific Railroad from Minneapolis to Portland and Tacoma was finally completed on September 3, 1883. Tacoma's residents were understandably delighted. Development since their choice as terminus in 1873 had been disappointingly slow, but migration picked up in anticipation of completion of the railroad, and by 1883 the population had spurted to some 2,500. This left it well behind Seattle's 7,000, but its residents were convinced that it was only a matter of time before it displaced its old, established rival as Puget Sound's leading city.

The response in Seattle was an entirely different story. Spokesmen congratulated Tacoma, but saw the completion of the Northern Pacific Railroad as an event that would stimulate the development of the entire region. The suggestion that it might lead to Tacoma's dominance was rejected as sheer nonsense. Seattleites reassured themselves that it was just a matter of months until tracks were laid to their city, and then migrants would continue their rail journey to a more logical destination. But as in the years after 1873, developments after 1883 would be sharply different from what they expected.

When we survey the history of Seattle and Vancouver prior to the completion of transcontinental rail links a number of basic themes stand out. The first is that although original settlement was similar and private initiative was dominant, public authorities played a much bigger role in the Canadian setting than in the American one. Thus the Denny-Boren-Terry party that landed at Alki in 1851 and the "Three Greenhorns" who investigated the Coal Harbour region in 1862 were very aware of possible future developments and rewards. And both parties preempted land in what they considered were ideal sites for future cities. But the American settlers had a free hand to choose as they saw fit; their counterparts in Canada faced partial, but nevertheless significant restrictions. Not only had the Royal Navy set aside extensive lands for townsite, Indian, and military reserves, but numerous public officials preempted land for their own purposes.

A second basic theme is that the early economic life of these communities was dominated by the lumber industry, and this activity in turn shaped the evolution of the cities themselves. Both Yesler's mill in Seattle and Hastings in Vancouver's "Gastown" provided a focal point for early development. Within a few years it was clear that propertied and professional persons in Seattle tended to gravitate to areas north and northeast of the mill, and mill workers settled nearby or to the south. A comparable pattern unfolded in Vancouver, though here it was a west-east division with the city's more prosperous elements moving west and workers east. In both, the alignments established in the mid-nineteenth century would be sustained.

Finally, it bears emphasis that the difference in the development of the two cities was largely a reflection of the difference in the development of the two regions. Whereas the entire lower mainland of British Columbia had some 5,000 white settlers in 1880, the Puget Sound region had four times that number. This basic difference had many ramifications. Granville was still a primitive lumber town of 300 in the early 1880s. Seattle with 7,000 residents was a much more complex community with local government, churches, schools, and hospitals. Along with its lumber industry it had a healthy supply trade with the Puget Sound region, and a substantial coal trade with San Francisco. Equally important, it had an identity and sense of self shaped by its prolonged struggle to get the local and national rail lines it so ardently sought. The lag in the Canadian city's development would continue, but it would be sharply reduced with the completion of a transcontinental railroad.

2

Two Transcontinental Railroads

The completion and impact of transcontinental railroads on Seattle and Vancouver are at first glance virtually identical processes. In 1883 the Northern Pacific Railroad was completed to Tacoma, and in 1884 extended to Seattle. Similarly, the Canadian Pacific Railway reached tidewater at Fort Moody in 1886 and was extended to Vancouver in 1887. Both cities enjoyed unparalleled growth and prosperity in the following years. Between 1886 and 1892 immigrants poured in, lumber output expanded, construction of homes and office buildings soared, electric streetcar lines opened up new districts and sharply extended the range of the two cities. Population growth was especially dramatic. Seattle more than quadrupled from 11,000 to 50,000, while Vancouver's population went up fifteenfold from 1,000 to 15,000. By 1893 this great surge was over and both cities were quite different communities from what they had been just a decade earlier.

Yet these apparently identical developments disguise almost as much as they reveal. Seattle was a substantial community of 7,000 and the leading city on Puget Sound well before the completion of the Northern Pacific. The railroad link obtained in 1884 was not all what its citizens had hoped for and would prove to be very disappointing. Not only did the main line go directly to Portland, but the terminus was at Tacoma. The branch to Seattle was over an inferior roadbed and did little more than link existing local coal lines. Similarly, rather than an impressive new railroad station, the passenger and baggage depot of the Northern Pacific was a small unpretentious building acquired from the previous owners. The railroad undoubtedly contributed to regional and city growth, yet it had little direct impact on Seattle itself. As an additional new facility, the Northern Pacific had to adapt to an established city whose economy, property ownership, land use, politics, and society were already clearly outlined.

Vancouver, on the other hand, was little more than a lumbering village of 300 to 400 when the Canadian Pacific Railway announced its decision to locate there. The CPR immediately assumed a powerful role in the community and virtually created a new city. With its arrival the pattern of land-ownership was significantly changed, and over time the CPR would determine Vancouver's basic street layout and land-use pattern as well as shape the real estate market, municipal politics, and local society.[1]

The sharply different experiences of the two cities can be seen in the response to the actual completion of the rail lines. The people of the entire Puget Sound region were pleased with the completion of the Northern Pacific to Tacoma in 1883, but the extension to Seattle in 1884 was almost ignored. There were no enthusiastic editorials, no speeches, no official ceremonies, and no celebration. Nor was there even any notice of the arrival of the first transcontinental train in Seattle. Instead only a minor change appeared in the long-standing advertisement that the Columbia and Puget Sound Railroad ran in the Seattle *Post Intelligencer*. Besides the usual schedule of trains between Seattle, Renton, and Newcastle, the July 10, 1884, advertisement pointed out that connections were also available for Puyallup and Tacoma. This obscure change marked Seattle's attainment of a transcontinental railroad.

Later developments would justify this lack of enthusiasm. During 1884 Seattle's friend Henry Villard was forced to resign as chairman of the Northern Pacific and new management under R. Harris and C. B. Wright clearly favored Tacoma over Seattle.[2] During their regime, service on the line that linked the two cities was so inefficient and inconvenient that it was dubbed "The Orphan Road." Freight seldom came direct. It was usually handled at Tacoma and sometimes transferred to boats to make the last 30 miles of its journey. Seattle was not a terminal point so freight charges were well above those at Tacoma. Eastern passengers often did not know that it was possible to go by rail from Tacoma to Seattle, and scheduling was inconvenient with long stopovers and trains leaving at odd hours. It was not at all what Seattle wanted from its transcontinental rail line.

Vancouver's experience was decidedly different. At 1:00 P.M. on Monday, May 23, 1887, CPR locomotive no. 374 pulled into Vancouver and almost the entire city turned out to witness the event.[3] Businesses were closed, city council adjourned its regular meeting, steam whistles tooted merrily, the fire brigade was in uniform, and the city band led the procession. After the polished and decorated locomotive was brought to a halt, Mayor Malcolm MacLean gave a brief welcoming address. Then Harry Abbott, general superintendent of the Pacific Division of the CPR spoke. He recounted the many difficulties that the CPR had overcome in order to build to Vancouver, but added, "Here we are, and here we will remain." The crowd loved it, and left no doubt that they realized it was a significant day for Vancouver.

Vancouverites were also thrilled three weeks later when the CPR liner *Abyssinia* arrived from Yokohama with cargo destined for New York and London. It marked the beginning of a regularly scheduled steamship service to China and Japan and was taken as one more piece of evidence that Vancouver was destined not only for national but indeed international stature.[4]

During the mid-1880s railroad matters dominated the life of both Seattle and Vancouver, whether it was rumors about expected moves, actual construction of the lines, or later policy decisions by management. But before examining the distinctive consequences of the Northern Pacific for Seattle, and the Canadian Pacific for Vancouver, I will turn to another significant issue of the mid-1880s, namely, the anti-Chinese riots of that era. These riots provide a vivid example of the fact that in racial attitudes and convictions there was little to distinguish the American city from the Canadian one. It is true that the 1885–86 riots in Seattle occurred during a period of economic recession, whereas the 1887 outbreaks in Vancouver coincided with economic recovery, but otherwise there was little to distinguish them. The attitudes, arguments, and events were virtually interchangeable.

The years 1884, 1885, and 1886 were difficult for Seattle. In addition to the problems associated with the Northern Pacific, the city also felt the impact of the national depression. A collapse in the demand for the Pacific Northwest's raw materials led to heavy unemployment for the region's loggers, fishermen, and miners who quickly turned to the city in hopes of finding jobs. Here they encountered not only unemployed city clerks and carpenters, but also substantial numbers of unemployed Chinese workers, who had been discharged after the completion of the railroad. In such a situation the Chinese were an automatic scapegoat.[5] Racial contempt, hatred, and fear, never far below the surface, were quick to assert themselves. A minor news item in the Seattle *Daily Chronicle,* four years before the actual riots, provides a revealing insight into prevailing ideas. Under the bizarre caption "Cheerful News," it read:

The cheerful intelligence has been received at Portland of the wreck on the coast of China of the steamer *Mary Tatham,* bound for this country with a cargo of 700 Chinamen. The officers and crew were saved, but, fortunately, not one of the 700 Chinamen survived. As yet no meeting of Pacific Coast citizens has been called to draft fitting resolutions of heartfelt grief. Philadelphia and Boston, however, are yet to be heard from.[6]

Such accounts, letters, and editorials leave no doubt that most residents saw the Chinese as inherently inferior, unreliable, debased, and immoral, given to gambling and smoking opium. Many were "diseased with syphilis, smallpox and the terrible maladies that are the resultants of four thousand years of poverty, hunger and neglect."[7] Not only did the Chinese worker differ in looks and actions, but the white worker was at a complete disadvantage in attempting to compete with them. "The workman who can subsist on a few handfuls of rice and a rat a day, as a Chinaman can, can of course cut under a white laborer who must at least live like a human being. The Chinamen have no business in this country."[8]

Although there was general agreement in Seattle that "the Chinese must go" there were considerable differences of opinion as to how this should be achieved. A radical element, headed by a local branch of the Knights of Labor, argued that they should be forcibly ejected, and the sooner the better.[9] The radicals were opposed by a moderate faction dubbed the "Opera House group," or as they preferred to call themselves, the Law and Order Society.[10] Led by Thomas Burke, a prominent attorney, and Henry Yesler, businessman and mayor, they clearly appealed to Seattle's more prosperous elements. While expressing no great fondness for the Chinese they stoutly opposed the violent measures advocated by the Knights, and argued that if all employers discharged their Chinese help, and if the entire community refused to hire them in any capacity whatever, the Chinese would leave voluntarily.

Threatened by the radicals and looked on unsympathetically by the moderates the Chinese could do little. Tensions increased steadily throughout 1885, especially in the small coal-mining towns south and east of the city where operators employed a number of Chinese in a variety of low-paying jobs. In September 1885, the first violence occurred near Newcastle, when a group of rampaging whites demolished living quarters of the Chinese and drove some thirty from the community. Over the next few weeks Chinese were driven from Black Diamond and Wilkinson, and by November the contagion had spread to Tacoma. During these tension-filled months a number of Chinese voluntarily left Seattle, but on February 7 and 8, 1886, the long-expected riot occurred. In the melee five men were shot, Chinese stores and living quarters were destroyed, and 200 Chinese were driven on board a ship bound for San Francisco. By March 1886, after federal troops restored order, virtually the entire Chinese community in Seattle, some 500 in all, had been eliminated.

In the ensuing municipal elections of July 1886, Seattle voters indicated general approval of the action by returning an almost solid slate of candidates of the anti-Chinese People's party.[11] Yet racial issues faded into the background with the return of economic prosperity in 1887.[12] In that year, the recently successful People's party was soundly defeated. Chinese were quietly and unobtrusively readmitted to Seattle, but not until the early 1890s did the Chinese community regain the size it had prior to the riots.

Vancouver too revealed bitter racial tensions during the 1880s, and though the actual expulsion of Chinese did not occur until 1887, the basic attitudes and events in the Canadian city closely paralleled those in Seattle. Like their American counterparts few Vancouver residents had to be convinced that Chinese by nature were a filthy, debased, immoral lot who represented a threat to the working man and to society. Anti-Chinese sentiments were given vigorous support by the strident editorials and news items in the *News Advertiser.* "Those pests" who "cut rates" and "kill enterprise" had to be "obstructed."[13] As in Seattle, spokesmen of the Knights of Labor led the anti-Chinese outburst, and what little support the Chinese received came from the business community and propertied interests in the city.

The decision by a local contractor in January 1887 to use twenty-four Chinese laborers for a land-clearing project in the West End precipitated the crisis. According to the *News Advertiser* such a step was an "infamous outrage," that threatened "the peace, goodwill and prosperity of the community."[14] Violence began on January 15, when a mob knocked down the temporary shacks and tents that had been erected on the job site, and before the day was over the Chinese were herded aboard a ship bound for Victoria. Over the next month a series of incidents occurred, and after an attack on the more settled Chinese community on False Creek an additional eighty-six men and women were driven out. Newspaper readers learned "there cannot be many remaining in town now." But as in Seattle overt hostility faded quickly. Provincial legislation temporarily curbed Vancouver's police powers and established special constables for the city. These enabled the Chinese to return and resume work.[15] By May 1, just four months after the original expulsion, the *News Advertiser* could matter-of-factly point out that 320 Chinese were employed in land-clearing operations in the West End.

Such anti-Chinese episodes erupted periodically, but the fundamental issue that concerned most Vancouverites during these years was the completion of a railroad link with eastern Canada. Under the terms of union by which British Columbia joined Canada in 1871 it had been agreed that such a railroad would be built and that it would be completed within ten years.[16] But over the years there were many exasperating delays. And even after construction began in their province in 1880 British Columbians worried about future routes, freight rates, and terminal points. Federal authorities had stated that the main line of the railroad would terminate at Port Moody at the eastern end of Burrard Inlet. It was rumored that the terminus would be changed to a more westerly location on the inlet, but not until the CPR's announcement in 1885 that the terminus of the railroad would be "in the immediate vicinity of Coal Harbour and English Bay" was all uncertainty removed.[17] With this announcement the stature of the little village of Granville was instantly transformed. No longer was it merely an isolated lumbering community, but rather the future terminus of a major transcontinental railway. The previous trickle of workers to the area soon became a steady stream of enthusiastic settlers.

The year 1886 was especially memorable. In April the City of Vancouver was officially incorporated. Just two months later a devastating fire destroyed most of the city, and twenty persons died. Yet migrants continued to pour in and recovery was rapid. The CPR trains reached Port Moody in July, and from there it was only two hours by steamer to Vancouver. Survey crews, road gangs, home builders, and real estate agents were busy throughout the year, and by Christmas the city's population had reached 2,000—more than four times what it had been when the year began. And in 1887 the arrival of the first CPR train on May 23 thrilled the entire community and seemed to guarantee the city's success.

In a less dramatic way and at a less hectic pace, the entire period from 1886 to 1892 followed the pattern of 1886–87. During this boom period the city absorbed some 12,000 migrants and reached a population of 15,000. City officials supervised the clearing and grading of some 60 miles of streets, provided schools and teachers for 2,000 students, established police and fire departments, and developed water lines, sewers, parks, and hospitals. The city's businessmen expanded the output of lumber and shingles, carried out construction valued at some $4 million, built a 13-mile electric streetcar system, created a variety of foundries, machine shops, and small manufacturing plants, and installed up-to-date lighting and telephone systems. Year by year the little lumbering village of Granville faded into the background, and the new city of Vancouver was created. A great variety of individuals and institutions contributed to this process, but the Canadian Pacific Railway was of fundamental importance.[18]

First and foremost, the CPR ended Vancouver's isolation and provided a quick, convenient means of moving there. The very existence of its transcontinental rail line and its trans-Pacific steamship service helped shape a whole set of expectations about the city's future. Thousands of people reasoned that with such facilities Vancouver was destined for inevitable prosperity. The city would surely become the depot for prairie grain exports, the processing and export point for British Columbia's lumber, fish, minerals, and manufactured goods, as well as the Canadian port that would handle passengers and freight from the entire Asian and Pacific region. Throughout the 1880s newcomers poured in from eastern Canada, Britain, and the Orient. By 1891 the federal census showed that Vancouver had soared to a population of 13,709.

Beyond contributing to population growth, the CPR played a major role in determining the city's street layout and general land-use patterns. The government of British Columbia had agreed in 1885 that in return for the extension of the main line from Port Moody to Coal Harbour and English Bay, it would grant the CPR some 6,000 acres of land in the vicinity of the new terminus.[19] On 13 February 1886, two significant Crown grants were issued to Donald A. Smith and Richard B. Angus as trustees of the CPR.[20] The first, amounting to some 480 acres, granted the former government reserve on Coal Harbour to the two trustees. This grant included thirty-nine specific lots (about 8 acres) in the Granville townsite. The second, a great tract of untouched forest south of False Creek, amounted to 5,795 acres.

Private owners in the city also made donations. They realized that real estate values would soar if Vancouver got a transcontinental railroad. Even though it might have been painful to make voluntary contributions to an already large and powerful organization, they undoubtedly saw it as an appropriate move that would help assure future gains. These scattered grants lying east and west of the Granville townsite amounted to about 175 acres.[21] Figure 5 shows those grants.

The system of public and private grants to encourage railroad construction was a familiar practice in both American and Canadian cities, yet it is noteworthy that the CPR received much more land in Vancouver than in other western Canadian cities. Winnipeg, for example, contrib-

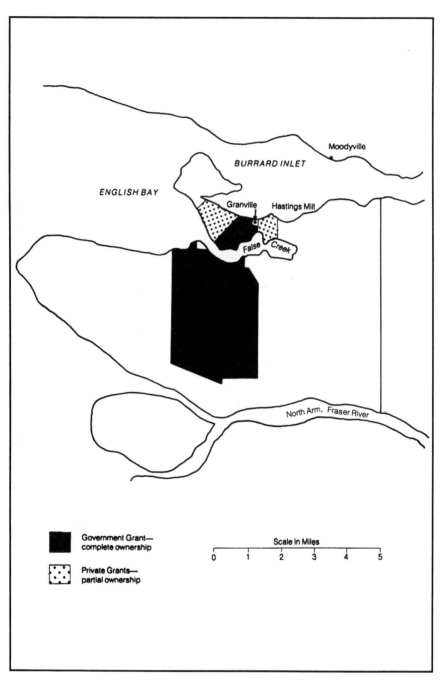

Figure 5—Canadian Pacific Railway Land Grants in Burrard Inlet, English Bay Region, 1886. *Source:* "The Canadian Pacific Railway Agreements with the Government of British Columbia," Archives of British Columbia, and adapted by author.

uted a city-built bridge, a $200,000 cash bonus, approximately 30 acres of land for station and stops, and a permanent exemption from taxation on railway property.[22] In Regina and Calgary the CPR obtained only the alternate sections of land that were bestowed under the original federal charter. Had the Canadian government originally fixed on Coal Harbour rather than Port Moody as the terminus of the CPR, the standard federal land grants would have applied all the way to Vancouver. But the choice of Port Moody, and later extension to Vancouver, meant that special arrangements were made with the government of British Columbia. The CPR was undoubtedly aware of the steps taken by various American cities on the Pacific Coast. Thus, San Diego offered the Santa Fe Railroad some 15,000 acres, and although Seattle's impressive offer to the Northern Pacific Railroad in 1873 had not landed the desired prize, the technique itself was an old and familiar one.[23]

Regardless of the rationale for these grants, the CPR's acquisition of 6,458 acres, some 10 square miles in the heart of the future city, marked the most significant land transaction in Vancouver's entire history. The CPR immediately became the largest landowner in Vancouver and for the next fifteen to twenty years would be the single most important agency in shaping the city.

The task of preparing a plan for the future city fell largely on L. A. Hamilton, the CPR's surveyor, and later land commissioner. He had already surveyed Regina, Moose Jaw, Swift Current, and Calgary for the CPR. Under his direction, along with H. Cambie and H. Abbott, the entire area was surveyed in 1885 and 1886. Existing arrangements in the old Granville townsite and the West End determined the location of many streets, but the CPR's detailed plans ultimately shaped the layout of much of the city.[24] The placement of the CPR station, office, wharf, and Hotel Vancouver along the Granville Street axis was especially significant, for it pulled the center of the city well to the west of the existing townsite. This western section of the city would be less heavily populated in the early years, but it attracted a more prosperous clientele, commanded the highest prices, and held the greatest prestige.[25] South of False Creek in the area of the CPR's main land grant, Hamilton established a system of east-west avenues and north-south streets. Granville Street itself was extended across False Creek to run through the center of the land grant, and was clearly destined to be one of the city's main thoroughfares. Hamilton's detailed plan reached a half-mile south of the creek, but over the years his basic system would be followed and extended all the way to the Fraser River, some 4 miles further south.[26]

Both in his role as town planner for the CPR and as an alderman for Vancouver, Hamilton played a significant role in the city's acquisition of the military reserve at First Narrows. At a meeting of city council in 1886 he introduced a motion that the federal government be requested to turn over the reserve to the city for park purposes.[27] The CPR had originally hoped to get an extensive slice of that reserve for its own use, but Hamilton and others argued that the entire reserve should be set aside as a public park. Approximately one year later the request was granted and Vancouver acquired a superb 950-acre peninsula, just a brisk twenty-minute walk from downtown. Officially named Stanley Park, it immediately became and would remain the focal point of the city's entire park system.

The long-range impact of the CPR's land grants, plans, and decisions was pervasive. Vancouver's central business district with its banks, offices, department stores, and theaters was firmly delineated. The placement of CPR rail lines and wharves on the inlet, and the choice of the north shore of False Creek for freight yards and repair shops, helped shape the industrial character of both areas. Similarly, the arrangements in the street pattern of the West End helped set that district off as a distinct residential area. With the clustering of prominent businessmen and professionals there, it was soon identified as the most prestigious area in the city. It would maintain this preeminence for some twenty years until displaced by the opening of the CPR's Shaughnessy Heights in the heart of the land grant south of False Creek. Of course, residential development continued in other areas of the city as well, but it is significant that the eastern edge of the CPR land grant became an unofficial dividing line between the more affluent established west side of the city and the less prosperous working-class east.

During the boom years from 1886 to 1892, all components of the local economy prospered, but the CPR quickly became and remained the city's largest employer.[28] The construction of its lines, wharves, station, and hotel created much employment in the 1880s, and this increased with the development of its passenger and freight services. By 1892 its 600 laborers, mechanics, trainmen, freight handlers, engineers, and cooks far exceeded employment at the Hastings mill.[29] In addition, CPR officials such as William Van Horne and Donald Smith developed private residential and commercial properties.

In the exuberant atmosphere of the late 1880s, with people pouring into the city and with newcomers and residents alike aware of the opportunities in a booming real estate market, no single organization could dominate the entire field.[30] The city had some thirty real estate firms, with Oppenheimer Bros., Ross & Ceperley, Berwick & Wulffsohn, Innes &

Richards, R. G. Tatlow, and C. D. Rand being especially active. Occasionally, groups of investors found it advantageous to incorporate as land companies, as the combined assets made it possible to deal in larger units of land. The Vancouver Land and Improvement Company, predominantly a group from Victoria, was the largest organization of this type. A great variety of individual investors were also active: Dr. I. W. Powell, C. T. Dupont, C. G. Major, and J. Robson were especially prominent. But even with this diversity, the CPR was in a class by itself. As can be seen in Table 1, the value of its land holdings was some six times as large as its nearest competitor, and no firm or individual could ignore its approach or prices.

Canadian Pacific management followed a cautious, long-range policy in the sale of its extensive holdings. They sold lots only in the city proper during the 1880s and 1890s and buyers had to meet very stiff terms. The usual requirement was one-third down, one-third in two months, and the balance in twelve months. Discounts of 20 to 30 percent were offered if buildings were erected on the property within twelve months.[31] According to D. C. Rand, the memories of the catastrophic slump in Winnipeg real estate after the great boom of 1881–82 were still very fresh, and the approach in Vancouver was to avoid the kind of "dishonest speculation" that had led to that setback.[32] The CPR's predominance in the local economy and real estate is especially revealing because its prudent policies in these areas undoubtedly retarded the kind of boom-bust cycles that hit many cities in the American and Canadian west. It provides a classic example of the important role played by a major, semipublic agency in the Canadian setting.

Vancouver's transformation in the six fat years between 1886 and 1892 suggests that it was an "instant city" which shared much in common with the explosive growth experienced by San Francisco and Denver some thirty years earlier.[33] In all three cities changes that normally evolved over a generation or more were telescoped into a few short years. Gold and silver discoveries were the magnetic attraction for the thousands who poured into San Francisco in the 1850s and Denver in the 1870s, whereas in Vancouver it was the completion of the CPR that created opportunities for the fit and nimble-minded.

Yet British Columbia's "instant city" differed significantly from those in California and Colorado. Unlike the incredibly diverse groups that flocked to the American cities from all parts of the globe, most of the newcomers to Vancouver were either Canadians or from the British Isles. New arrivals in San Francisco and Denver had a free hand to pursue their interests as they saw fit; those in Vancouver were always aware of the overwhelming presence of the CPR. The frenzied free-for-all that personified

Table 1   Major Real Estate Owners in Vancouver 1887, 1889, 1891, with Assessed Value of Holdings (in Thousands)

1887		1889		1891	
CPR	1,000	CPR	1,700	CPR	2,000
Hastings Saw Mill	250	Van. Improvement		Van. Improvement	
Oppenheimer Bros.	125	Co.	225	Co.	330
Brighouse &		Oppenheimer Bros.	150	Oppenheimer Bros.	200
Hailstone	100	Isaac Robinson	125	Isaac Robinson	200
Major Dupont	75	J. W. Horne	125	J. W. Horne	156
Dr. Powell	75	Dr. Whetham	100	A. G. Ferguson	140
John Morton	60	A. G. Ferguson	100	Whetham Estate	125
H. V. Edmonds	50	Berwick & Wulffsohn	60	C. E. Perkins	120
J. W. Horne	40	H. A. Dewindt	60	Street Ry. Co.	110
G. E. Corbould	30	Town & Robson	60	H. V. Edmonds	100
C. G. Major	25	John Morton	55	Van Land & Sec. Co.	100
E. Crow Baker	25	Sam Brighouse	50	C. T. Dunbar et al.	100
W. B. Wilson	25	Wm. Hailstone	50	Maj. Gen. Twigge	
Royal City Plan. Mills	25	H. V. Edmonds	50	et al.	100
R. H. Alexander	25	I. W. Powell	50	Waterworks Co. Ltd.	100
Gilmore & Clark	20	C. T. Dupont	50	S. Brighouse	75
A. G. Ferguson	20	C. G. Major	50	J. Mulligan et al.	75
Dr. Milne	15	Jonathon Miller	40	B. C. Mills	63
Abrahams & Co.	15	Hon. John Robson	40	P & W Thompson	60
Jos. Griffith	15	H. Bell Irving	35	H. W. Chamberlain	60
E. McKendry	10	Springer &		H. Hodden	60
John Dougall	10	Van Bramer	35	Hon. F. G. Vernon	56
Gideon Robertson	10	J. M. LeFevre	30	J. Miller	56
B. Springer	10	Harvey Hayden	30	Berwick & Wulffsohn	50
Wm. Power	10	Hon. L. G. Veron	30	H. Abbott	50
		F. C. Innes	30	B. W. Crownshilds	50
		Hastings Mills Co.	30	A. G. Delbruck	50
		George Turner	30	H. Bell Irving	50
		A. W. Sullivan	30	F. C. Innes	50
		J. M. Spinks	25	Gilmore & Clark	50
		C. D. Rand	25	L. A. Hamilton	50
		Inman & Thompson	25	Bodwell Bros.	50
		L. A. Hamilton	25	J. H. Ferguson	50
		Thos. Dunn	25	H. J. Chambers	50
		Jos. Griffins	25	C. G. Major	45
		A. G. Delbruck	25	Rand Bros.	45
		Gilmore & Clark	25	Springer &	

Table 1   (*continued*)

1887	1889		1891	
	New York Block	25	Van Bramer	45
	W. C. Van Horne	25	J. M. Forbes	40
	R. G. Tatlow	22	H. A. Jones	40
	Royal City Plan. Mills	20	George Turner	40
	Joseph Mannion	20	H. P. McCraney	40
	McLennan &		J. C. Keith	40
	McFeely	20	John Morton	40
	H. A. Jones	20	Inman & Thompson	40
	George Black	20	E. Courage	40
	J. M. Holland	15	W. Hailstone	39
	Hudson's Bay Co.	15	A. Cochrane	35
	R. H. Alexander	15	J. T. Mahon	35
	J. D. Townley	15	W. C. Van Horne	32
	G. E. Corbould	15	J. D. Townley	30
	M. Costello	15		

Source: The 1887 data are from M. Picken, *Vancouver Handbook* (Vancouver: Daily News, 1887). The 1889 and 1891 data are from unidentified newspaper clippings, circa March 1889 and circa September 1891, available in Bell-Irving MSS, vols. 1 and 5, Vancouver City Archives.

the American cities was far more subdued in Vancouver. In his *Instant Cities* Gunther Barth writes, "San Franciscans and Denverites were out to make themselves rich, not to build cities."[34] Such a proposition would not apply to the boom years in the Canadian city. Vancouverites were also out to make money, but most of them shared the CPR's conviction that this was no mere speculative opportunity, but rather that they were laying the foundations of a future metropolis.

When we turn to Seattle we see that it too underwent dramatic change between 1886 and 1892. The historian can uncover the basic picture from newspapers, city directories, U.S. census material, and published secondary accounts. But, as mentioned earlier, the limited documentary evidence for Seattle during the 1880s and 1890s is inevitably reflected in the written account. What might appear as a simpler, less complex process in Seattle largely reflects the paucity of material.

Throughout the late 1880s and early 1890s Seattle's newspapers poured out reams of statistics on population growth, lumber production, bank clearances, and business incorporations. As one writer pointed out in the *Post Intelligencer,* "The year just passed has been the most remarkable in the history of Seattle. It witnessed greater commercial activity, greater development of industry, and greater growth of population than any previous year and the city has easily maintained its prestige as the metropolis of Washington. . . . The transformation is marvellous."[35] This particular statement applied to 1890, but it would also be appropriate for 1887, 1888, 1889, or 1891.

The timing of the boom in both cities was identical and prosperity was fueled by railroad construction and the resultant surge of immigrants. Nevertheless, no single railroad or agency dominated Seattle's growth in the way that the CPR dominated Vancouver. The Northern Pacific was an asset for Seattle, but the city was well established before the arrival of that railroad, with property ownership, land use, and the economy already clearly outlined. Seattle's evolution was shaped by a host of institutions, including railroads, real estate concerns, streetcar companies, and municipal authorities.

This diversity is evident when one considers the railroad network that served Seattle by 1893. Besides the main line of the Northern Pacific via Portland and Tacoma, Seattle was also served by the Cascade branch of that railroad completed in 1887. In addition a network of small local lines was important. The Columbia and Puget Sound Railroad, that is, the old Seattle and Walla Walla of 1873–74 fame, linked the city with nearby coal districts. The Puget Sound Shore Railroad, built by Oregon capitalists, provided direct access to the agricultural region south of the city. Finally the 100-mile Seattle, Lake Shore and Eastern Railroad served the north and east. These locally sponsored railroads made up about 175 miles of line and assured the continuation and growth of the city's supply trade. On a typical day in 1890, for example, these local lines delivered about 900 tons of freight to the city and shipped out about 200 tons of general merchandise.[36]

The railroad that generated greatest interest in Seattle during these years was James J. Hill's Great Northern. Shortly after he gained control of a number of midwestern lines, and organized his railroad in 1887, Hill announced his intention to extend the system all the way to the Pacific Coast. Although no immediate commitment was made as to the future terminal site, Seattle was automatically a leading candidate. For a brief interlude it seemed that the Great Northern might choose Everett, but Hill announced in 1892 that his railroad would terminate in Seattle.

The completion of the Great Northern in 1893 marked a significant point in Seattle's history for it ended a preoccupation with railroads that had begun almost forty years earlier. The fact that a railroad terminus had eluded it for such a long time made Hill's choice just that more satisfying. By this time the Northern Pacific had granted Seattle equality in rates with both Portland and Tacoma, but the long and bitter experience with that railroad was not forgotten. The Great Northern was welcomed with open arms and seen as Seattle's friend and supporter. Not only did an appreciative city council grant it a 60-foot right of way along the waterfront, but also supported the construction of a large new union depot on King Street.[37]

No single concern dominated the Seattle real estate market, either. The Northern Pacific Railroad was the largest single landowner, but it had many rivals and could not control the local market. As can be seen in Table 2, a number of Seattle's founding fathers—the Dennys, Yesler, Bell, and the Terry family still had substantial holdings in the city. When this landowning pattern is compared with Vancouver's (see Table 1) it is clear that property ownership was somewhat more evenly distributed in the American than in the Canadian city; for example, the Seattle holdings of Arthur Denny, Henry Yesler, and David Denny together exceed that of the Northern Pacific. This made for a more competitive, volatile market than in Vancouver, where the massive holdings of the CPR tended to curb dramatic fluctuations.

The greater diversity of facilities in Seattle was also evident in the

Table 2   Major Real Estate Owners in Seattle, 1884,
with Assessed Value of Holdings

Northern Pacific Railroad	$592,345
Arthur A. Denny	266,155
Henry L. Yesler	225,315
David T. Denny	206,506
W. C. Squire	152,715
Puget Sound Railroad Co.	130,000
Terry Estate	124,830
Dexter Horton & Co.	115,640
W. N. Bell	111,325
Thomas Burke	103,565
Schwabacher Bros. Co.	102,530

Source: Bagley, *History of Seattle,* 3:547.

street railway system. Prior to 1888 it had relied on horse-drawn street-cars, but with the development of an effective electrical distribution system, electric street railways quickly made their appearance throughout the United States and Canada.[38] By 1892 Seattle had thirteen different street-car companies that provided 48 miles of regular electrical lines and 22 miles of cable lines. Company directors were as concerned about opening up new districts and selling real estate as they were in providing transportation facilities, and lines were constructed into Queen Anne, Madison Park, Lake Washington, the Rainier Valley, and West Seattle. These unsettled districts of the mid-1880s were substantial suburbs by the early 1890s.[39] During these years much the same pattern unfolded in Vancouver though on a reduced scale. By 1892 its Vancouver Electric Railway and Light Company had a 13-mile system in the downtown core.

Before the Seattle Fire of June 6, 1889, municipal authorities played a minor role in shaping Seattle's features. City debt was small and civic activity focused mainly on grading and planking streets and providing basic municipal services.[40] Park development was limited and relied primarily on private gifts of land, and not until 1887 did the city purchase a 40-acre tract that would ultimately evolve into Volunteer Park.[41] Such limited activity changed dramatically after the great fire of June 6. This conflagration wiped out sixty blocks in the heart of the city and municipal authorities were immediately called on for a great variety of work.[42] In the following eighteen months city officials purchased additional land, realigned streets to eliminate the flaws of the original Denny-Boren and Maynard plats, rebuilt wharves, constructed sewer lines, purchased the privately owned water system, and placed it under municipal control. The necessary bond financing for these diverse steps was overwhelmingly approved by city voters.[43]

During these busy years an unprecedented amount of construction was carried out. By the early 1890s, with its population approaching the 50,000 mark, Seattle's land-use pattern was clearly defined. A narrow strip along the waterfront, about a mile in length, contained the city's wharves, railroad depots, coal bunkers, warehouses, and freight sheds, and was the center of the wholesale trade. As Frederick J. Grant described it in 1891, "the locality itself is not enrapturing, being the sootiest, most crowded and most unpretentious. . . . But the businessman who gloats over long trains of coal, or freight cars crowded with bales of produce, hogs or cattle, or flat cars laden with stone and brick, the grime and stench are no objection. It savors of enterprise."[44] Before the fire, this area also included most of the city's sawmills. But after 1889 most of these lumber and shingle mills were moved north to Salmon Bay, Ballard, and Lake Union, where they had convenient water transportation, as well as lower land costs.[45]

Seattle's main business district was also permanently established by the early 1890s. It began about two blocks from the waterfront and reached up the hill to Fourth Avenue, stretching from Jackson Street in the south to Pine Street in the north. In total it was about a quarter of a mile in width and a mile in length and included the general retail and merchant blocks, banks, hotels, and offices. The reconstruction after the 1889 fire was almost exclusively of brick and stone and some buildings now reached five to eight stories.

There was no abrupt demarcation between the city's business and residential districts. But as one moved north of Pine or east of Fourth Avenue the area was overwhelmingly residential with a ring of suburbs—Belltown, Queen Anne, Ballard, Fremont, Green Lake, and Lake Washington. Population was much thinner in the southern sector of the city, but South Seattle and West Seattle were well established. According to Grant, the typical home revealed "comfort, decency and elegance rather than lavish expenditure or ambitious display." Many were simple cottages, but luxurious mansions also abounded. Flats of two and three stories of ambitious design were near the business section; in general residences were not crowded but rather laid out on a generous scale with ample room for lawns.[46]

Though the range and diversity of activity in Seattle was far greater than in Vancouver, by 1892 both cities were essentially complex service centers, with the typical worker a store clerk, waitress, or real estate agent.[47] In both cities 70 to 75 percent of the work force were in such locally oriented service activities. Each city had a great variety of small machine shops, bakeries, and printing plants, but only the occasional lumber or shingle mill employed more than 100 workers. Such manufacturing activity, along with skilled hand trades, accounted for 20 to 25 percent of total employment. Primary industry such as logging, fishing, mining, and agriculture still dominated the regional economies, but only about 5 percent of the Seattle or Vancouver work force were directly engaged in such activity.

The stream of migrants coming into Seattle and Vancouver in the wake of transcontinental railroad connections boosted population. With over 40,000 residents in 1890, Seattle was three times as big as Vancouver. Both were essentially white, native-born, English-speaking, Protestant

Table 3   Birthplace of Native-Born and Foreign-Born
in Seattle, 1890, and Vancouver, 1891

Seattle 1890			Vancouver 1891		
Birthplace	Number	%	Birthplace	Number	%
Northeast	6,871	16.0	Maritimes	860	6.3
South	1,889	4.4	Quebec	480	3.5
East North Central	6,842	16.0	Ontario	2,420	17.7
West North Central	4,893	11.4	Prairies	220	1.6
Pacific, Mt., other	8,686	20.3	B.C., other	4,572	33.4
U.K. & Ireland	3,700	8.6	U.K. & Ireland	2,543	18.6
Europe	6,345	14.8	Europe	372	2.7
Canada	2,714	6.3	United States	870	6.4
China & Japan	501	1.2	China & Japan	1,065	7.8
Other	396	0.9	Other	307	2.2
Total population	42,837		Total population	13,709	

Source: U.S. Census, 1890, vol. 1, Pt. 1, p. 580; *Census of Canada, 1891,* vol. 1, p. 332. The Vancouver data are estimates only and are accurate to $+/-$ 10 percent. They were extrapolated from New Westminster district data for 1891, with allowance made for the approximate number of British Columbia-born Indians in that district. See also *Annual Report, Department of Indian Affairs, 1892,* pp. 311–15.

communities. Over the years the source of native-born populations would change steadily, but the major foreign-born groups would still be evident fifty years later (see Table 3).

As can be seen in Table 3, some two-thirds of the population of both cities were native-born migrants, most from comparable regions of the United States and Canada. Most Americans who settled in Seattle were from New England, New York, Ohio, and Illinois, as well as from Washington itself. Vancouver at this time got most of its Canadians from the Maritimes, Ontario, and especially British Columbia. It is clear that both cities had a fairly representative sample of the entire population of their respective nations, and regardless of what characteristics one ascribes to "typical Americans" or "typical Canadians," they found expression in Seattle and Vancouver.

When one considers foreign-born immigrants much clearer distinctions appear. As early as 1890 Seattle had a much higher proportion of Europeans than Vancouver, with Scandinavians and Germans especially prominent. During these years such migrants provided much of the manpower for Seattle's sawmills, shingle factories, and logging and fishing operations.

Swedes, Norwegians, and Danes tended to locate in the northern and eastern sectors of the city, especially in Ballard where they established churches, clubs, newspapers, and communal organizations. Although numerically significant, Scandinavians did not have a major impact on Seattle's business or political world, however. With public education, marriage outside the ethnic group, movement into new occupations, and a strong desire to become Americans, assimilation in the new environment was rapid.[48]

Vancouver, on the other hand, had a very small European element, but a much higher proportion of British and Chinese immigrants than Seattle. Of all foreign-born groups the role of the British merits special attention. Not only did they account for one out of five Vancouverites in 1891—and one out of three by 1911—but they quickly assumed importance in the new community. The great majority of these British immigrants were of working-class origin, with some 15 percent of middle- and upper-class background. All carried their class association, values, and behavior to Vancouver, although these became somewhat muted in the Canadian environment. They nevertheless lent a distinctive ambience, a somewhat more formal, structured, class-conscious quality than was true of Seattle.

During these years Seattle was essentially a native-born, English-speaking, Protestant community.[49] Seattle had some 3,000 Scandinavians and 2,000 Germans, but less than 5 percent of the entire population could not speak English. The great majority of these residents lived comfortably, yet a substantial number of propertyless men huddled in "Shanty Town," along the water's edge in Belltown just north of the city: "Shanties of the most scant proportions and of poor materials have been erected as thick as they can stand. . . . Some are burrowed in the ground, some set on stilts along the beach, some are built on drift logs. There are hundreds of them."[50] In much the same way, some 300 Chinese and 150 Japanese were isolated in "Chinatown" south of Yesler. But with these conspicuous exceptions, social and cultural distinctions were not profound in Seattle.

Vancouver shared many of these characteristics, with blocks in the West End symbolizing the heights and "the Rancherie," a cluster of shacks east of Hastings mill, representing the depths. But it too was a decidedly homogeneous community that did not suffer intense social cleavage. At least 85 percent of the population spoke English. Anglicans, Presbyterians, Methodists, and Baptists dominated the religious realm, and property ownership was widespread. In 1888, 70 percent of the 1,536 persons on the voters list were identified as "owners." By 1892, owners accounted for 76 percent of the 5,303 eligible voters.[51] Only in Ward 2 with its concentration of boarding houses and hotels did the number of tenants approach the number of owners. This basic homogeneity, and wide range of property ownership, made for an orderly, stable, secure society with few outsiders. Vancouver's Chinese were the one major exception to this preponderance of white, property-owning, English-speaking Protestants. Concentrated in a few blocks around Dupont Street, the Chinese were well outside the mainstream of society. An outbreak comparable to the riot of 1887 would not occur for another twenty years, but in their editorials and letters, local citizens left no doubt that they saw Vancouver as a white-man's city and were adamant that it would remain so.

Throughout the late 1880s CPR officials maintained prominence in all aspects of Vancouver's life. When General Superintendent Harry Abbott built a handsome residence in the West End, the entire district was soon identified as the city's most prestigious area. By 1889, Abbott was president of the Vancouver Lawn Tennis Club.[52] The CPR officials also sponsored the establishment of the Vancouver Opera House and were some of its leading patrons. In much the same way "CPR Aldermen" were active in the city council,[53] and the council did everything possible to meet the company's needs and wishes. All were aware that Vancouver's prosperity resulted from the CPR's completion, and all agreed that any steps that would bind the railway to the city were not only sensible but desirable. In 1886, 1887, and 1888 few would challenge the assertion that "what's good for the CPR is good for Vancouver."

As Vancouver increased in size and strength, the relative importance of the railway declined. By the 1890s, CPR officials were becoming exasperated by what they considered the assertive, unappreciative behavior of the city. Harry Abbott reminded the city council in 1891 that Vancouver property owed its value "almost entirely . . . to the existence of the CPR." He argued that the company derived only a "small income" from Vancouver business, and that the connection there was "immeasurably in favour of the city."[54]

But city officials were not impressed. In 1892 the council authorized, and voters approved, the granting of a $300,000 bonus to the Burrard Inlet and Fraser Valley Railway. This line was to go from Vancouver to the U.S. boundary at Sumas, where it would link up with the Northern Pacific Railroad. It meant that the CPR would have to share Vancouver traffic with a major American rival and was an especially painful blow to CPR directors who still considered Vancouver "their City." Although the contemplated line was not built at that time, the incident revealed that by the early 1890s Vancouver had enough strength and economic clout to proceed as it saw fit.[55] It could not ignore the CPR, but the utter dependence of the 1880s was clearly a thing of the past.

There is no doubt that the transcontinental railroads provided a major stimulus to the growth of Seattle and Vancouver. The Canadian city was virtually created by the CPR, but Seattle already had a population of 7,000 before the arrival of the Northern Pacific and was over six times that size when the Great Northern was completed. Neither railroad shaped Seattle's physical environment, economy, politics, or society to the extent that the Canadian Pacific shaped Vancouver.

But in the realm of ideas and opinions, Seattle's experience with railroads had a decided impact. These experiences shaped a set of convictions and an image of the city that would be sustained for years. Visitors and locals alike continually emphasized the energetic, hard-working, businesslike quality of the city. A Portland visitor in 1882 considered it a "self-reliant, determined, well-governed" community with "exceptional public spirit."[56] About the same time a local journalist wrote, "This city of Seattle is just the liveliest, busiest, thorough going town in the Northwest," and both would agree that it was "the local citizenry" who "laid the foundations."[57] Ten years later, when the city had over 50,000 residents, the theme was much the same. A writer for the *New England Magazine* stressed the "marvellous enterprise" of Seattle's residents and added that it was a veritable "paradise" for anyone willing to work hard.[58] Another Massachusetts visitor, after a tour of the major communities on Puget Sound, pointed out that Seattle had "few flowers, less laughter and a scarcity of tennis courts." But in "dogged determination and energetic push Seattle reminds me most strongly of Chicago."[59]

Residents claimed it was the "Seattle Spirit" that gave the city its distinctive energy and drive. Just who coined the term is unknown, but after 1874 it was used steadily. The secretary of the Seattle Chamber of Commerce later insisted that "the Seattle Spirit . . . is a word of inspiration from San Francisco to Victoria."[60] Whether one noted the courageous work of the pioneers, the conflicts with local Indians, or the recovery from the great Fire of 1889, a lengthy list of examples could be provided to show the Seattle Spirit in action.

But it was the prolonged and successful struggle for railroads that was the essence of the Seattle Spirit, and spokesmen never tired of pointing out how the city's "unconquerable citizens" had surmounted all difficulties.[61]

The basic theme and self-portrait went something like this. "Our city can't be stopped for the 'Seattle Spirit' can overcome any obstacle. The Northern Pacific tried to stop us when they chose Tacoma in 1873, so we all rolled up our sleeves and built a railroad ourselves. After the Northern Pacific completed their line to Tacoma they deliberately ignored us, but we persevered in spite of them. Our own Tom Burke built the Seattle Lake Shore and Eastern, and we've done it without outside help or special favors. When Jim Hill brought his Great Northern here it was the sensible thing to do, for we are the biggest, most significant, most prosperous city in the entire state. We've had our ups and downs in the past, but we've always overcome our difficulties and we will do it again."

Images of Vancouver were also shaped by its experiences with a railroad. But as these experiences were so different from Seattle's, it is not surprising that the resultant image was also different. For American observers at least, there was not much in Vancouver to get excited about. At best, it was a pale, insipid imitation of its American counterparts. Shortly after the arrival of the CPR in 1887, for example, one Seattle resident noted that it was "a plucky and enterprising city, even if it is not very big."[62] Americans agreed that the tone and pace of life was much slower. To an observer from Oregon, the people of Vancouver "take life easier . . . the ceaseless hurry and worry that characterises so many American cities is almost entirely absent there. The business of the city does not get fairly to moving until 10:00 o'clock in the morning and very little is done . . . after 5:00 or 6:00 in the evening." But, at the same time, "the people are genial" and "seem to believe in enjoying life."[63] The harshest verdict of all came from a visitor from Boston, Massachusetts. "It is the CPR's town. The railroad controls everything, and is about the only aggressive factor, save a few transplanted Americans making what progress they can against British stolidity. It is a splendid town for Englishmen and Canadians but a poor place for Americans." He concluded with the observation that despite vigorous competition with American cities for trade with the Orient, there was little bitterness or hostility associated with it. Rather a "friendly, comfortable" feeling prevailed.[64]

Observers from Britain saw a substantially different Vancouver. The relaxed, sedate quality scorned by the Americans was admired by the Britisher. "The people . . . have retained their eastern and English habits. On Sunday the place has an aspect of quiet respectability like that of an English cathedral town."[65] Over and over again British observers contrasted the orderly, law-abiding quality of Vancouver with the harsh, rowdy patterns they associated with the American city. To a correspondent of the

London Times, Vancouver had "never known anything of the roughness of the new towns across the border."[66] Another added that Vancouver "was never like Seattle. There has been no Pacific Coast rowdyism, no revolvering, no instance or need of lynch law."[67]

Vancouverites themselves had yet another viewpoint as to the "real" Vancouver. The conviction that it was a uniquely endowed community, destined for both national and international greatness, was emphasized over and over. Editorial writers, city publicists, Board of Trade officials, and real estate promoters continually listed the characteristics that assured such greatness. On the day of the arrival of the first CPR train, the editor of the *News Advertiser* touched on them all: "As the actual terminus of the only transcontinental line under one management, and with the company running that line interested in our townsite, as the home port of a line of steamers to China and Japan . . . as the point from which a new submarine cable is to be laid . . . as the centre of the lumbering community unsurpassed on the continent, with immense resources of coal and iron in our immediate vicinity . . . with fertile valleys on one side and the sea teeming with all kinds of fish on the other, we can see nothing that is wanting."[68] This conviction of uniqueness and inevitable greatness received its classic statement by David Oppenheimer, city businessman, alderman, and mayor. "At no time in the history of the world," he pointed out, "has there been a city whose prosperity has been so marked or its future promises so bright as the City of Vancouver."[69]

An integral component of the Vancouver self-image was the fundamental importance of its political, social, and economic link with Britain. Such sentiments were sincerely revealed in times of international tension and conflict, but they were decidedly florid at the inauguration of a newly subsidized steamship line, the consideration of an imperial drydock, or the development of a preferential tariff scheme. Vancouverites also underscored the difference and indeed the superiority of their community to American cities. "The class of population which is being attracted to our shores," one particularly chauvinistic Canadian asserted, "is on the average a far better class than that which is going to the United States. The riff-raff of Europe, the anarchists, the assassins . . . find a more secure and congenial refuge in New York or Chicago than in the smaller but more orderly and peaceful cities of the Dominion."[70] Most were convinced that Americans as a group were a boastful, aggressive, hard-driving lot, lacking in charm or civility. The fact that Victorians viewed Vancouverites in much the same light could be ignored.[71]

3

The Klondike Gold Rush

During the 1890s Seattle and Vancouver revealed remarkable symmetry in their growth and development. Up to 1892 both cities surged in the wave of prosperity initiated by the railroad construction of the previous decade. By 1893, however, the railroad booms were over, and for the next five years both cities endured sharp depressions. The discovery of gold in the Klondike in 1897 caused intense excitement in both cities and the ensuing gold rush to the north, coupled with national economic recoveries, led to another spurt of good times that would be maintained into the new century.

The depression of the mid-1890s extended throughout North America, but was especially difficult in Seattle and Vancouver because of the exceptional prosperity of the previous years. Migrants continued to arrive, but when compared with the vigorous growth of the late 1880s and early 1890s, the advances were modest. Thus, between 1892 and 1897 Seattle rose from 50,000 to 56,000, whereas in 1888 alone the population had jumped by 12,000. The slowdown in Vancouver was not as drastic, as the population went from 15,000 in 1892, to 20,000 in 1897. But when compared with the era of the CPR boom, it too was disappointing.

The slowdown in population growth and the subsequent decline in demand for houses, stores, and office buildings, had a dramatic impact on the economy of both cities. Total construction activity in Seattle in 1896 amounted only to $200,000, or roughly one-tenth the level of 1890.[1] With such a slump, sawmill workers, carpenters, and laborers all felt the pinch; there were periodic layoffs and wage cuts.[2] It was an especially trying time for unions. Before the depression was over, the Shingle Weaver's Union, one of Seattle's largest, had disintegrated and the price for packing shingles had dropped from ten cents a thousand to three cents a thousand.[3] In Vancouver the pattern was similar. According to a report given to the August 1893 meeting of the Vancouver Trades and Labour Council, there was a large number of idle workmen. For bricklayers—"about half their number is idle," stone cutters—"no prospects of improvement," carpenters—"about two-thirds of their number at work." As for the printing trade, it "was never worse."[4]

Throughout the mid-1890s, Seattle's city officials struggled to maintain services while faced with a steady decline in tax revenues.[5] Staff was reduced, appropriations for various departments cut, and a whole variety of necessary work postponed. Planked roads expected to be replaced every four or five years were allowed to go for ten years, and "were rapidly wearing out."[6] Construction work on the Cedar River water supply system was delayed. Little was done to remedy the sewerage facilities in the city's seventh ward after the Board of Health warned "the water was polluted . . . their only sewers are three immense ditches carrying the sewerage of 10,000 people into Lake Union."[7] Even with these drastic measures, Seattle could not meet its financial obligations. It was especially painful to be told by eastern bankers, "If Seattle thinks it can neglect or refuse . . . to pay warrants . . . and retain a place among respectable financial cities, it is mistaken."[8]

Seattle's business firms were equally hard-pressed. The Northern Pacific Railroad pointed out in its annual report for 1893–94 that it was one of the most trying periods in the company's entire history. Seattle's banks also had problems. Many of their loans were based on the security of real estate holdings, and with the decline in real estate values, many were in difficulty. By 1896, five private banks in the city and one national bank had collapsed.[9] "Help Wanted" advertisements in local papers got shorter and shorter, and more and more tax sales occurred.

It was much the same in Vancouver where business firms, property owners, and city hall all felt the impact of the depression. The locally owned street railway company was taken over by the London-based British Columbia Electric Railway Company in 1897.[10] The city itself took over both the privately owned waterworks and the electric lighting system.[11] Henry Collins, drygoods merchant, city alderman, and mayor during 1895 and 1896, was declared bankrupt in 1896.[12] Real estate values fell and there were more frequent sales of property for unpaid taxes.[13] All of these conditions posed problems for city hall, for while it had heavy obligations from previous commitments, tax revenues dropped and tax arrears rose steeply.[14]

A host of suggestions was offered on how to improve economic conditions. The Vancouver Board of Trade argued that a system of preferential tariffs would revitalize trade throughout the British Empire.[15] Individual businessmen and journalists proposed a variety of bonus schemes to encourage the construction of smelters, foundries, and manufacturing plants.[16] A cowboy from Salt Lake City offered to provide women to Vancouver, to meet that scarcity.[17] But the most typical advice was that suggested by the editors of the *News Advertiser* who continually lamented that the city's debt was too large and its expenditures too great. Only prudent, conservative government, with a cutback in city staff and salaries, postponement of works projects, and a reduction in debt would solve the problem.[18] City council substantially agreed, and followed such a program throughout the mid-1890s.

Businessmen in Seattle also came up with suggestions on how to reinvigorate the local economy. One idea was to build a canal from Puget Sound to Lake Washington.[19] It would create employment and provide additional docking facilities on a fresh water lake. Another proposal was for the construction of a hydroelectric complex at Snoqualmie Falls. But after brief flurries of enthusiasm, little came of either venture.[20] Similarly, local lumbermen were delighted in March 1893 when the Great Northern Railroad announced a significant freight rate reduction of all eastbound lumber shipments.[21] But in the depressed economic conditions of the mid-1890s, freight rate reductions by themselves provided little incentive to eastern lumber buyers.

These were difficult, disappointing years for both cities, yet there were some significant developments. In Vancouver, a kind of settling down and maturation occurred. The erosion of dependence on the CPR and the assertion of city rights continued, as city officials became more and more aware of their powers. In 1893, the city strongly opposed the granting of additional foreshore rights to the CPR. Tax rates on railway property were raised. According to CPR President Van Horne, the level of taxes on CPR property was "unknown anywhere else in the Dominion."[22] City officials also pursued a long and bitter legal struggle to obtain the right of public access to the waterfront, across CPR property. Originally, the Supreme Court of British Columbia upheld the city's claim. But the decision was later reappealed to the Appeal Court of British Columbia, the Supreme Court of Canada, and ultimately to the Judicial Committee of the Privy Council, which ruled in favor of the CPR.[23] Though this particular battle was lost, the city's fight with the CPR over the rights of public access would continue for years.

Seattle's achievements during these years were also modest. The pro-

longed attempt to develop a wheat and flour trade began to have some success. In 1895, eastern interests took over management of the local grain
elevator, and after a prominent English shipper, Balfour, Guthrie and Company, established a branch in the city, flour exports picked up steadily.[24]
The other promising development of the mid-1890s was the establishment
of regular steamship connection with the Orient. A working agreement
was hammered out between James J. Hill of the Great Northern Railroad
and the Nippon Yusen Kaisha line of Tokyo. Monthly service was inaugu-
rated on August 31, 1896.

Such developments provided a minor stimulus to Seattle. But the arrival of the steamer *Portland* from St. Michael, Alaska, on July 17, 1897,
was an entirely different story. On board were sixty passengers, most of
whom had spent the previous year prospecting for gold in the Klondike region of Canada's remote Yukon Territory, and every one of them seemed to
have struck it rich.[25] The *Portland* was not the first ship to publicize the
news of the Klondike discoveries, for two days earlier the *Excelsior* had
docked in San Francisco with a group of miners from the same region. The
arrival of these vessels set in motion North America's last "old-fashioned"
gold rush, and in the process pulled Seattle and Vancouver out of the economic doldrums they had suffered for five long years.

From the beginning of this stampede, Seattle's spokesmen claimed
that their city was the only logical gateway to the goldfields, and that it controlled practically all the trade to the Klondike. On July 28, the editor of the
Post Intelligencer asserted:

> Seattle . . . is the present terminus of every single line to the Yukon
> country now in operation. It was at Seattle that the present population
> of the Klondike procured their supplies; it was to Seattle that the first
> returning miners came, and from Seattle it was that the news has
> gone out to the world of the wonderful discoveries which have been
> made. Naturally and inevitably, the great bulk of adventurers who pro-
> pose to seek fortune in the new gold fields will flock to Seattle as the
> point of final departure for the Yukon.[26]

This claim was challenged by every major seaport on the Pacific Coast.
San Francisco, Portland, Tacoma, Vancouver, and Victoria all asserted they
had excellent facilities to offer. Lesser ports like Bellingham, Nanaimo, and
Juneau sought a share in the trade, while interior cities like Edmonton,
Calgary, and Spokane also tried to establish themselves as outfitting centers. Although all these cities shared in the Klondike trade, not one of
them overcame Seattle's early dominance.

In the scramble for business and profits, one of the most intriguing rivalries was that of Seattle and Vancouver.[27] Over the years they had been largely indifferent to each other. The Klondike Gold Rush offers one of those infrequent episodes when they were deeply aware of each other and in direct competition. An examination of this competition not only shows an interesting urban rivalry, but indicates the ways Americans and Canadians responded to an economic opportunity. It also shows how cities in both nations played an important role in shaping the policies of their respective federal governments. In 1897, Seattle was much larger than Vancouver, 56,000 to 20,000, but both were well-established lumber and trading centers, with substantial transportation networks. Businessmen, politicians, and publicists in both cities showed some distinctive traits in the way they pursued the gold rush trade, but the overall similarity in their approach was unmistakable.

An examination of the Alaska-Yukon region prior to 1897 helps explain Vancouver's difficulties and Seattle's early dominance of the gold rush trade. Up to the time of the Klondike discoveries, most Americans had little interest in the area and thought of it as an isolated, barren region fit only for polar bears and Eskimos. By the 1880s, the Alaska Commercial Company of San Francisco had steamers operating on the Yukon River and had extended its posts well into the Canadian Yukon.[28] There was considerable seasonal work in the salmon canneries of southeast Alaska, but even as late as 1890, Alaska had a permanent white population of under 5,000.[29] What little trade there was with the outside world was monopolized by San Francisco, and the only regular transportation was provided by the Pacific Coast Steamship Company of that city.[30] A few Portland-based firms sent the occasional vessel to Alaska, but on the whole, San Francisco's dominance was largely unchallenged.[31]

It was not until 1891 that Seattle merchants began to seek out Alaskan business. In that year, McDougall & Southwick, Fisher & MacDonald, and the Seattle Hardware Company, three of the city's largest wholesale firms, sent representatives to Alaska.[32] These agents usually ignored the large firms which got their supplies from their San Francisco owners, and concentrated on the independent merchants and canneries in Sitka and Juneau. Seattle had definite advantages as a possible supply base for Alaska's merchants. The city was nearer Alaska than either San Francisco or Portland, and it could therefore offer lower freight rates and faster service. In 1891, for example, the Pacific Coast Steamship Company charged $10 per ton of freight from Seattle to Sitka, $11 from Portland, and $13 from San Francisco. While the average steamer took about seven days to go from San Francisco to ports in southeast Alaska, those from Seattle made the trip in four days.[33]

With these advantages, Seattle's foothold in the Alaska trade was steadily enhanced. In 1892, the Pacific Coast Steamship Company of San Francisco shifted its center of operations from Portland to Seattle.[34] In the same year, the North American Transportation and Trading Company, which had a number of trading posts on the Yukon River, also made Seattle its base. A locally owned line, the Alaska Steamship Company, was organized in Seattle in 1895. City firms obtained the government contract for carrying mail, and in 1895 and 1896, Seattle also served numerous gold miners who were headed for Alaska.[35] In its annual business survey for 1896, the *Post Intelligencer* could claim that 75 percent of all Alaska's trade was controlled by Seattle.[36] The claim might be an exaggeration, but there can be no doubt that Seattle had the experience, business contracts, and regular shipping facilities for trade with Alaska well before the gold rush started.

Canadian contacts with the Alaska-Yukon region were very limited before 1897.[37] The one business concern that might have given Canada a solid foothold for the Yukon trade ceased operations in 1889. In that year, the Hudson's Bay Company, which had been active in the Yukon Valley, withdrew completely from the area when it discovered that its trading post on the Porcupine River was in America, rather than British territory. What little contact there was between Canadian ports and southeast Alaska depended on American facilities. When the Canadian government sent the original party of twenty officers and men of the North West Mounted Police to establish its authority in the Yukon in 1895, the group left from Seattle and went by way of St. Michael and the Yukon River on board American vessels to reach its destination at Fort Cudahy.[38] After the first year and until 1898, this group purchased its supplies from the Alaska Commercial Company and the North American Transportation and Trading Company, both American concerns. Much of the mail came via Seattle.[39]

The net result of this lack of Canadian facilities was that when the *Excelsior* and the *Portland* publicized the exciting news of the Klondike gold finds, Vancouver had to start virtually from scratch in its attempt to capture some of the trade. Seattle on the other hand, could concentrate on expanding a trade that it had been cultivating for seven years. By early August 1897, Alaska-bound vessels carrying 100 to 1,200 tons of cargo were leaving Seattle wharves at the rate of about one a day.[40] Vancouver, at this time, could send one steamer a week to Dyea, with about 100 tons of merchandise.[41]

In the following three years, Vancouver struggled to capture the trade of the Canadian Yukon. Although it did not succeed during the peak years of 1897 and 1898, its basic approach was much like that of its American rival. In some cases, Vancouver's techniques were modeled on Seattle's example, but on the whole, the Vancouver entrepreneur made his decisions quite independently of his Seattle counterpart.

One similarity in the approaches of Seattle and Vancouver was that both carried on vigorous advertising campaigns in order to publicize their facilities and attract potential Klondikers. In this sphere, Seattle's efforts dwarfed those of Vancouver. In fact, almost five times as much advertising material came from Seattle as from Vancouver, Tacoma, Portland, or San Francisco.[42] Most of this was generated by a committee of the Seattle Chamber of Commerce under the energetic leadership of Erastus Brainerd. With a steady stream of cash from local business firms, Brainerd spread the message that Seattle was the only logical place for any gold hunter to outfit and begin his trip north. Most of this money was used to place advertisements in syndicated newspaper lists that covered the Midwest. Illinois alone had 488 different weekly newspapers carrying a Seattle advertisement.[43] National periodicals, such as *Munsey's, McClure's, Cosmopolitan, Harper's,* and *Scribner's* also carried Seattle ads.[44] Migrants to the Pacific Northwest were urged to write their hometown newspapers about their good treatment in Seattle. If one found writing difficult, Brainerd provided the stationery, postage, and even the message itself. All the "author" had to add was his signature. On one occasion, Brainerd persuaded Washington's secretary of state to sign one of the Chamber of Commerce circulars. It automatically became an official proclamation. The most ambitious undertaking was an eight-page special Klondike edition of the *Post Intelligencer* published on October 13, 1897. Altogether, 212,000 copies were printed. Every postmaster and public library in the United States got a copy. Hundreds of additional copies were sent to newspapers, businessmen, and railroad executives. Through newspaper advertisements, letters, journal articles, and official proclamations, the message that Brainerd and his associates pounded home was consistent, "Seattle is the gateway to Alaska."

Vancouver's advertising efforts were inundated by the stream of material that came from Seattle, but a number of steps were taken. In August 1897, Vancouver's Board of Trade established a committee to advertise the city's advantages as an outfitting point for the Klondike.[45] Businessmen in the city promptly subscribed $7,545 for the campaign, but in the first year only $4,514 was actually collected. Advertisements were placed in Canadian, British, American, and Australian newspapers. A variety of pamphlets were prepared, the *Vancouver World* turned out a Klondike edition, and a small agency was established in Seattle to drum up business in the rival camp. In addition, a number of Vancouver firms distributed brochures, while city council and local newspapers emphasized the need for effective advertisement. But the Vancouver campaign never achieved the volume, coordination, or impact of that of Seattle. It was particularly humiliating for Vancouverites to read in British newspapers and journals that Seattle was the outfitting center for the Klondike.[46] Brainerd's message on behalf of Seattle had obviously been effective.

A further similarity in the approaches of Seattle and Vancouver was the way both appealed to their respective federal governments for policies that would protect and benefit them. The policies ultimately adopted in both Ottawa and Washington, D.C., reflected the wishes of Pacific Coast cities. Governmental action probably assumed greater importance for Vancouver than for Seattle, but both cities sent out a steady stream of letters, telegrams, lobbyists, and legislators asking for consideration of their particular needs.[47]

Within a week of the first news of the Klondike strike, the Vancouver *News Advertiser* was criticizing the federal government for not having customs officials in the Yukon. "The country is losing large amounts of revenue," it pointed out, "while the business which should come to British Columbia merchants is being done in Seattle and other American towns."[48] When Clifford Sifton, Canada's minister of the interior, visited Vancouver in November 1897 after an inspection trip of the Yukon, he received a detailed series of recommendations from Sol Oppenheimer, vice-president of Vancouver's Board of Trade. These called for telegraph communication with Dawson, subsidies for railroads and shipping lines, establishment of special postal facilities, modifications of the mining regulations, issuance of miner's licenses in Vancouver, development of special escort systems, systematic and coordinated advertising, and the use of federal facilities to acquaint British authorities with Vancouver's special advantages for Yukon outfitting.[49] The Canadian government was definitely interested. Within three years many of these recommendations were implemented.

The issue of greatest concern for both Vancouver and Seattle centered on customs regulations. The overwhelming majority of people bound for the Klondike in 1897–98 took a steamer from a Pacific port to Dyea or Skagway in southeast Alaska. A rugged 25-mile hike across the mountain passes followed. After reaching the Yukon Territory, a boat was built to navigate a series of lakes and rivers for another 600 miles to reach the main goldfields in the Klondike. Customs duties, whether levied by American authorities in Alaska or Canadian officials in the Yukon, accounted for a significant proportion of any miner's expenses and often determined where he bought his original outfit. All outfitting centers were therefore very conscious of any regulation that might affect their chance of getting a share of the supply business.

From the start of the rush, Seattle and Vancouver each sought customs regulations that would benefit itself, but the stampede of miners caught both nations largely unprepared. A scarcity of officials, ambiguous regulations, and the need for on-the-spot improvisation led to much bitterness. For about eight months, newspapers and politicians in Vancouver, Victoria, and Seattle exchanged a voluminous series of threats, boasts, charges, and countercharges. Minor victories were accepted with glee, setbacks looked upon as the forerunners of a complete loss of trade. In the first month of the rush, Canadian customs duties were seldom collected simply because there were no customs officials in the Yukon. By September 1897, a customs post was established at Lake Tagish, but exemptions on miners' outfits were quite liberal.[50] To the great irritation of Vancouver's merchants, Seattle newspapers suggested that virtually no Canadian customs whatever would be collected on goods purchased in the United States.[51]

Vancouver merchants in the meantime were advertising that Canadian goods could be landed in Skagway in bond and then taken across the mountain passes to Canadian territory without paying any American duties. This too was premature as many who bought their supplies in Vancouver discovered.[52] Although Dyea had been made a subport of entry for British goods, and theoretically no duty had to be paid on them, American officials in Alaska developed an ingenious convoy system.[53] In practice it meant that a man with a Canadian outfit could either pay an American official about nine dollars a day to trudge along the trail with him, and "convoy" his goods to Canadian territory, or else pay the regular American duty of about 30 percent of the value of the goods landed in Dyea. It was usually cheaper to pay the regular American duty and most miners with Canadian outfits did precisely that.

With the establishment of regular Canadian duties on January 1, 1898, and the continuation of the American convoy system, irritation increased on both sides. While the Vancouver Board of Trade bombarded the Canadian minister of the interior for clarification of the regulations and for retaliatory action, Vancouver and Victoria newspapers accused the American government of deliberate delaying tactics so as to benefit Seattle. Though the U.S. secretary of the treasury announced new regulations on February 2, 1898, it was not until May 15 that the American convoy system was abandoned.[54]

Though seldom reaching the intensity of the customs controversy, both Vancouver and Seattle interests approached their respective governments on a host of other issues. Quite understandably, the two cities took opposite positions on the desirability of establishing a subport of entry at Dyea. Vancouver urged Ottawa to issue Yukon miners' licenses only at selected Canadian cities, while American interests pushed equally hard for issuance of the licenses at the passes or at British consulates in American cities. Both cities also sought and obtained government assay offices, mail subsidies, and federal support for transportation companies. The Canadian government, with some support from Vancouver and Victoria, also sought to build a railroad to improve transportation to the Yukon. This proposal for a Stikine River-Lake Teslin railroad, however, was defeated.[55]

Another way Seattle and Vancouver showed a similar response was that businessmen and journalists in both cities used questionable tactics to secure benefits for themselves or their community. Not unexpectedly, businesses in each city claimed to be able to provide supplies and equipment to the prospective Klondiker at prices lower than their competitors. Specific prices were seldom given. From the welter of conflicting testimony, it seems fair to conclude that there was no substantial difference in Canadian and American outfitting costs, especially for food and general provisions.[56] On woolen goods, and especially blankets, Vancouver apparently had the edge, whereas in general hardware, Seattle was cheaper. Much depended on the relative quality of the goods concerned. Miners' outfits cost about $200 to $300, but as they ranged from $100 to $1,000, valid comparisons of outfitting costs are difficult to determine.

The most consistent thorn in the side of Vancouver and Victoria was that Seattle's merchants and newspapers played down or ignored the fact that the Klondike was in Canadian territory and that American goods were subject to Canadian duty.[57] Though Canadian papers endlessly proclaimed the real state of affairs, few Americans heard or heeded. Petty harassments and distortions abounded. The Seattle *Times* refused to print a Victoria advertisement, and the *Post Intelligencer* urged the Seattle city council to place a $500 monthly license fee on Canadian agents in Seattle. A steamship of the Washington and Alaska Steamship Company was magically transformed into a vessel of the British Columbia and Alaska Steamship Company when it was advertised in the Vancouver *News Advertiser.*[58]

Canadian papers were not outdone, however. On July 20, 1897, Victoria's *Colonist* gave a detailed, enthusiastic description of the departure of the steamer *Al-ki* for the north. She carried 110 passengers and 350 tons of merchandise along with 30 horses, 65 head of cattle, and 900 sheep. The general implication of the article was that most of this cargo had originated in Victoria. The *Colonist* conveniently ignored the fact that the *Al-ki* belonged to a Seattle firm and that it had obtained virtually all of its passengers and freight in that city. In fact, most of the column itself was cribbed word for word from the Seattle *Post Intelligencer* of the previous day. Except for some cattle that were loaded in the Canadian city, Victoria's total contribution to the cargo consisted of the following: 1 sack of onions, 1 sack of potatoes, 1 bundle of shovels, 1 bundle of axes, 3 bundles of pack saddles, and a few packages of general hardware. Altogether this weighed somewhat less than 350 tons.[59]

It was not until early in 1898 that Vancouver shared significantly in the Klondike trade. Beginning in February and lasting for about four months, the city's merchants and businessmen experienced the prosperity that had been so often prophesied. A number of factors contributed to this expansion. Not only had a convenient bonding system been established for carrying Canadian goods through Alaska, but Canadian customs were now regularly collected on American goods entering the Yukon. Vancouver-owned steamship lines had expanded their operations, and numerous Puget Sound-based steamers now stopped at the city for additional passengers and freight on the way north.[60] Victoria's steamship companies had also expanded operations. Most important of all, the Canadian Pacific Railway had transferred two ocean-going steamers, the *Tartar* and the *Athenian,* to the Vancouver-Skagway run. Both of these vessels were big, fast, and comfortable. The *Tartar* was 4,425 tons gross register and could make the run to Skagway in under three days.[61] For one short period during the entire gold rush, Vancouver had the shipping facilities it wanted.

The flurry of activity proved to be brief. By late summer it was over and merchants were disappointed to find themselves heavily overstocked with goods.[62] It was only after the peak of the stampede that Vancouver and Victoria clearly replaced Seattle as the supply center for the Yukon. Seattle retained dominance in Alaska, but the completion of the White Pass and Yukon Railway from Skagway, Alaska, to Whitehorse, Yukon, in July 1900 changed the pattern of Yukon trade.[63] In that year approximately 75 to 80 percent of the goods entering the Yukon came from Canada, whereas in 1898 about the same proportion had been from the United States.[64] Unfortunately for the Canadian cities, the population of the Yukon declined steadily in the next decade as individual prospectors were displaced by highly capitalized mining concerns.[65]

Vancouver's inability to capture a larger share of the Klondike trade in 1897–98 can be explained by its lack of a substantial, Vancouver-based line of steamers, and its heavy dependence on vessels that started their voyage in San Francisco, Seattle, or Victoria. American economic dominance of the Yukon Valley and the contacts, knowledge, and experience gained by Seattle in the years before 1897 also played a part. It is also significant that 65 to 80 percent of the prospectors in the Canadian Yukon were Americans. A careful count of Dawson, Yukon Territory, in 1899 showed 3,205 Americans out of a population of 4,445.[66] Whereas Canada's Dominion Day on July 1 was practically ignored, the glorious Fourth of July saw an immense celebration that lasted the entire day. Most of these Americans in the Yukon outfitted in an American city, usually Seattle; few but British subjects chose to outfit in Vancouver or Victoria.[67]

Although Vancouver never threatened Seattle's early dominance of the gold rush trade, the response of the Canadian city was remarkably similar to that of its American rival. From the summer of 1897 onward, Vancouver was aware of the stakes involved, and of the possibility for a lucrative supply trade, especially because it was the nearest major port to the goldfields. Its early advertising campaigns, lobbying efforts with the federal government, pursuit of better transportation facilities, and willingness to exaggerate its services or understate its prices were all quite like the reaction in Seattle.

The only basic difference was one of timing and degree. Seattle had begun its supply trade with Alaska long before the gold rush. Because it was much larger and better supplied than Vancouver, and because most gold seekers were Americans, it was logical that they would outfit themselves there. Beyond this, however, Seattle's businessmen were faster off the mark, more aggressive, and more willing to commit resources and effort to the task than were their Vancouver counterparts. Canadian businessmen worked hard, yet the sense of urgency that permeated the Seattle scene was never as intense in British Columbia. On August 14, 1897, the editor of the *Vancouver Province* warned prospective miners of the difficulties inherent in a trip to the Klondike, and added, "there is plenty of time . . . the gold won't run away. It has been there for several million years already, and will no doubt wait a month or two longer." No such cautious sentiments came from Seattle in the summer of 1897.

There is a little doubt that the gold rush of the 1890s stimulated both national and city economies. Seattle, the unquestioned leader in the Alaska-Yukon trade, grew significantly. It had 42,837 residents in 1890 and reached 80,671 by 1900. For the decade as a whole, its population rose by about 88 percent. Tacoma, with little gold rush business, virtually stagnated in the 1890s, its population creeping from 36,006 to 37,714. A somewhat similar pattern was evident in British Columbia. When the decade opened, Victoria was still ahead of Vancouver 16,841 to 13,709, but during the gold rush years Vancouver grew rapidly and by 1901 had left Victoria well behind with 27,010 to 20,919. One might argue from such evidence that it was the gold rush business of the late 1890s that enabled both Seattle and Vancouver to become the dominant cities of their respective regions.

But when we look further afield, a somewhat different picture emerges. As can be seen in Table 4, Portland and Vancouver, neither of which had seriously challenged Seattle's control of the gold rush trade, both grew at a faster rate in the 1890s than did Seattle. Similarly, Los Angeles and Spokane, which had only the slightest of connections with the gold rush, also jumped dramatically. San Francisco and Victoria, on the other hand, both of which had considerable business in the early months of the rush, only increased by 15 percent and 25 percent, respectively. It is also significant that Seattle had drawn well ahead of Tacoma in the early 1890s, and that Vancouver exceeded Victoria's population by 1896, well before the Klondike gold finds were even announced.

It seems reasonable to conclude that Seattle, and to a lesser extent Vancouver, both got a boost from the Klondike-Alaska gold rush. The re-

Table 4   Population Growth in Selected Western Cities, 1890–1900

City	Population		Increase 1890–1900	
	1890	1900	Number	%
Los Angeles	50,395	102,497	52,102	103
San Francisco	298,997	342,782	43,785	15
Portland	46,385	90,426	44,041	95
Tacoma	36,006	37,714	1,708	5
Seattle	42,837	80,671	37,834	88
Spokane	19,921	36,848	16,927	85
Vancouver	13,709	27,010	13,301	97
Victoria	16,841	20,919	4,078	24

Source: U.S. Census, 1900, Population, vol. 1, Pt. 1, pp. 430–32; *Census of Canada, 1891, 1901, Population.* The data for Vancouver and Victoria are for 1891 and 1901.

sultant activity buttressed their lead over their nearest rivals, and helped consolidate their regional dominance. But like other West Coast cities, their growth in the 1890s resulted primarily from the fact that thousands of migrants still observed Horace Greeley's old advice, "Go West, young man, go West."

4
Critical Growth Cycles

———

During the first decade of the twentieth century Seattle and Vancouver enjoyed a growth and prosperity that surpassed anything they had experienced in the past. With only periodic slowdowns this growth was sustained until the eve of World War I. Both cities showed a dramatic increase in population as migrants arrived in unprecedented numbers. Both extended their lead over their nearest rivals and indisputably established preeminence in their respective regions. Thousands of homes, stores, and warehouses altered the appearance of these cities, while the construction of roads and streetcar lines, along with the development of new residential districts and suburbs, extended their physical range. Both cities also became more and more integrated with their respective nations and lost much of their small-town quality and local orientation. This whole set of developments profoundly modified the cities of 1900, and by 1914 had left an imprint that would not be lost for years—any fifty-year-old residents of either Seattle or Vancouver on the eve of World War II would still recognize the same basic city they had known twenty-five years earlier.

If one factor can be said to be basic to all the changes that took place at this time it was rapid population growth. Such a process was not unique to Seattle and Vancouver alone, for while they were forging ahead much the same thing was happening to other western cities. All felt the consequences of a stream of immigrants from Europe, as well as a heavy westward migration of Canadians and Americans. Thus Los Angeles tripled its population between 1900 and 1910, jumping from 100,000 to over 300,000.[1] Portland doubled, Spokane tripled, while Calgary and Edmonton with populations under 5,000 at the turn of the century went up tenfold. The patterns in Seattle and Vancouver are outlined in Table 5.

Table 5   Birthplace of Native-Born and Foreign-Born in Seattle and Vancouver, 1900–01, 1910–11

SEATTLE

Birthplace	1900 Number	%	1910 Number	%
Northeast	10,907	13.5	23,743	10.0
South	3,637	4.5	10,765	4.5
E. North Central	12,341	15.3	41,432	17.5
W. North Central	9,124	11.3	35,857	15.1
Pacific, Mt., other	22,659	28.1	57,941	24.4
U.K. & Ireland	4,905	6.1	11,721	4.9
Europe	9,234	11.4	35,242	14.9
Canada	3,786	4.7	10,708	4.5
China & Japan	3,457	4.3	6,476	2.7
Other	621	0.8	3,309	1.4
Total population	80,671		237,194	

VANCOUVER

Birthplace	1901 Number	%	1911 Number	%
Maritimes	1,460	5.4	5,698	5.7
Quebec	640	2.4	2,170	2.2
Ontario	3,950	14.5	16,663	16.6
Prairies	530	2.0	3,925	3.9
B.C., other	9,788	36.2	15,522	15.5
U.K. & Ireland	4,304	15.9	30,689	30.6
Europe	834	3.1	6,141	6.1
United States	1,840	6.8	10,401	10.4
China & Japan	2,810	10.4	5,205	5.2
Other	854	3.2	3,987	4.0
	27,010		100,401	

Source: U.S. Census, 1900, vol. 1, Pt. 1, pp. 686–89, 710, 713; *U.S. Census, 1910,* vol. 1, pp. 730–34, 770–71. *Census of Canada, 1901,* vol. 1, pp. 416–18. The Vancouver data for 1901 are estimates only and are accurate to +/− 10 percent. They were extrapolated from Burrard District data for 1901 with allowance made for the approximate number of British Columbia born Indians in that district. See also *Annual Report, Department of Indian Affairs, 1901,* pp. 158–66. The 1911 data are from *Census of Canada, 1911,* vol. 2, pp. 426–28, 440–41.

Seattle virtually tripled its population between 1900 and 1910, jumping from 80,671 to 237,194. Yet the basic makeup of this population remained much like that of the early 1890s. About 70 percent of its newcomers were native-born Americans, from the north-central section of the nation, stretching in a broad band from Ohio to Nebraska and Kansas. Seattle's early Scandinavian flavor was strongly reinforced with the arrival of some 15,000 Swedes, Norwegians, Danes, and Finns. A new element in Seattle consisted of about 10,000 Russians, Hungarians, Italians, and Greeks. But 1910 marked the peak of Eastern European migration and in the following years it gradually declined.

Vancouver's growth was equally dramatic with the population almost quadrupling. Approximately 45 percent were native-born Canadians, but unlike Seattle most of Vancouver's newcomers were from outside the country, especially from the United Kingdom. During these prosperous years, 16,000 English and Welsh, 9,000 Scots, and 2,000 Irish, along with a sprinkling of Australians, New Zealanders, and South Africans gave a decidedly British cast to Vancouver's population profile. By 1911 there were 33,995 such Britishers out of a total city population of 100,401. A substantial American contingent and diverse Europeans and Asians also settled in Vancouver during the decade and together accounted for approximately 20 percent of the Canadian city's population by 1911.

The stream of migrants from the British Isles was especially significant—it both sustained and reinforced a group that had long been established in the city. With a third of its population from Britain, Vancouver had a style and ambience quite unlike that of Seattle. The prevalence of British accents among its store clerks, schoolteachers, and policemen was but one indication of that role, as were the number of British papers in newsstands, the abundance of Tudor houses, and the popularity of flower gardens. British immigrants would account for a disproportionately large number of Vancouver's business leaders and civic bureaucrats, and over time would help shape the city's economy, labor organization, political life, and educational system.[2] Such immigration would not match the pre–World War I level but it would continue to play an important role in the city's life.

A further indication of growth during these years was the strong expansion of urban transportation networks. The depression of the mid-1890s had entailed severe financial difficulties for the locally owned streetcar companies in both cities. In 1897 the British Columbia Electric Railway assumed complete control in Vancouver. After a series of bankruptcies and reorganizations, the eleven existing companies in Seattle were taken over by the Stone-Webster interests of Boston in 1900, and renamed the Seattle Electric Company.[3] Both organizations began major construction programs early in the century and sustained them for years. Heavily traveled routes in the downtown core were double-tracked, and lines pushed out in all directions to new residential areas and suburbs. Between 1900 and 1912 streetcar trackage in the Canadian city rose from 13 miles to 106 miles, while in Seattle it went from 71 miles to 239 miles.[4] Whether the Vancouverite lived in West Point Grey, Shaughnessy Heights, or South Vancouver, or his American counterpart in West Seattle, Laurelhurst, or the distant reaches of Rainier Beach, he was within easy walking distance of a streetcar line and a quick ride downtown.

A major extension of interurban lines also increased the range of activity and settlement.[5] Two lines linked Seattle with areas to the south. One, the Seattle and Rainier Beach Railway, was extended to Renton by the early 1900s. The other was completed to Tacoma by 1902 and provided frequent service to a string of small communities. This Puget Sound Electric Railway could make the 36-mile trip between Seattle and Tacoma in seventy-five minutes. The Everett and Interurban Railway provided service to areas to the north. Taken over by Stone and Webster in 1908, it acquired a number of local lines and by 1912 extended to Snohomish, some 35 miles north of Seattle.

Interurban lines appeared somewhat later in the Canadian city, and were oriented primarily eastward to the Fraser Valley, but otherwise the pattern was similar. The CPR constructed the Lulu Island line in 1902 which connected the city with the fishing center at Steveston. By 1914 three separate lines connected Vancouver with New Westminster and that city in turn was linked with the farming centers at Abbotsford and Chilliwack. The result of all this construction was that Vancouver became the focal point of a thriving regional transportation network. For all practical purposes anyone living within an 8-mile radius of downtown could get there in thirty-five minutes, while a rush order from Chilliwack, 40 miles away, could be delivered within a few hours.

The new districts that received streetcar service in the great surge of construction between 1900 and 1914 were not as thinly settled as their counterparts of the early 1890s. Yet these facilities often preceded any significant population concentration; it was the expectation of rapid growth and a rise in real estate values that influenced both companies and private speculators in their decisions.[6] The municipality of Point Grey, for example, had 16 miles of tramway by 1912, with a population of under 5,000.[7] Interurban lines showed much the same pattern with lengthy sections of track stretching through farmland or forest. Revenues from passenger and freight service seldom met operating expenses and financial crises and reorganizations seemed endless. Yet although these urban and interurban lines exceeded immediate needs, they encouraged many citizens to settle on the outskirts of the city, and tended to reduce the population concentration in the central city.

Along with the development of these urban and interurban railway lines went an incredible amount of construction. Building activities had been reasonably vigorous in the early 1900s but as the decade unfolded construction raced ahead at an unprecedented rate. Each year of the decade seemed to set some kind of record only to be exceeded by an even greater volume of activity the following year. Some idea of the size, growth, and cyclical nature of this activity can be gathered from the graph in Figure 6. This graph reveals variations in the timing and amount of construction in the two cities. It also captures the essential similarity in the boom-bust cycles that both experienced in the early twentieth century. The construction boom of 1900–12 and the slump during the World War I years were more intense in Vancouver. The construction boom of the 1920s and the subsequent slump in the 1930s, on the other hand, were more severe in the American city.

Such construction played a large part in sustaining the growth of both cities. Editorial writers and city publicists were inclined to ignore construction and provide reams of data on lumber and shingle shipments, bank clearances, and population growth. But year in and year out the construction of homes, apartment buildings, offices, stores, and warehouses was critical. Not only did such activity create a demand for local lumber and shingles, but it also provided employment for thousands of migrants as well as for resident carpenters, laborers, and real estate agents.

Vancouver's construction boom in the decade before World War I was especially energetic. At that time it had less than half Seattle's population, yet its construction approached and in some years exceeded that of its counterpart. Some idea of the magnitude of this activity can be gained from the fact that in the entire period from 1900 to 1945 it was only in the banner year 1929 that the value of construction in Vancouver exceeded that achieved in 1912. This sustained activity expanded and consolidated the structure outlined by earlier cpr decisions and would define Vancouver's basic land-use patterns for years to come.

Construction was citywide, ranging from small bungalows on 33-foot lots to massive department stores in the central business district. The great bulk of it consisted of single family houses in the West End, Kitsilano,

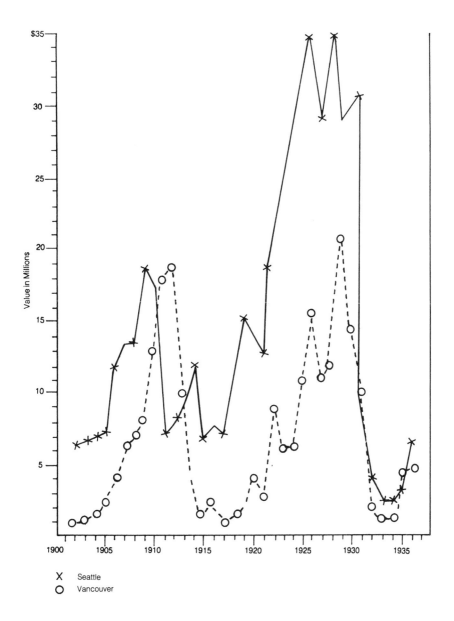

$35

30

25

20

15

10

5

Value in Millions

1900   1905   1910   1915   1920   1925   1930   1935

X   Seattle
O   Vancouver

Figure 6—Value of Construction in Seattle and Vancouver, 1902–1936. *Source: Vancouver Annual Report 1936*, "Report of Building Inspector," 91, lists the yearly value of building permits issued in the city from 1902 to 1936. See also *Seattle Building Department, Statistical Report of Building Permits 1936*. The data refer to the city proper, and do not include construction in suburban districts.

Fairview, Mount Pleasant, and Hastings. In 1906 alone, 23 houses were constructed on Sixth Avenue in Kitsilano, 35 on Seventh, 47 on Eighth, 31 on Ninth, and 30 on Tenth, while Comox, Robson, Nelson, and Barclay in the West End each had about 20. In the peak year 1912, 2,224 houses, 217 factories and warehouses, 293 offices and stores, and 218 apartments were built.[8] The land was bought from provincial authorities, the CPR, real estate concerns, or private owners, and was usually subdivided on a grid-iron pattern and sold in an unimproved state to individuals. Only infrequently was a block developed by one owner. In 1905 typical housing lots sold for $100–$200. A modest bungalow on a 33-foot lot sold for under $1,000 but the majority of houses fell in the $1,500–$2,500 range. A very few on large lots in prime residential areas sold for over $3,500.[9]

The central business district underwent dramatic changes. Whereas three- and four-storied frame and stone buildings dominated at the turn of the century, by 1914 Vancouver's downtown had been transformed with scores of eight- to fourteen-storied stone, brick, and concrete structures.[10] Much of this construction consisted of office blocks built by investors for rental to a variety of small concerns; banks, hotels, insurance companies, and shipping concerns usually built for their own use. The Hudson's Bay Company, Woodward's, Spencer's, and Birks either built anew or enlarged their stores, while the court house, post office, Hotel Vancouver, Carnegie Library, and the World Building provided prominent new landmarks.

Besides this private construction, authorities in both cities built new roads, sidewalks, water lines, sewage systems, parks, playgrounds, and schools. In 1901, for example, Seattle had a total of 120 miles of road. But as population increased and people moved further and further from the center of the city, a major extension of the street system was called for. In 1902, 15 miles of street were added, 1903—19 miles, 1904—18 miles, 1905—51 miles. As the city engineer exclaimed, "This is really an astounding rate of growth."[11] Much the same pattern was evident in the opening of new schools, the construction of water mains, the paving of sidewalks, and the provision of additional branch libraries. This type of growth and the desire to have superior water and sewage facilities led to a series of annexations. Between 1907 and 1910, Ravenna, Roosevelt, Ballard, Georgetown, West Seattle, South Seattle, and South East Seattle were all annexed. This boosted the city's population by about 48,000 and added some 37 square miles of territory. One of the biggest projects of all was the Denny Hill regrading. Beginning in 1908 pumps poured tons of water against gravelly hillsides and washed them into Elliott Bay. By the time the project was completed in 1911, this great obstacle north of the central business district was removed, and both pedestrians and street-cars could handle the gentle slopes with ease.[12] From 1900 to 1912 some 200 miles of streets were paved, 400 miles of water mains laid down, 525 miles of roads built, as well as 800 miles of concrete sidewalk.[13] Little wonder that merchants could exclaim "business has been phenomenal."

With immigrants arriving in unprecedented number, tramways opening new districts, and construction booming, real estate promotion and speculation became an integral part of the Vancouver business world. Hundreds became real estate agents—the *Vancouver Directory* of 1910 listed some 650—thousands of Vancouverites participated. Whether they dabbled or plunged depended on personal whim and available resources, but few were indifferent. As one exuberant promoter exclaimed, "Do you know how I would write a dissertation on 'How to be rich in Vancouver?' Take a map of the lower peninsula, shut your eyes, stick your finger anywhere and sit tight."[14]

Such activity was not a new phenomenon for Vancouver. At the time of the original boom of the late 1880s many who had speculated in real estate reaped handsome returns. But in the period from about 1890 to the early 1900s prices rose only modestly, about 6 percent per year.[15] The real surge began about 1904 and continued unabated to 1912. In an annual business survey the *News Advertiser* pointed out,

> With the real estate dealers 1909 has been a banner year in Vancouver. Three years ago it was prophesied that the real estate business had reached its apex and must decline; today prices have doubled and trebled and real estate brokers have probably made more money in 1909 than even in the early days of the great real estate movement about 3 years ago. Five years ago lots might have been purchased within the city limits for $50 each; now it would be difficult to secure a single lot anywhere in Vancouver for less than $600.[16]

With appropriate changes in prices the comment made about 1909 could be repeated for 1904, 1907, or 1912.

Among the numerous examples of profitable real estate transactions was the small 26-foot lot on Pender Street that was purchased from the CPR in 1887 for $480. The original owner held it for three months and sold for $600. By March 1888, it sold again for $1,500. It did not change hands again until 1904, when it sold for $4,000, and just two years later it sold once more, this time for $6,000.[17] Similarly, a 52-foot lot on Hastings Street owned by former Mayor C. S. Douglas, was sold in 1904 to the real estate firm of Martin and Robinson for $26,000. They held it for four years and sold in 1908 to N. Morin for $90,000 and he in turn sold it just one year later for $175,000.[18]

Even the U.S. consul in Vancouver felt the impact of surging real estate prices. Anxious to get a raise in pay he pointed out to his superiors in Washington, D.C., that the new landlord had increased his rent from $40 to $45 per month. He also sadly announced that the house he could have bought for $3,800 in 1897 had sold for $6,000 in 1905 and that the present owner had declined an offer of $10,000 for it in 1906.[19]

The boom in real estate peaked in 1912, and for those who held out for still higher prices it was a painful experience to see their paper profits suddenly evaporate. Although evidence abounds of the robust profits between 1887 and 1889 and from 1904 to 1912, it is not surprising that few people were willing to divulge the extent of their losses after 1912. No one liked to admit that he had failed to exploit a "sure thing" or—even worse—that he had lost heavily. Yet we do have some examples of the downslide. One owner of an expensive corner lot on Robson and Granville who had refused an offer of $250,000 in 1910, sold for $122,500 in 1916; another disillusioned investor sold his Granville-Helmcken lot for $40,000 in 1917, having rejected an offer of $125,000 in 1912.[20]

During these years a number of districts became firmly identified as "residential," "commercial," or "industrial." To appreciate this development one might consider Vancouver at the height of the Klondike Gold Rush in 1897–98. At that time the city occupied the small peninsula of land between Burrard Inlet and False Creek. It was strongly oriented to the waterfront with about 80 percent of its population of some 22,000 living within a mile of the CPR's depot, yards, and wharf near the foot of Granville Street.[21] The tramway along Granville, Hastings, and Main clearly identified the city's core and most of the city's retail businesses concentrated in that area, especially on Water, Cordova, and Hastings streets. Two industrial districts could also be distinguished, one on the waterfront with the CPR facilities, the British Columbia Sugar Refinery, and the Hastings sawmill, another on the north side of False Creek with lumber and shingle mills, wood-working plants, as well as the freight shed and roundhouse of the CPR. Homes were scattered throughout the community and some settlement had spread into East Hastings, Mount Pleasant, and the West End. Legally Vancouver covered some 10 square miles, but essentially the city was concentrated in 2 square miles: almost everyone could walk to work or to downtown stores in fifteen to twenty minutes.

By 1912 the patterns hinted at in 1898 were clearly delineated, and there was no doubt about the future layout of the entire city. Population had jumped to 115,000 and was spread over much of the peninsula from Burrard Inlet to the Fraser River, some 30 square miles in all. The legal city now amounted to 16 square miles. Business was still concentrated in the same core, but the cramped and limited quarters of Water and Cordova had evolved into a wholesale and warehouse district. Hastings, Pender, Granville, and Main were now the main business thoroughfares, and each had been extended and improved. The West End, early recognized as a desirable residential area, was heavily settled. Settlement had also followed the British Columbia Electric lines into Fairview, Kitsilano, and Point Grey, while Fourth Avenue and Broadway had acquired a variety of small retail outlets. Although no construction had taken place, extensive lands had been set aside for the future University of British Columbia. To the south Kerrisdale was developing, while Shaughnessy Heights, in the center of the CPR's land grant, was being hailed as the city's most elegant area. Throughout these years the long-established tendency for prosperous, socially prominent Vancouverites to settle in the western sections of the city, and for skilled workers and laborers to gravitate eastward continued. In the East End where lots were smaller and cheaper, with parks and playgrounds more limited, dynamic expansion occurred as well. Grandview and Collingwood had grown and the annexation of Hastings townsite in 1911 extended the eastern boundary of the city to some 4 miles from downtown. All of these districts were overwhelmingly residential, with single family frame houses nearly universal.

Industrial districts too were clearly delineated. Shipping facilities on the waterfront had been expanded, but most industrial activity concentrated in the False Creek Basin. In the 1890s it seemed likely that industry would remain localized on the north shore of the creek, and that the higher land of the south shore would evolve into a prime residential area. A number of substantial houses were built in Fairview and Mount Pleasant, but as the decade unfolded significant changes occurred. The CPR constructed a branch line along the south shore of the creek in 1902, and this hastened the industrial development of the entire area.[22] By 1903 the British Columbia Mill, Timber and Trading Company had shifted its major plant from the north to the south shore and this was followed by a host of lumber and shingle mills, machinery depots, and gravel and cement plants. The construction of additional freight lines and marshaling yards by the Great Northern and the Canadian Northern, the filling in of the tideflats east of Main Street, and the creation of Granville Island in 1914 marked the culmination of the industrialization of the False Creek area. Marpole, on the north arm of the Fraser River, also evolved as an industrial area. Its growth was aided by interurban rail facilities while the low land costs and the availability of river transport hastened the development of lumber and shingle mills, an abattoir, and a flour mill.[23]

The rapid growth of both Seattle and Vancouver during these years made it a difficult time for all administrators and elected officials. City hall bureaucrats were responsible for the roads, zoning changes, new schools, and permits for plumbers and electricians; the work seemed endless. Elected officials were ever conscious of a host of reform proposals. In Seattle's case voters approved municipal ownership of lighting plants, a telephone system, and the street railway system. Proposals to improve efficiency and economy and to make municipal government more "business-like" were also common. A commission form of government with city manager was proposed in 1914, but ultimately rejected. Another series of reform proposals sought to make municipal government more democratic and return city hall to "the common people." Municipal use of the initiatives was approved in 1908, and in 1910 the election of councilmen was changed from a ward system to an at-large system. There was also a prolonged fight against saloons, vice, and prostitution. Under the leadership of the Public Welfare League with strong support from Protestant churches, that fight peaked during the administration of Mayor Hiram Gill. Portrayed as an advocate of a "wide-open town" and as a menace to its moral climate, Gill was removed from office in the recall election of 1911. Though defeated in 1912 and 1913, Gill was returned to the mayoralty in 1914.[24]

City administrators in Vancouver found these years equally hectic, and it is not surprising that many resigned.[25] In 1906, for example, City Clerk A. McEvoy resigned his office while urging city council to appoint additional staff. By 1907 he was followed by the chief of police, then the city engineer, then the city solicitor. The mayor and city council felt the strain of the city's mushrooming growth too. Meetings and committee assignments took more and more time, but although aldermen complained of overwork there was at the same time a sense of excitement and satisfaction with the city's growth. Like their counterparts in other West Coast cities, the aldermen of Vancouver delighted in this growth, for it meant more people, more jobs, bigger payrolls, and greater opportunities for all. Many of them were directly involved in the city's business life—of the 1912 council of sixteen, for example, at least ten were in real estate or general business—so it is not surprising that they wanted this growth to continue.

Ten different mayors and some eighty different aldermen served Vancouver between 1900 and 1914, but with the exception of the administration of Louis D. Taylor, the general guidelines were consistent. Beyond the conviction that growth was desirable was the equally strong conviction that property owners should be free to develop their property as they saw fit, and that private enterprise should provide the basic municipal services and utilities. Vancouver owned and operated its own water works system, but this was the exception rather than the rule. The British Columbia Electric Railway provided both streetcar service and electric lighting. After 1904, it provided gas service as well.[26] Although complaints about inadequate service and high prices were perennial, and although rates charged were apparently much higher than in comparable Canadian and American cities, city council's opposition to municipal ownership was shared by the public. When plebiscites were held seeking authorization to borrow funds for the purchase of these facilities, they were decisively defeated.[27]

In line with the idea that private enterprise should be given free rein was the council's belief that city government should function primarily as a profitable, efficient, businesslike concern. Their task was not to direct or plan city growth, but to see that municipal services were available, that city regulations were met, and that funds were spent in an honest, impartial manner. Many considered the mayor-council system both unwieldy and inefficient, especially as new wards were added to the city and the number of aldermen increased from ten in 1902 to sixteen by 1912. Various charter amendments and new forms of city government were proposed, all of which aimed at withdrawing power from elected ward representatives and concentrating it in a small, highly centralized board. In 1907, for example, Mayor A. Bethune suggested that the city be managed by a board of control consisting of the mayor and three councillors. In 1910 Mayor Taylor supported a similar proposal and in 1911 extensive discussions were held on the desirability of establishing a commission form of government.[28] The plebiscites on these issues drew support from the business community and the city's more prosperous wards, but did not receive the necessary two-thirds majority. Similarly, a Royal Commission of 1912 investigated municipal government, and in 1914 the idea of a board of control was again brought forward.[29] None of these proposals were implemented, yet their recurrence suggests that municipal government was hard-pressed to keep up with the demands of rapid growth and change.

While city council favored private ownership and private enterprise, during these years a sense of public needs and public rights was also beginning to assert itself.[30] This was especially evident in council's insistence on the public's right of easy access to waterfront facilities. Local residents had long used the beaches along English Bay as public bathing areas, but the precise legal status of those areas was cloudy.[31] In 1902 the city began a policy of purchasing private lots for public swimming and picnic areas. By 1904, English Bay beach was ascertained to be in city hands, and in 1907 voters approved a bond issue for significant improvements to that beach.[32] The steady acquisition of a variety of parklands, the resistance to attempts to establish a lumber mill on Deadman's Island, and the vigor with which both council and public responded to any suggestion that Stanley Park might be developed or improved all indicate that the dominant philosophy did not go unchallenged.[33]

In Seattle too the years 1900 to 1914 were exciting as population, housing, streetcar lines, and businesses all expanded sharply. But as an older, more established city, changes were not as dramatic as in the younger, smaller Vancouver. By the turn of the century, for example, Seattle had over 80,000 residents and its 70-mile streetcar system already linked outlying residential and industrial districts to the downtown core. The construction of 165 miles of additional streetcar lines merely elaborated an already well-established system. During these years the American city also led the Canadian one in a significant extension of its park system, and in an early attempt, though ultimately unsuccessful, at comprehensive city planning.

In 1903 the regents of the University of Washington hired a firm of landscape architects—the Olmstead Brothers of Brookline, Massachusetts—to advise them on an appropriate layout for the university grounds.[34] The plan impressed university officials, and in time many of its recommendations were implemented. City officials were also impressed, for they hired the same organization to study Seattle's park needs.

The investigation and subsequent report on Seattle's parks was done by John Olmstead. He shared his famous father's conviction that parks should be a basic component of any urban environment.[35] The Olmsteads believed that parks should be adapted to the local topography, utilize the area's trees and shrubs, and be available to the entire community. They especially emphasized the need for natural, serene settings where harried urban dwellers could periodically escape from the city. The essence of the Olmstead park plan was to develop a continuous driveway, 20 miles long, that would tie together a whole series of parks, playgrounds, and parkways.[36] At appropriate sections along the main drive would be bicycle paths, picnic sites, and bathing beaches. In some places, especially along Lake Washington, the boulevard would be 150 feet wide, to accommodate "tens of thousands" of people, whereas in difficult terrain or less scenic spots it would be much narrower. There would be local parks and squares, too, but all of this was meant to supplement the major driveway, which was to remain the unifying factor for the entire system.

City council adopted the Olmstead Report on November 16, 1903, and it automatically became the master plan for the city's park system. Prior to this report Seattle's park development was very limited and funding meager. As late as 1898, when the city had a population of 65,000, total parkland amounted to only 70 acres, nearly half of this the gift of wealthy benefactors.[37] All this changed after the report. Between 1907 and 1913, city voters offered a series of special bond issues amounting to $4 million.[38] With such unparalleled sums at their disposal, with the Olmstead guidelines to follow, and with the added incentive of wanting to have the city at its best for the Alaska-Yukon-Pacific (AYP) Exposition of 1909, the Parks Board bought aggressively. By 1913 Seattle had twenty-five parks amounting to 1,400 acres, as well as 400 acres in playgrounds, pathways, boulevards, and triangles. More lands would be added in the future, but for all practical purposes it was the great surge of 1907–13 that established Seattle's park system.

There can be little doubt that the Olmstead Report of 1903 was one of the basic determinants of the city's park system, and that it fully exploited Seattle's beautiful lakes, ravines, waterways, and hilltops. Anyone who has visited Volunteer Park, walked through Ravenna Park, the Arboretum, or driven along Lake Washington Boulevard is thankful for Olmstead's insight, and for the Park Board's perseverance in implementing his ideas. Yet this sustained channeling of resources into the creation of a "continuous scenic drive" meant that parks in the downtown area were slighted. Similarly, Olmstead's conviction that the public could best be served by providing a view of the natural and the picturesque downplayed the need for public recreational facilities. It is true that the 1903 report did not ignore such facilities, but they were given a decidedly secondary role.

Vancouver too expanded its park facilities during these years with the expenditure of over $1 million for the purchase of diverse sites and bathing beaches. But their purchases essentially elaborated and extended a system that had begun in 1887 with the city's acquisition of Stanley Park. That 950-acre peninsula was so prominent and well established that it tended to shape and monopolize later expenditures, and to link them to that major park. Though this led to very desirable facilities accessible to the downtown region, it tended to cater to middle-class interests on the west side and to downplay the needs of the less-prosperous east side.

This pattern was upheld by the remarkable continuity of membership in the Vancouver Parks Board. From the 1890s through the 1920s terms of six, eight, ten, and more years were not uncommon.[39] As a group these park commissioners were well-to-do businessmen aware that attractive parks and especially Stanley Park would boost adjacent real estate values, provide a significant tourist attraction, and serve Vancouver's more prosperous elements. Their commitment to the acquisition of waterfront property for public use can bring nothing but praise, but it would not be until the post–World War II years that Vancouver's working-class east side would begin to get the parks and recreational facilities long enjoyed by the more prosperous west side. Park development in Vancouver during the pre–World War I decade was significant, yet it essentially continued a long-established pattern without the abrupt change occasioned by the Olmstead Report in Seattle.

During the years that Seattle's officials were implementing Olmstead's park plans they became increasingly convinced that not only the city's parks but the city's streets, schools, hospitals, transportation systems, and housing arrangements could all profit from such planning. But rather than treat each component separately, a comprehensive city plan should be developed that would provide a guide for city officials to follow. Such a plan would make for a more orderly development of the city's diverse districts, reduce conflict over land use, improve transportation facilities, and generally make Seattle a more attractive and functional community.

In 1910 the city hired Virgil R. Bogue, a widely experienced engineer and planner, to make a detailed study of Seattle and provide guidelines for its future development. At a time when Seattle had a population of about 250,000 and covered some 70 square miles, Bogue was directed to plan in terms of a region of some 150 square miles and a future population of a million.[40] With the help of a small staff he spent a year collecting material and preparing the analyses and ultimately submitted a hefty 191-page report.[41]

Bogue's *Plan of Seattle* (1911) treated five major issues. The first focused on realignment of improvement of the city's streets and the development of an arterial highway system. A number of major north-south highways were suggested as well as arterials to the downtown business district. A second and critical component was the construction of a major civic center at Fourth Avenue and Blanchard Street. It would bring together federal and municipal buildings and act as a focal point for the entire community. "It must have the air of far-seeing urbanity," he stressed, and "cannot be manifested within narrow limits." Bogue's engineering background and approach were especially evident in his treatment of

Seattle's harbor and port facilities. In his analysis of the central waterfront, Lake Union, and the Duwamish waterway, he outlined in meticulous detail the precise facilities to be constructed. A fourth area of concern focused on park facilities and beautification projects. Bogue considered the existing facilities adequate for Seattle itself, but suggested the acquisition of 3,000 additional acres of parkland beyond the city limits. These were to be connected by an extensive parkway network along the lines already developed by Olmstead. A final section suggested a variety of improvements for the city's railroad network. Two new railroad stations were recommended, one to the north for passengers, one to the south for freight. In addition, a 90-mile rapid transit system was proposed.

Although public attention subsequently focused on Bogue's proposal for a civic center, such "City Beautiful" suggestions made up only a small proportion of the total report. About 30 pages of the report were devoted to the civic center, parks, and beautification projects. But Bogue's real convictions about urban planning came out in the other 160 pages, where step by step and item by item he treated the location of streets and highways, the establishment of water channels, the construction of docks and freight sheds, and the development of an appropriate transportation system. The report left no doubt that such steps would transform Seattle into a functional, efficient city.

Though one might admire Bogue's technical expertise, his plan was not as comprehensive or as thorough as he had hoped. His concern with highways, railroads, freight sheds, and dock facilities gave little attention to the housing needs of thousands of Seattleites, let alone their social or cultural aspirations. The very precision of his recommendations made for a certain "take it or leave it" attitude and the expectation that his recommendations could be implemented without any special legislation or administrative powers revealed a rather naive view of the political process.

The *Plan of Seattle* was given wide circulation and publicity. Vigorously supported by the Municipal Plans Commission, Seattle Municipal League, Protestant churches, and prominent officials like City Engineer R. H. Thomson, it also faced united opposition.[42] Downtown business interests were especially active. They disliked the location and concept of the civic center, did not approve of the new railroad depots, and saw the plan as one that disrupted business and threatened property values. Organized labor also opposed the plan. When presented to the voters for a final decision in the municipal election of 1912 it was overwhelmingly defeated by a vote of 24,996 to 14,506. In not one of Seattle's fourteen wards did it receive majority support.

Analysts and authors have had a field day explaining why the Bogue Plan was defeated. The Municipal League's *Newsletter* suggested that the defeat was caused by a lack of public understanding, a conviction that the plan was too rigid, and a fear of possible consequences of the plan for individual property owners. Others suggested that the Municipal Plans Commission had done a poor job of packaging the proposal, and that it was last among the forty-two other issues that crowded the ballot. James A. Barnes of the Seattle City Planning Commission wrote in 1954 that such plans lacked "financial realism." [43] Roger Sale, in his sensitive and perceptive *Seattle: Past to Present,* sees it as but one more symbol of the indifference of an older, established generation of Seattleites, who had withdrawn to the comforts of suburbia and were no longer concerned with the problems of the city. [44] William H. Wilson argued in 1984 that Bogue disregarded Seattle's natural topography, and that his plan was "hopelessly extravagant." [45]

All these suggestions have merit, but at the core of the issue one must emphasize that there never had been a major commitment to planning in Seattle. As such, the Bogue Plan marked a sharp departure from the past. It is true that middle-class professionals saw merit in such a plan, but for thousands of owners, big and small, it represented a potential threat to their property, and a curb to their individual freedom. It is probably fair to say that the truly remarkable thing about the vote on the Bogue Plan was not that it was defeated by a two to one margin, but that some 15,000 Seattle voters supported this drastic break from the past. This degree of support possibly reflected the mood of the Progressive Era but not until the Depression of the 1930s would such a large body of people again look kindly on the desirability of planning.

While Seattleites were debating the merits of the Bogue Plan, Vancouver was considering planning proposals, though at a much more modest level. In 1912 the Vancouver Parks Board hired Thomas Mawson, an English landscape architect, to prepare a comprehensive design for the entrance to Stanley Park and the whole Coal Harbor area. After an unsuccessful attempt to have the scope of his work extended, Mawson proposed a variety of schemes. The most grandiose involved the creation of a large fresh water lake, with a 180-foot statue at its center. Adjacent to the lake was a massive city stadium, as well as a museum, playgrounds, and restaurants. Like his even more elaborate proposal for Calgary in 1914, little came of Mawson's plan, and with the outbreak of war it was soon forgotten.

The growth and change in Seattle and Vancouver during these years went beyond the accumulation of more people, more parks, more streetcar lines, and more plans for the future. Other less tangible but significant change occurred as well. The small-town and regional outlook so typical of these communities at the turn of the century was gradually lost. Both cities evolved into diverse, metropolitan centers more and more integrated into a national economy and a national culture. The process unfolded somewhat earlier and faster in the American than in the Canadian setting, but there is no doubt that the Seattle and Vancouver of World War I were very different from what they had been at the time of the Klondike Gold Rush.

In one sense at least, both cities revealed a continuity with previous decades. The majority of their workers still gained their livelihood providing the goods and services needed by fellow urbanites and residents throughout the region. Clerks, secretaries, schoolteachers, and real estate agents were still the representative occupations. In both Seattle and Vancouver some 75 to 80 percent of the work force were in such trade, transportation, and service activities.[46] Manufacturing accounted for about 15 percent of the work force, with most of it concentrated in lumber and shingle mills, along with a great number of small, locally oriented plants that turned out bakery products, beer, confectionery, and specialized machinery. Workers in primary activities like mining, forestry, fishing, and agriculture accounted for about 5 percent of the work force.

The change from folksy small town to metropolitan center was especially rapid in Vancouver. The chatty, local columns that had been a staple item in the eight-paged local papers of the 1890s faded into the background as the 1900s unfolded. By 1912 weekend editions ran from forty to sixty pages. National and international events dominated the news, special sections treated business, sports, society, and entertainment. One might still recognize a prominent lumberman or real estate broker as he strolled along Hastings or Granville, but this became the exception as years went by. There were just too many new companies, new offices, new faces, and new millionaires. Unless one belonged to the Vancouver Club or the Terminal City Club or was active in the Board of Trade, one had little chance to know who these men were, let alone recognize them. The visiting salesman from Montreal, Chicago, or London would still consider the city a comfortable, prosperous, low-keyed community. But for the resident who had arrived at the time of the Klondike Gold Rush, or possibly even before the CPR, Vancouver had been transformed. Now that the city was three times as large as Victoria, the heated competition of the 1880s and 1890s could be dismissed as that "era of parochial rivalry."[47] The general scope of the city's activities had also broadened. Many prominent businessmen now worked as managers, agents, or salesmen for national companies, and national products. But as Vancouverites promoted mines in the Kootenays, publicized investment opportunities in the Okanagan, or sold timber and shingles on the prairies, there is no doubt that they operated far beyond the city's boundaries.

Seattle's nationalizing process was hardly new—it had been under way since the city's founding in the 1850s and had been speeded up with the transcontinental rail links of the 1880s. By 1910 Seattle still catered to the needs of the Puget Sound area, but it was becoming an integral component of a national system, tied to the characteristics, requirements, and fluctuations in that system. Here too the city's newspapers were a clear reflection of this phenomenon. No longer did local events dominate the news, rather attention focused on national and international events. Congressional developments were closely followed, and statements by Presidents Theodore Roosevelt and Woodrow Wilson treated at length. Sports and comics were displayed prominently, but now it was the big game between Harvard and Yale that got the attention rather than the baseball series between Seattle and Tacoma. The Seattle housewife, like her counterpart in Atlanta, Omaha, or Sacramento, was continually reminded that she could buy Campbell's tomato soup, Post's cereal, Westinghouse light bulbs, or Ivory soap (99 and 44/100 percent pure) from her neighborhood store. Her husband could drive a Buick or Studebaker, use Standard Oil products in his car, listen to an Edison-Victor phonograph, or enjoy a bottle of Blatz's Milwaukee beer at a corner tavern. The fact that as a lumber broker he also kept a close watch on prices in Minnesota, North Carolina, and Texas all suggested that Seattle's isolation from the rest of the nation was now a thing of the past.

The Alaska Yukon Pacific Exposition of 1909 provides a convenient symbol of Seattle's dramatic growth in the decade before World War I. Held on a specially developed site on the University of Washington campus, and supported by substantial state and federal funds, as well as by $500,000 raised in one day by a spectacular reassertion of the "Old Seattle Spirit," the AYP Exposition dominated Seattle for much of the year. Between June 1 and October 16 almost 3 million people visited the fairgrounds to examine the diverse exhibits and enjoy the amusements, games, and rides. At one level the AYP Exposition was a fairly standard one, with its exhibits, displays, and usual complement of promoters anxious to make some money. But beyond this, the exposition also symbolized and dramatized Seattle's growth. Thousands of Seattleites were excited by this growth, anxious to publicize the city's achievements, and convinced that the exposition would be a springboard to even more development. Yet although Seattle would continue to grow in the following years the rate would decline, and the enthusiasm of 1909 would soon be lost in the dislocation and tension of the war years. Rather than marking the takeoff into a new and even brighter future, the AYP Exposition marked the end of an era.

One might view the establishment of the Half Million Club in Vancouver as analogous to the AYP Exposition. In 1905 an organization of businessmen calling themselves the Hundred Thousand Club had coined the slogan "In 1910, Vancouver then, will have 100,000 men." As population surged in the latter part of the decade they awaited the results of the Canadian census with lively anticipation. According to city hall Vancouver already had a population of 111,245, but since these were local figures, and open to the charge of distortion, the Hundred Thousand Club was delighted when the census of 1911 officially revealed that Vancouver had 100,401 residents. Flushed with success and aware that this meant that Vancouver had almost quadrupled in ten years, the organization was renamed the Half Million Club. There was little doubt in the minds of these businessmen that the growth of the previous years would continue and that by 1917 greater Vancouver would reach that mark. The year when greater Vancouver actually reached 500,000 was never precisely identified, but rather than taking five or six years it actually took about thirty-five years. The Half Million Club's boosterism is understandable given the nature of the previous decade. But 1912, rather than marking the beginning of vigorous new growth, actually marked the end of one of the most significant growth cycles in Vancouver's history.

5

A Generation of Business Leaders

It is highly unlikely that Frank Whitney Baker and Robert Purves McLennan ever met each other or even knew each other existed. Both were prosperous businessmen who lived just 150 miles apart and both had comparable backgrounds, associations, and achievements. But although Baker's career in Seattle and McLennan's in Vancouver evolved in similar ways, their lives and activities showed distinctive characteristics. An examination of their careers both before and after their arrival on the West Coast offers insight into the nature of a whole generation of business leaders. No one person can be considered typical of a city's entire business community, but Baker and McLennan are reasonably representative of the generation of business leaders that shaped these cities in the expansive period from the 1880s to World War I, when both cities mushroomed from relative obscurity to substantial metropolitan status.

Like many young people before and since Frank Baker was both excited and apprehensive about leaving home in 1868.[1] He was then sixteen and except for occasional visits to nearby Niagara Falls and Buffalo had never been away from Youngstown, New York. His family was quite comfortable financially, for the move away from home was for Frank's further education. He was first sent to Genessee Wesleyan Seminary in Lima, New York, and later to Eastman Business College in Poughkeepsie, New York. After finishing his business training, Baker became a schoolteacher. But in his early twenties, he decided to abandon both New York and teaching and start anew farther west. He lived for a while in Greenville, a small town in central Michigan, where he was employed by a retail hardware merchant. Baker profited from his experience, and after a few years accepted a position as bookkeeper for the Black Hardware Company of Detroit. In December 1888, he returned briefly to New York to marry Jennie Godfrey of Lima.

It is quite possible that the newlyweds would have settled permanently in Detroit but for the Seattle Fire of June 6, 1889. This spectacular blaze gutted a large part of Seattle. Baker's employers, Clarence, Frank, and Charles Black, decided it might be opportune to transfer their operations to that Puget Sound city. Seattle had a population of about 30,000, and was expanding rapidly. The Blacks reasoned that the normally heavy demand for hardware in a growing community would be vastly increased as a result of the fire losses. Sometime in late 1889 or early 1890 they purchased controlling interest in the Seattle Hardware Company. Baker was invited to come as bookeeper for the new firm and accepted promptly.

He was thirty-eight years old when he arrived in Seattle in March 1890. Though his progress was not spectacular, it was steady. By 1894 he had advanced from bookkeeper to manager of the credit department. Three years later he was treasurer of the Seattle Hardware Company, and would hold that position until he resigned from the firm in 1910. During this period he became increasingly more interested in a wide variety of financial concerns. In 1906 he organized and became president of the Title Trust Company, which did both general banking and trust business. In 1920 he was chosen vice-president of the newly organized Commercial State Bank. He retained this position and a directorship after its reorganization as the National City Bank. From 1914 on he was treasurer of the Sparger Construction Company, and in 1918 became treasurer of the Occidental Land Company. He was also active in business ventures in Alaska.

Baker's success in the Seattle business world was mirrored in the successive changes in his residence. He and Mrs. Baker first lived at 804 Columbia Street, about six blocks from the Seattle Hardware Company at First Avenue and Marion Street. In 1901 they moved to 1221 Minor Avenue, which still allowed ready access to the business district less than a mile away. The Bakers remained there for seven years, then in 1908 moved to their newly constructed home at 1212 Highland Place, a prosperous residential neighborhood on Queen Anne Hill.

Outside of the business world, Baker was active in a number of social and charitable organizations. He belonged to the Rainier, Arctic, Commercial, Seattle Golf, and Seattle Athletic clubs. In addition, he was a member of the Seattle Chamber of Commerce, the Masons, Shrine, Nile, and Fine Arts Society. He and Mrs. Baker were also active in the Charity Organization Society of Seattle, of which he was chairman. Baker was a Protestant, and in politics a Republican. He never ran for public office, though he was suggested as a possible candidate for mayor. During his later life Baker was in poor health, and from 1915 on was in semiretirement. He died March 13, 1919, at the age of sixty-seven. His estate, valued at $260,000, was left primarily to his wife, as they had no children. Lesser amounts were also willed to a number of charitable organizations.

Baker's Vancouver counterpart, or at least a representative business leader in the Canadian city, was Robert McLennan.[2] In many ways McLennan is better known than Baker, for he established a wholesale firm that still plays an important role in Vancouver, yet the basic similarity in the backgrounds and careers of the two men is quite striking. McLennan grew up in Pictou, Nova Scotia, a small town of about 2,000 in a predominantly Scotch-Presbyterian environment. He attended the regionally renowned Pictou Academy until about fifteen, then took his first job in a hardware store in town. He remained for two years, then moved to River John, a shipbuilding village about 10 miles away. Shortly after, like countless other Nova Scotians who found limited opportunity in the region, McLennan decided to leave. In 1882, when he was twenty-one, he headed for Winnipeg, then on the threshold of rapid expansion. After two years in the hardware business there, he returned home. But finding little changed, he decided to move again, this time to the West Coast. After a trip on the recently completed Northern Pacific Railroad, he worked briefly in the United States but finally opted for Victoria, British Columbia, in 1884.

He opened a small establishment where he made and sold a variety of tinware and building supplies. Business proved good and within a year he invited Jim McFeely, an old Winnipeg friend, then working in Minneapolis, to join him. The two young partners were aware of the expected completion of the Canadian Pacific Railway and in 1885 established an additional store in Vancouver. Throughout the 1880s and early 1890s both branches prospered. In 1896 the main center of operations was transferred to Vancouver and the firm incorporated as McLennan, McFeely and Company Ltd. With the Klondike Gold Rush of the late 1890s McLennan moved once again, this time to Dawson in the Yukon Territory where he opened another general hardware store. He remained there for six years and served a term as mayor of Dawson before returning permanently to Vancouver in 1904. His timing was good, for Vancouver was just beginning a major boom that would last for the next eight years.

Besides his success in the business world McLennan was active and prominent elsewhere. He served on the Board of Governors of the University of British Columbia and of McGill, ran as a Liberal candidate for a seat in the provincial legislature, was a member of the prestigious Vancouver Club and Terminal City Club, and served a term as president of the Vancouver Board of Trade. He and his wife, the former Bessie McKenzie of River John, Nova Scotia, had nine children. A number of his sons were active in the family business.

The careers of Baker and McLennan are distinctive in their own right but they also reveal many of the characteristics of the generation of businessmen who shaped Seattle and Vancouver in the late nineteenth and early twentieth century. Both grew up in small-town eastern environments. Both benefited from education beyond the public school system. Baker had considerable business experience in Detroit and McLennan in Winnipeg. Both were relatively young when they arrived on the West Coast, and both would qualify as self-made men. Both were Protestant and members of elite social clubs. Baker was a Republican, but McLennan, unlike most Vancouver businessmen, supported the Liberal party. It is also significant that the Vancouver businessman was much more active politically than his Seattle counterpart, for not only did McLennan serve a term as mayor of Dawson, but also ran for a seat in the British Columbia legislature. Both men left substantial estates, with most of it willed to their immediate family.

In the remainder of this chapter similar findings will be presented on a large number of Seattle and Vancouver business leaders, though in a much briefer fashion than for Baker and McLennan. Some comparisons will be made between the local business leaders of this 1885–1915 generation, and the national business elite of that same era. In addition, the probated wills of a large number of these business leaders will be analyzed to gain further insights into their careers and values.

The basic prerequisite for qualification as a Seattle business leader in my sample was that the individual be president of a firm in the city. This requirement eliminated those who were vice-presidents, general managers, or superintendents. These officers held responsible positions, and in some instances probably were more influential than was the president in guiding the destiny of the firm. But in the greater number of cases such officers were responsible to others for basic policy decisions. By restricting entry to presidents only, the sample tended to center on the dominant men in Seattle business firms.

Not all company presidents or heads of organizations qualified automatically. The business leader must have promoted or controlled some form of economic activity that had significant consequences for Seattle's total employment or total productivity. Thus heads of manufacturing plants, bank presidents, promoters of railroads or steamship lines, and wholesale merchants qualified as business leaders. On the other hand, proprietors of grocery stores, contractors, presidents of legal firms, or heads of real estate concerns, were not considered business leaders.

With these qualifications in mind, eighteen biographical sources were covered in detail to obtain a list of Seattle business leaders who were active between 1885 and 1915.[3] These sources consisted of the biographical volumes of local histories, local *Who's Who,* and a variety of reference works. Because the biographical information on those included in only one or two sources was often scanty, such listings were excluded from the sample. This elimination not only reduced the working sample, but focused on those men who had received attention from many editors. On this basis eighty-seven men qualified as business leaders.

This particular approach for obtaining a sample has obvious drawbacks. The most serious objection is that many borderline cases must be decided on scanty evidence. Should a real estate agent with a small staff be rejected as a business leader, while another man who ran a shingle mill with a similar-sized work force be included? Should a prosperous building contractor be classified as a business leader? On what specific grounds should the president of a painters' supply house be rejected, while the president of a wholesale grocery is included?

It should also be stressed that the works from which the biographical details have been obtained are far from ideal source material. Many of these volumes were prepared on a subscription basis.[4] If an individual would not pay for his biographical sketch and portrait, he was not included. Consequently, some legitimate business leaders are missing in our sample of eighty-seven men. Baily Gatzert, for example, a prominent Seattle banker, merchant, and reputed millionaire, is conspicuously absent from these biographical volumes. On the other hand, some men were undoubtedly included because they were willing to pay the subscription fee, rather than because of their accomplishments. In addition, the articles in these volumes are almost invariably laudatory, and the "rags to riches" story is presented with numerous variations.

Regardless of the shortcoming of these biographical volumes, or the definition of business leader followed here, it is highly likely that these eighty-seven men would form the nucleus of any study of Seattle's business leaders in the late nineteenth and early twentieth centuries.

Seattle Business Leaders 1885–1915

Edward W. Andrews, banker
P. F. Apfel, electrical equipment manufacturer
Morris A. Arnold, banker
Manson F. Backus, banker
Frank W. Baker, banker, merchant
J. F. Ballaine, railroad promoter
William R. Ballard, banker, promoter
D. W. Bass, lumberman
Alden J. Blethen, newspaper publisher
W. M. Bolcom, lumberman
D. W. Bowen, sheet metal manufacturer
J. S. Brace, lumberman
Albert M. Brookes, food manufacturer
A. Buhtz, lumberman
Thomas Burke, railroad promoter
E. E. Caine, steamship line promoter
Ernest Carstens, meat packing
Herman Chapin, banker
Andrew Chilberg, banker
John E. Chilberg, financier, promoter
C. H. Clarke, fish packing
C. H. Cobb, lumberman
James M. Colman, lumberman, railroad promoter
George Danz, iron manufacturer
Arthur A. Denny, merchant, banker, manufacturer
Nathan Eckstein, merchant, banker
J. C. Eden, cement manufacturer
C. F. Farnsworth, merchant, manufacturer

James C. Ford, steamship line
William R. Forrest, clay manufacturer
John M. Frink, steel manufacturer
G. F. Frye, merchant, lumberman
Jacob Furth, banker, promoter, manufacturer
D. Gilman, railroad promoter
James P. Gleason, banker
Albert J. Goddard, iron manufacturer
T. J. Gorman, fish canning
E. O. Graves, banker
E. I. Grondahl, banker
John T. Heffernan, machinery manufacturer
Alvin Hemrich, brewer
Andrew Hemrich, brewer
Louis Hemrich, brewer
Martin J. Henehan, railroad equipment manufacturer
Horace C. Henry, railroad construction, financier
James D. Hoge, banker
Dexter Horton, banker
J. Isaacson, iron manufacturer
G. James, iron manufacturer
John W. Kahle, food manufacturer
Wilmer J. Kahle, food manufacturer
Daniel K. Kelleher, banker
A. S. Kerry, lumberman
Edward C. Kilbourne, street railroad promoter
C. W. Kucher, iron manufacturer
Frank S. Lang, stove manufacturer
Norval H. Latimer, banker
John Leary, lumberman, promoter

Charles H. Lilly, seed merchant

James D. Lowman, stationery manufacturer, merchant

A. MacKintosh, banker, promoter, lumberman

James A. Moore, steel manufacturer, real estate

Robert Moran, shipbuilder

E. Neufelder, banker, merchant

Frank H. Osgood, street railroad promoter

W. D. Perkins, investment securities

William Piggott, steel manufacturer

P. Polson, farm equipment manufacturer

John E. Price, banker, promoter

Albert J. Rhodes, merchant

William L. Rhodes, merchant

J. Rosene, promoter of commercial companies

Thomas Sanders, lumberman

J. Schram, merchant, banker

E. Shorrock, banker

Henry O. Shuey, financier, real estate promoter

A. B. Stewart, wholesale druggist

Charles D. Stimson, lumberman

Frederick K. Struve, banker

Elbridge A. Stuart, dairy products manufacturer

M. Thomsen, flour milling

H. W. Treat, financier

Lester Turner, banker

Frank Waterhouse, steamship line promoter

Robert G. Westerman, iron manufacturer

O. Williams, lumberman

W. Wood, promoter of transportation lines

A number of valuable sources exist for a study of Vancouver's business leaders during these years, but the biographical volumes and local *Who's Who* are not as numerous or comprehensive as those available for Seattle.[5] Consequently, the techniques used to identify business leaders in the Canadian city are somewhat different than those followed for Seattle. I am greatly indebted to R. A. J. McDonald's comprehensive study "Business Leadership in Vancouver 1890–1914," for not only does it identify a specific group of business leaders, but it also provides a great number of ideas and insights on that group.[6]

McDonald focused on business leadership during two periods of rapid expansion, 1890–93, and 1910–14. If an 1890–93 company had $100,000 in assets, or a 1910–14 company $500,000, its president was automatically identified as among the city's business elite. Where company assets were unknown, more subjective interpretations and standards were applied. Thus the size of a work force and a contemporary account of a businessman's role or a company's influence qualified others. Under this procedure a business elite of 21 was established for 1890–93 period, and 90 for the years from 1910–14. On the basis of this group of 111 persons (21+90) I carried the selection process one step further, to make the final sample more directly comparable with the group of Seattle's business leaders studied. All persons who were vice-president, treasurer, director, and so on were eliminated from the Vancouver sample. In addition, presidents engaged only in real estate activity were excluded, as were those for whom no significant biographical data could be obtained. On this basis a final sample of 36 persons was obtained, and it is this small, select group who will be studied here.[7] During 1885–1915 Seattle's population was about two and a half to three times as large as Vancouver's. Consequently, samples of 87 business leaders from Seattle and 36 from Vancouver are approximately proportionate. Since the definition of business leader was also similar, we have reasonably comparable samples from the two cities.

Vancouver Business Leaders 1885–1915

Harry B. Abbott, railroad management
Richard H. Alexander, lumberman
Alvo von Alvensleben, promoter, financier
W. H. Armstrong, construction
Henry O. Bell-Irving, fish canner
Frederick Buscombe, merchant
F. Carter-Cotten, financier, newspaperman
H. T. Ceperley, finance, milling
W. H. P. Clubb, merchant, banker
Charles Doering, brewer
Thomas Dunn, merchant
William Farrell, merchant, shipper
William Godfrey, banker
John Hanbury, lumberman
E. H. Heaps, lumberman
John Hendry, lumberman
R. K. Houlgate, financier
Andrew Jukes, banker
J. C. Keith, banker
Robert Kelly, wholesale merchant

T. Langlois, financier
Edward J. McFeely, merchant
J. W. McFarland, financier, promoter
Robert P. McLennan, merchant, banker
A. D. McRae, lumber, fisheries
William H. Malkin, wholesale merchant
A. R. Mann, construction
H. W. Maynard, coal mine operator
Edwin B. Morgan, banker
David Oppenheimer, merchant, promoter
Benjamin T. Rogers, sugar manufacturer
Jonathan Rogers, finance, construction
R. H. Sperling, street railway promoter
J. E. Tucker, lumberman
Alfred Wallace, shipbuilder
Charles Woodward, merchant

Table 6   Birthplace of Seattle's Business Leaders
and Total Population in 1900

| | Business Leaders | | Total Population |
	Number	%	%
New England & Mid Atl.	25	28.7	13.5
North Central	30	34.5	26.4
South	4	4.6	4.4
Mt. & Pacific	3	3.5	28.2
Scandinavia	5	5.7	5.8
Gr. Britain & Ireland	6	6.9	6.1
Canada	8	9.2	4.7
Germany	4	4.6	2.4
Other foreign-born	2	2.3	7.3

Source: U.S. Census, 1900, vol. 1, Pt. 1, pp. 710–13.

It is not surprising these leaders were all men—few women occupied executive positions in the business world at that time. It is also not surprising that virtually all of these leaders were migrants. Washington and British Columbia had not been settled long and the small local-born population were predominantly children or young adults. It is also noteworthy that almost all of these businessmen were married. Though these general characteristics were similar, the two groups of leaders show a number of distinctions when examined more closely. The distribution of these leaders by birthplace is shown in Table 6.

The data show that most of Seattle's business leaders were native-born Americans from a cluster of states in the northeastern section of the nation. New York State, for example, contributed eleven business leaders to Seattle, Wisconsin followed with eight, and Ohio with six. Although this older, more-developed section of the nation tended to be overrepresented, business leaders came from all regions of the United States as well as from Britain, Europe, and Canada. It is also noteworthy that twenty-five out of Seattle's eighty-seven business leaders were foreign-born, and as such corresponded closely with the percentage of foreign-born in the city's population. A look at comparable data on Vancouver shows a decidedly different picture; see Table 7.

The most striking feature in Table 7 is that persons born outside Canada accounted for over half of Vancouver's business leaders. The overrepresentation of persons born in Britain was especially significant. Although such migrants made up 16 percent of the population in 1900, they accounted for 44 percent of the business leaders. The sample is small, so one must be cautious about the significance of smaller groups. In each case the addition or subtraction of just one individual would make a sharp change in the relative importance of that group. Thus the drastic over-representation of German-born leaders is somewhat deceptive. David Oppenheimer of Bavaria, for example, was unquestionably important during Vancouver's early years, but he died in 1897. Similarly, Alvo von Alvens-leben achieved meteoric success following his arrival in 1904. But as an enemy alien during World War I he lost virtually everything and disappeared into relative obscurity in the United States. Only Charles Doering, who arrived in 1882, and later became president of Vancouver Breweries Ltd. achieved a long and successful career. He died a wealthy, prominent figure in 1927.

But even with these qualifications there is no question about the importance of immigrants from Britain, the United States, and Germany. If business leadership in Vancouver at the turn of the century was distinctive, it undoubtedly reflected the training, style, and values of persons born outside Canada, especially in England and Scotland. Seattle too had numbers of foreign-born business leaders, but such persons were not over-represented. Rather it was a decidedly "American" business community.

The men who became business leaders in these two cities were from a

Table 7   Birthplace of Vancouver's Business Leaders
and Total Population in 1901

| | Business Leaders | | Total Population |
	Number	%	%
Maritimes	2	5.5	5.4
Quebec	2	5.5	2.4
Ontario	10	28.0	14.6
Prairies	—	—	2.0
B.C. & other	—	—	37.0
Gr. Britain & Ireland	16	44.4	16.0
United States	3	8.3	6.8
Germany	3	8.3	0.7
Other Foreign-born	—	—	15.2

Source: Census of Canada, 1901, vol. 1, Table 14, p. 418. See notes 2, 5, 6 of Chapter 5 for sources of biographical detail.

somewhat different mold than the average American or Canadian citizen of that time. The importance of Englishmen and Scotsmen in Vancouver has been emphasized but, in addition, business leaders in both cities were much more likely to be the sons of businessmen, professionals, or skilled craftsmen then was true of the population at large. Between 1830 and 1880 some 60 percent of the U.S. population aged ten and over were engaged in agricultural pursuits.[8] Yet 65 percent of the fathers of Seattle's leaders were in nonagricultural pursuits. A comparable pattern was evident in the backgrounds of Vancouver's leaders. But as many of these leaders gave no information on their fathers' occupation, this point can not be made as precisely as in the Seattle case.

There is little doubt about the educational level of Seattle's business leaders, as data are available for all eighty-seven men. Among Vancouver's leaders, on the other hand, the evidence is incomplete and ambiguous. In many cases we learn only that the Vancouver leader "attended public schools" or "was educated in the local schools." Consequently, some distinctions in Table 8 are little more than a guess, based on the background and early working career of that particular individual.

The data indicate that the Seattle business leader had somewhat more formal education than his Vancouver counterpart. This was especially true of university graduates. Seattle had 14, Vancouver had but 2. Statistical data on the educational levels of Washington's residents are unavailable for the 1880s, 1890s, and early 1900s.[9] But in 1910 the United States had about 1 college graduate for every 100 men over the age of twenty.[10] There

Table 8   Education Level of Business Leaders

	Seattle		Vancouver	
	Number	%	Number	%
University graduate	14	16	2	7
University attended	21	24	6	21
High school or equivalent	30	34	17	58
Grade school only	22	25	4	14

Source: Bagley, *History of Seattle*, vols. 2, 3; Howay and Scholefield, *British Columbia from Earliest Times to the Present*, vols. 3–5. For a complete listing of the biographical sources see notes 1, 2, 3, and 5 of Chapter 5.

Note: Only twenty-nine of Vancouver's thirty-six business leaders provided information on their education. The percentage figures have been rounded out to the nearest whole number.

was 1 college graduate for every 7 men among Seattle's business leaders, so there is little doubt that they were much better educated than the nation at large. Vancouver's modest showing in this regard reflects the fact that university education in Canada, and especially in Great Britain, was limited to a much smaller segment of the population than was true in the United States.

The data also suggest that a higher proportion of Seattle's than of Vancouver's leaders had their education limited to grade school only. It should be noted, however, that the total impression from many biographical sketches was that the Seattle leader cited his limited schooling with a touch of pride, as but one more obstacle he had overcome in the struggle to achieve success. The Vancouver leader, on the other hand, seemed less willing to acknowledge limited formal education, and seven men provided no information whatever on their education.[11] If, as seems likely, these seven had attended grade school only, it would reinforce the conclusion that the Vancouver businessman had the more limited education.

The road to business success for those Seattle leaders with little education was a long, tough one. Most of these men started out as unskilled laborers. Some began as apprentice blacksmiths or machinists, and only a small minority started as clerks. But as the level of education went up, first jobs tended to be somewhat more pleasant. The most typical first job for one who had gone to high school was as a clerk in a store or office. The business leader with university education seldom started out as a manual worker. Of thirty-five college-trained men, only two began their working careers in such activity. Most of these men started their working careers in stores, offices, or banks, many of which were run by relatives. Some had a brief fling at schoolteaching. Lawyers and engineers commenced their professional careers immediately on graduation. Complete data are tabulated in Table 9.

In addition to starting in poorer jobs, the average individual with only a grade school education took much longer to become established than did his better-educated competitor. One convenient indicator of such achievement is the age at which the businessman assumed the presidency of his firm. On this basis, of the twenty-two business leaders who had attended only grade school, just nine had achieved a presidency by the time they were forty. Those with a high school education or university education did much better, for of these sixty-five men, forty-six were so established by the age of forty.

The available data on first jobs held by Vancouver's business leaders again are much scantier than that on Seattle's leaders, but the overall pat-

Table 9   First Jobs of Seattle's Business Leaders by Level of Education

Education	No.	Prof'l	Clerical	Labor & Semi-skilled	No Info.
University graduate	14	6	6	1	1
University attended	21	4	15	1	1
High school	30	3	15	10	2
Grade school	22	—	3	19	—
Total	87	13	39	31	4

Source: Bagley, *History of Seattle,* vols. 2, 3. For a complete listing of the biographical sources see notes 1 and 3 of Chapter 5.

tern is similar. In twenty-two cases of persons with high school or university education, eighteen started their working careers in some clerical, professional or skilled capacity, and only five in some unskilled laboring job, whether on a farm, construction project, or factory. Of two cases with grade school only, both started in manual laboring jobs.

Regardless of where these business leaders grew up or where they ultimately settled, they were clearly an energetic, adventuresome group of men who tried a variety of occupations and locations before they settled permanently. The biographical sources are sprinkled with phrases such as "worked for a brief period in New York," "supervised railway construction in Ontario," "taught school in Wyoming," "opened a clothing store in Winnipeg," "settled temporarily in California." On the whole these men averaged two such stopovers on the way to a West Coast city, but three, four, and five stopovers were not uncommon. Of the small minority who moved directly to either Seattle or Vancouver most had an established business which they quickly reestablished in the new locale.

The first move for most men from New England or the Middle Atlantic states was to the upper Mississippi Valley, from there they usually moved directly to Seattle. New Englanders often tried their luck in Boston or New York and then moved on to the Midwest. The migration of future business leaders from the Midwest and Great Plains shows no dominant pattern. Direct moves to Seattle, stopovers in nearby states, and stopovers in Pacific Coast states were all common. Seldom did foreign-born immigrants come directly to Seattle. Whether from Scandinavia, Germany, or Canada, they usually worked in a number of American states before settling in Seattle.

Britishers who wound up in Seattle had very often worked in Canada before opting for the United States.

The same basic patterns were evident among Vancouver's leaders. Maritimers and Quebecers frequently tried Ontario, the Prairies, or the United States. Some Ontarians moved directly to British Columbia, but stopovers in the Prairie provinces were more typical. The Scotch, Welsh, or Irish migrant almost invariably went to England first, then moved to Ontario or the Prairies. Work in the United States was quite typical for the Canadian-born or the German-born leader; the great majority of leaders born in the United Kingdom tended to come directly to Canada. Only three out of sixteen settled temporarily in the United States.

The years during which these future leaders arrived in Seattle, their ages at arrival, and the elapsed time from arrival in Seattle to success in their chosen fields show a variety of patterns. While one cannot be dogmatic, the evidence in the biographical volume suggests that of these eighty-seven business leaders, fifty-one founded their organization and achieved success in Seattle itself. They tended to be in their twenties and thirties when they migrated, and most of them appeared in Seattle before 1890. The other thirty-six were apparently well established in the business realm before their arrival in Seattle, and merely added to their wealth and stature there. As a group they came after 1890, and were in their thirties and forties.

The degree of career assistance these leaders received from family or relatives is an intriguing and significant issue, but one that is not easily determined. The biographical sketches imply that these business leaders were self-made men who achieved success entirely on their own merits. But if a young man started to work in his father's bank after college graduation and quickly became president, there is little doubt that family connections boosted his career. Such clear-cut cases are infrequent, however, and the estimate of career assistance becomes little more than an educated guess. The body of evidence suggests that of Seattle's eighty-seven leaders, twelve received major assistance, and eighteen received some assistance. The remaining fifty-seven (65 percent) apparently achieved their success independently and would qualify as self-made men.

Taking the entire eighty-seven leaders as a group it is noteworthy that the great majority of them came to Seattle when it was still fairly small. Fifty-three arrived in the 1880s or earlier, seventeen in the 1890s, and seventeen in the 1900s. The individual who arrived when the city was a small community apparently had a better chance for future business success, than did his counterpart who arrived after the city had grown to substantial size. In 1890, when the city had a population of 42,837, fifty-three of the business leaders were active. During the next twenty years, Seattle added more than 185,000 to its population, but only thirty-four to its business leaders.

One can only make very general statements about the career developments of Vancouver's business leaders, their patterns of success, and the extent to which they benefited from family support or personal contacts. Again, evidence in these matters is not readily available. As a case in point, of the thirty-six leaders treated here, the occupation of the father is known for only seventeen. It is clear that these men were fully aware of the significance of the completion of the CPR, for a full two-thirds of them, twenty-five out of thirty-six, arrived in the city during the CPR boom years from 1885 to 1892. Another five arrived before 1900. The median age at arrival was thirty-one. The available evidence also suggests that Vancouver's business leaders were predominantly self-made men. In only six cases is there a clear indication of significant family help. In thirteen other cases the education, first job, and career advances all suggest that the man acted independently and achieved success largely through his own efforts.

There is no doubt about the political preference of these businessmen. Among Seattle's leaders Republicans outnumbered Democrats by about a seven to one margin, whereas in Vancouver, Conservatives outnumbered Liberals four to one. During the late nineteenth and early twentieth century voters in Seattle tended to favor Republican candidates over Democrats. But even the landslide for President Theodore Roosevelt in 1904 did not approach the extent to which Seattle's business leaders supported Republicans. The preference of Vancouver voters fluctuated sharply during these years, but at no time did the ratio of votes for Tory candidates reach the four to one margin shown by the city's business leaders.

Only a small number of Seattle's business leaders sought elected political office, usually at the state level. Six of these men, all Republicans, held public office. One served as territorial delegate to Congress, two in the state House of Representatives, and three in the state Senate. Two other business leaders were members of the Republican State Central Committee. Most of these men held office before 1900.[12] Thomas Burke, one of the city's most prominent businessmen and paradoxically a Democrat, sought election to both the U.S. House of Representatives and the U.S. Senate, but was unsuccessful. In addition, John Leary, Robert Moran, and William Wood each served a term as the city's mayor. But with these exceptions, direct political activity by Seattle's eighty-seven business leaders was limited.

Vancouver's business leaders, on the other hand, played a much more prominent role in federal, provincial, and municipal politics. A. D. McRae served as a Conservative Member of Parliament (MP), and was later appointed to the Senate. Harry Abbott ran as a Conservative MP but was defeated. At the provincial level both Charles Woodward and R. P. McLennan sought seats as Liberal Members of Legislative Assembly (MLA) but were defeated. F. Carter-Cotten served as a Conservative MLA, and later became minister of finance in the provincial government. But it was at the municipal level that these businessmen were especially active. Seven of them served as city aldermen. One of these, Jonathan Rogers, headed the Board of Park Commissioners for eight years; another, David Oppenheimer, would serve four terms as mayor. In addition, Fred Buscombe and W. H. Malkin served terms as mayor.

One might argue that the greater political activity by Vancouver's business leaders is but one more example of the old adage that it is easy to be "a big frog in a small pond." But regardless of whether it was easier to win a seat in Ottawa than in Washington, D.C., or in Victoria rather than Olympia, it is clear that the commitment of the necessary time and energy was much more typical of the Canadian than of the American business leader. While the greater political involvement of the Vancouver business leader is obvious, it is striking that this was much more a "British" or a "European" phenomenon than a "Canadian" one. For of the eight leaders elected to municipal political office, three were Englishmen, two were Scots, two were German, and one Welsh. Without a close examination of the political careers of these eight leaders one can say little about the significance of their role. Yet the fact that nine out of thirty-six of Vancouver's business leaders served terms in elected municipal offices, while only three of Seattle's eighty-seven leaders did so, indicates an involvement and concern about city affairs that was not duplicated by Seattle's leaders.

As for religious affiliation, these business leaders were overwhelmingly Protestant. In Seattle, information was available on seventy men, and of these sixty-one (87 percent) were Protestant, seven were Roman Catholic, and two Jewish. Vancouver data revealed twenty-eight Protestants (90 percent), one Catholic, and one Jew. In order of importance the three leading Protestant denominations among Seattle's leaders were Congregational, Episcopalian, and Presbyterian, whereas in Vancouver it was Anglican, Presbyterian, and Methodist. The preponderance of Protestants among these leaders is notable; it reflected the basic religious makeup of the cities themselves. In 1909, for example, Seattle had 155 Protestant churches, fourteen Roman Catholic churches, and two Jewish synagogues.[13] Vancouver had some 86,000 Protestants, 10,000 Catholics, and 1,000 Jews.[14]

The number of social and fraternal organizations joined by these business leaders would indicate that considerable time and attention was devoted to these activities. Whether participation led to personal contacts, increased business, or merely provided pleasant evenings away from the more immediate cares of the world, these business men joined in numbers. The average business leader belonged to two or three clubs, though membership in six or more was not uncommon. Seattle's Rainier Club was by far the most prestigious in the city, and apparently everybody who was anybody in local business circles joined. Fifty-six of our eighty-seven leaders were members, and four served terms as president. The next most popular social group was the Seattle Golf Club, followed by the Chamber of Commerce, the Arctic Club, and the Masons, each of which had at least thirty business leaders among its members. The Seattle Yacht Club, University Club, Shrine, Elks, and Rotary also were popular with the business community.[15]

The Vancouver Club was clearly the most significant in the Canadian city. J. C. Keith was one of its founders, Harry Abbott an honorary president, and at least eighteen leaders held memberships. This was followed by the Terminal City Club and Jericho Golf Club with nine each, the Royal Vancouver Yacht Club with seven, and the Shaughnessy Golf and Country Club with six. Like their counterparts in Seattle, Vancouver's leaders belonged to a variety of the local clubs. But a substantial sprinkling of Vancouver's leaders also retained affiliations with clubs outside the city. The Union Club of Victoria was the most typical, but memberships were also held in the St. James of Montreal, the Albany of Toronto, the Rideau of Ottawa, and the Carleton of Winnipeg.

On the basis of the foregoing evidence, some comparison can be drawn between these local business leaders of the pre–World War I generation and national business leaders of the same era. A very extensive body of research has been done on the American business elite; comparable work on the Canadian business elite is much more limited.[16] The sampling techniques, range, and approach of this research differs, yet an examination of the literature reveals that on virtually all counts the business leader of Seattle and Vancouver shared the attributes of their more prominent counterparts of New York, Chicago, St. Louis, Montreal, and Toronto.

In background and training Seattle business leaders were quite similar to their more prominent counterparts in the national business realm. The general backgrounds of these two groups differed significantly on only one major point; the local business leader was much more likely to be the son of a farmer than was his national counterpart. Therefore the local business scene showed a higher proportion of "self-made men." Otherwise, local and national business leaders alike had fathers in business or professional fields, their education was well above average, they were predominately Protestant, they voted Republican, and a substantial number of them received career assistance. They tended to start their working careers in clerical occupations, they shunned formal business training, and most of them had attained success by their forties. One cannot be as explicit about local, and national business leaders in Canada, but the available evidence shows no major difference between these two groups. One could conclude with the observation that while Seattle's Bakers, Isaacsons, and Osgoods or Vancouver's McLennans and Hendrys did not achieve the preeminence of their counterparts who labored in downtown Manhattan or on Bay Street in Toronto, they were from much the same mold.

A further insight into the careers and outlook of these early leaders can be gained from examination of how they handled their personal estates. The precise details of any large estate are complex, and can be unraveled only by an analysis of a great variety of evidence; still, valuable information and insights can be obtained from the probated wills of these businessmen. Seattle, for example, has some 150,000 probates on record for persons who died before 1960, and Vancouver has about 75,000.[17] From this immense body of material, probates were found on sixty-two of Seattle's eighty-seven business leaders, and twenty-five of Vancouver's thirty-six leaders.

In some cases the probate records are thin, providing little more than the deceased's will and the total value of his estate. But in other cases they are very extensive as appraisers, trustees, lawyers, and beneficiaries each added their documents to the record. Many of these businessmen accumulated substantial fortunes, others died virtually destitute. Some estates were settled quickly and amicably, others entailed prolonged and bitter disputes. Love, compassion, and kindness are revealed in these records, as are jealousy, deception, and greed. But each probate is a story unto itself.

Before considering these probates, it is well to reemphasize that they focus on a tiny elite, at the very peak of a local economic pyramid. Ninety percent of these men were born between 1840 and 1880, and died between 1910 and 1950. All were prominent in the local business world at

Table 10   Value of Estates Left by Sixty-Two Seattle Business Leaders

	Number	Total Value	Average Value
Under $50,000	15	$ 230,000	$ 15,000
$50,000–$249,999	13	2,127,000	164,000
$250,000–$499,999	11	3,587,000	326,000
$500,000–$749,999	9	5,383,000	598,000
$750,000–$999,999	4	3,570,000	893,000
$1,000,000 or more	10	16,979,000	1,698,000

Source: Probate Section, Washington State Court House, Seattle.

some time between 1885 and 1915. In no way should they be considered typical of the total population of Seattle and Vancouver. The estates of these business leaders varied widely, but on the whole were substantial, as can be seen in Table 10 and Table 11.

When one compares the distribution of wealth within these two groups of business leaders, the basic similarity is clear. Both cities produced a number of millionaires. Three of Seattle's millionaires had estates of over $2 million, none in Vancouver reached that level. The largest estate of all amounted to $2,800,000. The opposite end of the financial scale is equally intriguing for it shows that a quarter of all these business leaders—fifteen of sixty-two in Seattle, six of twenty-five in Vancouver—ended their lives in modest circumstances. The probates of these men with estates under $50,000 reveal that many apparently wealthy leaders were actually in a very precarious financial position. A number died insolvent, with the family home representing the only significant asset in the entire estate. The great bulk of business leaders in both cities, however, fell between these two extremes. They were prosperous, and left substantial estates with the median value about $275,000.

In virtually all of these estates regardless of size, real estate holdings accounted for a quarter or more of the total value. Among the smaller estates, real estate holdings were especially significant. But as the size of the estate rose, the relative importance of landholdings usually declined. The one significant exception to this rule occurred in those estates whose owners had settled in Seattle or Vancouver when those cities were in their infancy.

To make this distinction clearer one should consider these leaders not as a single group, but rather as falling into two subgroups that might be labeled "Pioneers" and "Executives." The Pioneers make up almost a quarter of these leaders. As a rule they were older, and had settled in Seattle and Vancouver either before or shortly after the completion of the Northern Pacific or the Canadian Pacific railroads. Convinced of the inevitable growth of their city, they invested heavily in real estate and profited from the surge in land values that occurred with rapid population growth. Seattle Pioneers like Arthur Denny, Thomas Burke, Jacob Furth, Dexter Horton, and Frederick Struve all achieved substantial fortunes primarily on the basis of such investments. Similarly, Vancouver Pioneers such as Harry Abbott or Charles Doering also profited from their real estate holdings.

The Executives, on the other hand, tended to arrive in Seattle and Vancouver after 1890 and either organized new companies or managed branches of national organizations. While they too invested in real estate, they were much more likely to have their assets concentrated in the specific firm that they owned or managed. William Piggott's holdings in the Pacific Coast Steel Company, Benjamin Rogers's commitment to British Columbia Sugar, and Edward Andrews' concentration on the Seattle National Bank were all quite understandable because the firms were substantially the creations of these specific men.

Nearly all of these business leaders held a variety of common stocks. The occasional man had the majority of his estate in industrial securities—but the usual range was from 25 to 35 percent. Shares of well-known national firms predominated. General Electric, American Telephone & Telegraph, General Motors, and Standard Oil, for example, were all well represented. In Canada, the Canadian Pacific Railway, and the Bank of Montreal were popular. Securities of local or regional concerns (with the exception of stock in their own companies) made up only a very small portion of investment portfolios. When local firms were included, they were usually well known. Dexter Horton National Bank, Seattle National

Table 11   Value of Estates Left by Twenty-Five Vancouver Business Leaders

	Number	Total Value	Average Value
Under $50,000	6	$ 87,000	$ 14,000
$50,000–$249,999	6	1,087,000	182,000
$250,000–$499,999	5	1,738,000	348,000
$500,000–$749,999	3	1,954,000	651,000
$750,000–$999,999	2	1,798,000	900,000
$1,000,000 or more	3	3,571,000	1,190,000

Source: Probate Office, Supreme Court of British Columbia, Vancouver.

Bank, and Pacific National Bank were favorites in Seattle, whereas British Columbia Sugar and British Columbia Telephone were popular in Vancouver. Bond holdings tended to be "blue chip," especially government bonds and those of major national institutions. There were numerous exceptions, but Vancouver's businessmen tended to be somewhat more conservative in their investment strategies, with a slightly higher proportion of their estate in bonds, life insurance, and cash, than was true of their American counterparts.

Although the general range of assets held by these business leaders suggests that they were a prudent, no-nonsense lot, the abundance of worthless securities in their portfolios indicates that they were also capable of self-deception and wishful thinking. From the insolvent to the multimillionaire, they hoped to make some fast money and held an incredible variety of worthless "cats and dogs." Oil companies and mining concerns were especially popular speculations—the Bethlehem-Texas Oil Syndicate, Pine Creek Lead and Zinc Company, Uncle Sam Mining and Smelting, Dundee Gold Mine, and Empress Petroleum are representative. Others acquired shares of Hadlock Loganberry Products; Vancouver, Westminster and Yukon Railroad; the New England Apple Service Company; and Twentieth Century Fireplace. The conviction that "one of these is bound to pay off" was ever present.

If the allocation of their estates can be taken as a yardstick of these men's interests and values, one must conclude that they were responsible family men, but with little concern beyond the immediate family and a few close relatives. The small estates almost invariably went to the man's wife alone. Divisions of one-half or more to the wife, with the remainder divided among surviving children was also common. As estates increased in size, brothers and sisters were included among the beneficiaries, and at about the $200,000 level nieces, nephews, grandchildren, and friends tended to be remembered. But in many many cases, including eight out of thirteen millionaires, the entire estate went to the immediate family. Some form of trust fund with guaranteed annuity payments was usually arranged for the widow, but seldom was she granted much freedom to handle the estate herself.

Contributions were made to a variety of churches, hospitals, libraries, and orphanages, but the total of such contributions was miniscule when compared with the total value of the estates. One Seattle millionnaire left close to 10 percent of his estate to various charitable organizations, but this was a striking exception to the usual pattern. It is possible that many men made substantial contributions during their careers, or that their widows or children later did so. But the Seattle probates show that out of a total estate value of some $32 million, something in the order of $300,000 or about 1 percent went to charitable and philanthropic causes. The record of Vancouver's leaders was somewhat better. From estates valued at $10 million, about $330,000 would qualify as charity or philanthropy. But a large slice of this came from one prosperous man, a British immigrant, who granted almost half of his estate to such causes.

Colleges and universities were virtually ignored in the wills of these businessmen. Although the probates included men who had attended Yale, Harvard, Cornell, Williams, Wesleyan, Michigan, Notre Dame, Whitman, Oregon, and Washington, as well as the University of Toronto and McGill, I could not find a single man who willed money to the university he had attended. Three major contributions to educational institutions were noted. Whitman College was granted $100,000 by one Seattle millionaire, another granted $10,000 to Mills College. One Vancouver leader left $75,000 to the University of British Columbia. Another prosperous Seattle businessman willed $100,000 to the University of Washington, but in a codicil to his will withdrew it, pointing out that he had already contributed more than that amount to the university. These decisions suggest that support for any educational institution, whether public or private, received a very low priority in the thinking of these businessmen. In much the same way not a cent was left to the Rainier Club, the Vancouver Club, the Republican party, or the Conservative party. Only five leaders made significant contributions to religious organizations. All such affiliations might have been helpful in advancing one's career, but they were seldom considered worthy of support.

A variety of federal taxes, as well as state inheritance taxes or provincial succession duties, took a substantial slice from these estates. The exact amount of these taxes are often omitted from the probates, and where cited show wide variations depending upon the year of death, the type of assets, and the number of dependents. Total taxes, however, went far beyond the amount voluntarily contributed to charities. Through the 1920s such taxes in the United States remained low. In 1923, for example, a Seattle estate assessed at $256,000 paid $1,444 in inheritance tax, and $1,394 in estate tax. In 1944, a comparable estate of $247,000 paid $6,000 in inheritance tax and $40,000 in estate taxes. Both in the United States and Canada the estates of these business leaders were usually assessed taxes in the range of 2 to 5 percent of their total value. Taxes on estates of $1 million or more showed many variations but approximated 20 percent.

What kinds of conclusions can we draw about these men, and what do their careers tell us about the cities in which they achieved success? First and foremost the career patterns of these Seattle and Vancouver leaders were noticeably similar in their backgrounds, education, work experience, and achievement of business success. There was little to distinguish their political preference, religious affiliation, or social activities. In both cities they tended to be self-made men who as a group acquired significant financial assets and achieved upward social mobility. Even the proportion of relative failure among them was alike, for in both Seattle and Vancouver approximately a quarter of these apparently prosperous businessmen ended their lives in very modest circumstances.

Some distinctions can be drawn, however. The much larger estates left by Seattle's millionaires, for example, suggest that as a group Seattle's leaders were more aggressive and innovative, and that greater economic opportunities existed in that city than in Vancouver. Canadian business leaders were a more prudent and cautious group if we are to judge from their investment portfolios. At the same time they were also more socially conscious and politically minded. For not only were their philanthropic contributions somewhat higher, but their involvement in municipal, provincial, and federal politics was much greater than that of their Seattle counterparts.

Nevertheless, it is the similarities that are most illuminating. In both Seattle and Vancouver we see that business success was a transitory phenomenon. The overwhelming majority of these businessmen and their families of the 1885–1915 era did not sustain their power and influence beyond one generation. Substantial estates were passed on to wives and children and in some cases the businesses were maintained. But as a general rule the company was either absorbed by a larger organization, or disintegrated soon after the founder's death. In the very same way that there was little continuity between the Pioneers of the nineteenth century and the Executives of the early twentieth century, there was also little continuity in the makeup of subsequent generations of business leaders.[18] Each was an entity unto itself, which reflected the needs and characteristics of that particular era. Few family dynasties were established in either city.

There are some exceptions. Woodward's Department store still thrives in Vancouver and in the early 1980s was under the direction of C. N. "Chunky" Woodward, the grandson of the original founder. Rhodes Department store in Seattle was also still in existence, though under new owners and management. The names Denny, Moran, Burke, and Stimson are also still known in Seattle, though the usual association is with a street, park, playground, or museum. The social activities or business ventures of the descendants of Benjamin Rogers, William Farrell, H. Bell-Irving, or Alfred Wallace are still followed by some in Vancouver. But for most Vancouverites and Seattleites these early business leaders and their families are unknown.

When we review the careers and achievements of these two groups of business leaders, the substantial size of their estates and the inevitable hard work that this entailed certainly commands our respect. One can also understand and admire the care they took to provide for wives and families. Yet the distribution of their estates suggests that their commitment was not to nation, city, neighborhood, university, church, or political party, but to oneself and one's family only. The business community of this era whether in Seattle or Vancouver was a tough, competitive one where the successful were rewarded and the failures forgotten. But above all one had to look out for oneself. It may be unduly harsh, but these men would probably have nodded in agreement with the statement by George Nathan, drama critic of *The American Mercury* in the 1920s, "The great problems of the world . . . social, political, economic, and theological . . . do not concern me in the slightest. . . . What concerns me alone is myself, and the interest of a few close friends. For all I care, the rest of the world may go to hell at today's sunset." [19]

6

World War I and the 1920s

The impacts of World War I on Vancouver and on Seattle were decidedly different. In Vancouver's case it was immediate and direct. Britain declared war on Germany on August 4, 1914; Canada followed two days later, and Vancouver plunged into a host of wartime activities.[1] Volunteers flocked to recruiting stations to join the Seaforth Highlanders, the Duke of Connaught's Own Rifles, and the Irish Fusiliers of Canada. Enlistments in the navy reserves, the army service corps, and the field engineers were also heavy. Public spokesmen urged everyone to contribute as best they could, and the Reverend Dr. Mackay captured the thoughts of many when he announced "If ever there was a righteous war, this is one." Before the end of August, 1,400 soldiers had marched along packed city streets to the CPR station where they boarded trains for eastern training camps and service overseas.

But while Vancouverites were intensely aware of the war and closely followed developments in Europe, the local economy received no immediate stimulus. The prewar construction slump continued and not until late 1915 when local machine shops began the manufacture of artillery shells would the city's economy begin to recover. The depression of those years was especially evident in a steep decline in the city's population, the first such sustained decline in Vancouver's entire history. From a prewar peak of 122,000 in 1912, population slipped year by year to 96,000 in 1916.[2] In part the loss was caused by the outflow of unemployed workers. But after August 1914 enlistments in the armed forces became more and more significant. Such enlistments were especially heavy from that third of Vancouver's population born in "the Old Country." One survey of 761 recruits done in September 1915 showed that 45 percent were English, 22 percent Canadian, 19 percent Scottish, 6 percent Irish, 8 percent American and "other."[3] Enlistments in the British flying services are also revealing. They show that Vancouver had 3.50 enlistments per thousand population, and of all Canadian cities only Victoria with 5.05 enlistments per thousand exceeded the Vancouver rate.[4] Comparable data on urban enlistees in the Canadian Expeditionary Force are not readily available, but on a province-by-province basis only Manitoba had a higher proportion of soldiers than British Columbia.[5] According to the *Vancouver Sun* British Columbia contributed some 50,000 during the war, of which 28,000 enlisted in Vancouver.[6] On all counts there is little wonder why the city's population dropped so sharply.

During the first years of the war, employment in Vancouver shipyards was limited to repair work and the construction of wooden schooners and did not differ significantly from regular peacetime activity. But by 1916 the Imperial Munitions Board began to place substantial orders. Relations between this federal board and the province's businessmen were always strained.[7] Yet in spite of a host of conflicts over wage rates, work stoppages, and the conviction of the chairman that British Columbia's businessmen were "a hungry pack of wolves," the board ultimately spent some $50 million in British Columbia, most of it concentrated in Vancouver.

The first major contract was for the construction of *War Dog*, an 8,800-ton steel vessel launched from the Wallace Shipyards in North Vancouver in early 1917. The Wallace yards and the J. Coughlan yards on False Creek would ultimately turn out twenty-six additional steel vessels, while smaller yards throughout the province produced wooden vessels of various types and sizes. Much of this latter work was done by the Lyall Construction Company in North Vancouver.[8] Though the total output of the province's yards was impressive, with Vancouver accounting for about two-thirds of the 350,000 tons produced (approximately 50 percent steel and 50 percent wood), the shipbuilding boom was a relatively late wartime phenomenon that flourished briefly and then disappeared. Tonnage statistics tell the basic story. In 1916 less than 10,000 tons were produced, 1917—37,000 tons, 1918—134,000 tons, 1919—165,000 tons, and 1920 less than 10,000 tons.[9] It is especially noteworthy that almost half of this total tonnage was produced in 1919, after the war was over. By 1920 local shipyards employed about 500 workers, a far cry from the wartime peak of some 6,000.

The impact of World War I on Seattle was very different. Politicians, journalists, and the general public were sympathetic to the Allied cause, but most saw the war as a European struggle to be fought out by Europeans. "There is absolutely no chance of the United States being drawn into the struggle," the editor of the *Argus* pointed out, "and there is no chance for suffering in this country. We raise and manufacture everything which is essential to our needs. We also have goods to sell. . . . Should the European war be prolonged this country will prosper as never before."[10] Unlike Vancouver, Seattle's population increased steadily with no setback whatever. Even the U.S. declaration of war in April 1917 and the subsequent drafting of men did not interrupt the growth. For losses to the services were more than compensated by the rush of workers to Seattle's thriving shipyards, sawmills, and manufacturing plants.

The expansion of the city's shipyards was especially dramatic, with the first 8,800-ton steel freighter launched in September 1916, a full six months before the comparable event in Vancouver. In part this resulted from the experience gained in the construction of the battleship *Nebraska* some ten years earlier. But as with the Klondike trade of the late 1890s, Seattle's businessmen proved to be much more venturesome and opportunistic than were their counterparts in Vancouver.

Skinner and Eddy, a long-established lumber concern, was the first to move to steel shipbuilding and they were soon followed by J. F. Duthie and Company, Ames Shipbuilding, the Washington Shipping Corporation, and others, all of which were aware of the potential wartime demand for ships. By December 1917 the Skinner and Eddy yards had five ways in operation, and the entire Harbor Island area was transformed into a massive shipbuilding center with 22,000 workers. During the year these yards turned out nine steel vessels totaling some 80,000 tons. Seattle displaced San Francisco as the biggest shipbuilder on the Pacific Coast and became well established as one of the nation's major shipbuilding centers. During 1918, employment increased to 30,000 and output surged to sixty-one vessels, aggregating 535,000 tons.[11] The basic technology for the construction of steel ships was already well developed, but the rapid adaptation and the speed with which ships were produced were most impressive. By 1918 Seattle plants could put a standard steel freighter in commission in 100 working days. As one *Post Intelligencer* correspondent proclaimed, "When the shipbuilders of the Clyde were told of the Skinner and Eddy feat they were skeptical. They doubted the achievement. Said it could not be done. But it was done."[12]

When the United States declared war in April 1917 Seattle quickly acquired the wartime characteristics that had long existed in Vancouver. With the production of ships, the manufacture of shells, and the general intensification of work there was little to distinguish the economic life in the two cities. Similarly, the bond drives, victory gardens, and patriotic endeavors of woman's organizations were all quite alike. Yet on balance there is no denying that the American city came through the war years substantially unscathed, whereas the Canadian city was deeply and permanently scarred. The casualty lists printed in the *Vancouver Sun* following the Battle of Ypres in April 1915, and the need to cite the 10:00 A.M. List, the Noon List, the 1:30 P.M. List, the 7:30 P.M. List, or the Midnight List after the Battle of the Somme in October 1916 were not duplicated in Seattle. The complete listing of "Canadian Casualties" was later abandoned by local newspapers, but awareness of the heavy losses at Vimy Ridge, Hill 70, Passchendaele, and Amiens was an ever-present fact of life for all Vancouverites.

Precise casualty figures for the two cities are unavailable, yet the magnitude of the dissimilarity is unmistakable. With a prewar population of 235,000, Seattle had about 16,000 men in the armed services, of whom some 250 were either killed in action, or died from wounds or disease.[13] Vancouver, with a population just half that of Seattle, suffered about 1,600 deaths, a rate twelve times that of its American counterpart.[14] With virtually every neighborhood in Vancouver experiencing one or more war-related deaths, it is little wonder the memories and scars of that massive conflict were permanent ones. In Seattle, on the other hand, memories faded quickly and by the mid-1920s the Great War was largely forgotten.

One of the most significant but indirect consequences of World War I for Seattle occurred three months after the cessation of hostilities. This was the Seattle General Strike of February 6–11, 1919.[15] It entailed no violence or casualties, yet it had profound ramifications for the city's economy and politics and its impact on organized labor would be felt for years.

During the wartime surge in shipyard employment Seattle's union membership reached nearly 60,000 by 1919.[16] Though all union locals were formally part of the American Federation of Labor (AFL), the Seattle labor movement had a strongly regional outlook and a conviction that its own Central Labor Council was the ultimate authority on all union affairs. Within this broad consensus, however, a great range of opinion existed. A conservative wing of the movement focused almost exclusively on the traditional issues of better wages, hours, and working conditions. A radical wing, with support from the Industrial Workers of the World (IWW), looked forward to a major restructuring of American society in which labor would play an active role in politics, key industries would be nationalized, and industrial unionism promoted. The largest and most significant element of all fell between these two wings, with "Jimmy" Duncan, an able, energetic Scot, its undisputed leader. Pragmatic in approach and convinced that all could work together for the common good through the Central Labor Council, this moderate group dominated the Seattle labor scene.[17] It was their temporary loss of power that paved the way for the General Strike, and its disastrous aftermath.

Early in 1919 union representatives began negotiations on a new contract for the city's shipyard workers. Employers resisted their wage demands and when further negotiations proved fruitless a strike was called. On January 21, 28,000 workers left their jobs and the shipyards closed. The following weeks saw a quick escalation in tensions. Discussions within the Central Labor Council were especially heated, with radical spokesmen advocating a general strike of all Seattle workers. To the surprise of many, support for this proposition spread quickly, with local after local voting in favor of the move. The absence of Duncan and other moderate labor leaders, all of whom were in Chicago on union affairs, undoubtedly benefited the radicals. What seemed like a bizarre suggestion in late January had become a virtual certainty by early February.

Union support for a general strike was unquestionable but there was little agreement on how it should develop, or what it should achieve. Was it a sympathy strike on behalf of the shipyard workers? A demonstration of labor's power? The beginning of a movement to reshape American society? And would it last a day? a week? month? or more? Though no specific answers were ever given, Anna Louise Strong's highly publicized editorial in the February 4 edition of the *Union Record* opened up many possibilities. In part it stated, "We are undertaking the most tremendous move ever made by LABOR in this country, a move which will lead—NO ONE KNOWS WHERE." For middle-class Seattleites frightened by local developments, bombarded by anti-union propaganda, and distressed by postwar international turmoil, the "NO ONE KNOWS WHERE" editorial seemed to indicate that the upcoming general strike was the first step on the road to revolution.

Seattle was ominously quiet on February 6, 1919, when 60,000 organized workers failed to report to their jobs and the nation's first general strike was under way. Buses and trolleys remained idle, foundries, machine shops, bakeries, and cafes were closed, lumber mills were empty, and the waterfront silent. But while rumors abounded and people feared the worst—nothing dramatic happened. After some early confusion, labor's special Strike Committee organized a variety of necessary services. Milk deliveries were established, emergency food kitchens opened, and hospital services continued. Most city residents seemed prepared to wait it out.

The response of Ole Hanson, Seattle's flamboyant mayor, was decid-

Photographs
Seattle & Vancouver
1880–1985

1 Seattle in 1882. Photograph by A. Curtis, no. 16394, courtesy of Special Collections Division, University of Washington Libraries.
2 University on the hill, Seattle, early 1880s. Photograph by A. Curtis, no. 28836, courtesy of Special Collections Division, University of Washington Libraries.
3 The arrival of the CPR in Vancouver, May 23, 1887. Photo no. 1091, courtesy of Vancouver Public Library.

1

2
3

4

5

6

4   Howe Street with ten-
nis courts as seen from
Hotel Vancouver, about
1890. Photo no. 4864,
courtesy of Vancouver
Public Library.
5   Laying streetcar tracks
on Powell Street, Van-
couver, 1889. Courtesy of
Vancouver City Archives.
6   First Avenue and Yes-
ler, Seattle, 1900. Photo
no. 2130, courtesy of Special Collections Division,
University of Washington
Libraries.

7

7 Pioneer Place, Seattle, 1900. Courtesy of Museum of History and Industry, Seattle.

8 Klondike Fever, Seattle, 1898. Photograph by Webster and Stevens, no. 4712, courtesy of Special Collections Division, University of Washington Libraries.

9 Madison Avenue trolley to Lake Washington, Seattle, 1900. Courtesy of Museum of History and Industry, Seattle.

8

9

11

12

10 Second Hill, Seattle, about 1900. Photograph by A. Curtis, no. 4039-1, courtesy of Special Collections Division, University of Washington Libraries.
11 Canadian Pacific Railroad station and harbor, Vancouver, 1905. Photo no. 1867, courtesy of Vancouver Public Library.

12 Ballard sawmill, Seattle, about 1900. Photo no. 2132, courtesy of Special Collections Division, University of Washington Libraries.

13

14

13 A drizzly Vancouver day, about 1905. Photo no. 5222, courtesy of Vancouver Public Library.
14 Seattle waterfront, 1914. Photograph by A. Curtis, no. 30471, courtesy of Special Collections Division, University of Washington Libraries.
15 Catching a streetcar, Vancouver, 1905. Photo no. 2137, courtesy of Vancouver Public Library.

15

17

18

16   An elite residential district in Vancouver's West End, 1905. Photo no. 5266, courtesy of Vancouver Public Library.
17   Fuel wagons and modest housing, Vancouver, 1906. Photo no. 1874, courtesy of Vancouver Public Library.

20

20   Kitsilano Boardwalk, Vancouver, 1911. Courtesy of Vancouver City Archives.
21   Hastings Street looking west, Vancouver, 1910. Photo no. 51, courtesy of Vancouver Public Library.
22   A new subdivision, Kitsilano, Vancouver, 1909. Courtesy of Vancouver City Archives.

21

23

23 A messy, dangerous job in a Vancouver salmon cannery, 1913. Photo no. 2062, courtesy of Vancouver Public Library.
24 Fairview housing, south shore of False Creek, Vancouver, 1912. Photo no. 2999, courtesy of Vancouver Public Library.
25 Boeing craftsmen, Seattle, about 1925. Courtesy of Museum of History and Industry, Seattle.

24

26　Lumber mill, south
shore of False Creek, Vancouver, 1923. Photo no.
3672, courtesy of Van-
couver Public Library.
27　Second Avenue, Se-
attle, about 1930. Photo-
graph by Lee, no. 8152,
courtesy of Special Collections Division, University
of Washington Libraries.
28　The Boeing plant,
Seattle, June 1917. Cour-
tesy of the Boeing Com-
pany Archives.

27

28

29 Housing in the Grand-view district, Vancouver, 1922. Photo no. 7401, courtesy of Vancouver Public Library.
30 Tudor Court, Vancouver, 1933. Photo no. 5299, courtesy of Vancouver Public Library.
31 King Street Station and Smith Tower from the south, Seattle, early 1930s. Courtesy of Museum of History and Industry, Seattle.
32 Alaskan Way, Seattle, about 1935. Courtesy of Museum of History and Industry, Seattle.

30

31

32

33

34

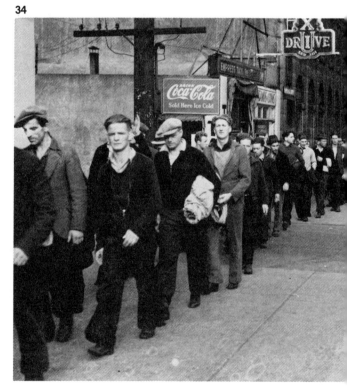

35

33 The opening of the Lake Washington floating bridge, Seattle, 1940. Photograph by A. Curtis, no. 65146, courtesy of Special Collections Division, University of Washington Libraries.
34 Unemployed workers demonstrate, Vancouver, 1937. Photo no. 1314, courtesy of Vancouver Public Library.
35 Hooverville, Seattle, 1937. Photo no. 2129, courtesy of Special Collections Division, University of Washington Libraries.

36   Children returning from school, Seattle, about 1960. Photo no. 2133, courtesy of Special Collections Division, University of Washington Libraries.
37   V-J Day celebration, Vancouver, 1945. Courtesy of Vancouver City Archives.
38   Twelfth Avenue South, Seattle, 1952. Photo no. 2134, courtesy of Special Collections Division, University of Washington Libraries.
39   1950s affluence, Seattle, about 1955. Photo no. 2131, courtesy of Special Collections Division, University of Washington Libraries.

37

38

39

40

40   Nelson Street, West
End, Vancouver, 1960.
Courtesy of Vancouver City
Archives.
41   Winter launch, Van-
couver, December 1976.
Courtesy of Vancouver City
Archives.
42   A downtown alley,
Seattle, about 1955. Photo
no. 2135, courtesy of Spe-
cial Collections Division,
University of Washington
Libraries.

42

41

43

44

45

43   Seattle waterfront,
1975. Photo no. 469,
courtesy of Special Collections Division, University
of Washington Libraries.
44   East end of False
Creek, Vancouver, about
1960. Courtesy of Van-
couver City Archives.
45   Aerial view of Van-
couver, September 1960.
Courtesy of Vancouver City
Archives.

46

47

48

46 False Creek, Vancouver, 1985. Courtesy of Vancouver City Archives.
47 Seattle from the south, overlooking Interstate-5, 1981. Photo no. 2125, courtesy of Special Collections Division, University of Washington Libraries.
48 The Space Needle from Queen Anne Hill, Seattle, 1981. Photo no. 2123, courtesy of Special Collections Division, University of Washington Libraries.

edly different. On the second day of the strike (February 7) the following notice appeared in a free edition of the *Seattle Star*.

PROCLAMATION

To the People of Seattle

By virtue of the authority vested in me as Mayor, I hereby guarantee to all the people of Seattle absolute and complete protection. They should go about their daily business in perfect security. We have 1,500 regular soldiers from Camp Lewis, and can and will secure if necessary, every soldier in the Northwest to protect life, business and property.

The time has come for the people in Seattle to show their Americanism. Go about your daily duties without fear. We will see to it that you have food, transportation, water, light, gas and all necessities.

The anarchists in this community shall not rule its affairs.

All persons violating the laws will be dealt with summarily.

OLE HANSON
Mayor

Hanson's proclamation was ridiculed by union spokesmen, but it reinforced the opinion that the strike was an attempted revolution and that tough steps had to be taken to suppress it. In the face of this public reaction defections soon appeared within the strikers' ranks. Streetcar service gradually resumed, individual shops, stores, and restaurants reopened, and by the third day of the strike all power plants were back in operation. To a reporter of the *New York Times* Hanson insisted, "We refuse to treat with these revolutionists. Unconditional surrender are our only terms."[18] As public hostility intensified, defections increased, and though union leaders insisted that the General Strike would continue, by the fifth day virtually all support for it had evaporated. At noon on Tuesday, February 11, the strike was declared officially over.

In the months that followed Ole Hanson catapulted into national fame. In a year-long speaking tour that netted $38,000, or five times his annual salary, Hanson pointed out over and over again how he had "upheld Americanism," "maintained law and order," and "whipped the Reds." But while Hanson benefited, the general strike was an unmitigated disaster for Seattle labor. Contracts for the construction of twenty-five ships were canceled, and employment in shipyards and machine shops plummeted. The traditional unity of city labor was also shattered with bitter disputes over the direction of the movement, and over the responsibility for the recent fiasco. Under the banner of the Associated Industries of Seattle the city's business community launched an intense anti-union drive that would be kept up for years. The editor of the *Argus* spoke for many in the fall of 1919 when he insisted that every union in the city was "in the hands of Bolsheviks, IWW's, or anarchists." By 1920 he was convinced that the University of Washington was a "seething cauldron of Bolshevikism," with professors "teaching doctrines that lead up to social revolution."[19]

Yet the ramifications of the General Strike went further still. The detailed references in the nation's newspapers to the "Revolution in Seattle" proved to many that drastic measures were necessary to suppress radicals and dissenters of all types.[20] The nation's "Big Red Scare" would flame out after two hectic years, but it would take fifteen years and the pro-union legislation of President Franklin Delano Roosevelt's New Deal administration before organized labor in Seattle would recover from the disastrous effects of its General Strike.

During the later years of the war Vancouver too experienced labor tensions and recurring strikes. Union membership had soared, and the increasingly radical stance of British Columbia labor with its opposition to wartime conscription, condemnation of capitalism, and periodic advocacy of a general strike caused much concern. Not only were such ideas considered unpatriotic, but many middle-class citizens saw them as a revolutionary threat to the entire social order. An indication of such tension occurred in August 1918 following the fatal shooting by police of "Ginger" Goodwin, union official, pacifist, and "draft dodger." The resultant protest demonstration endorsed by the Vancouver Trades and Labour Council has been labeled "Canada's first full general strike." But while longshoremen, street railwaymen, construction workers, and metal tradesmen stopped work, many unionized workers remained on the job. A march of returned soldiers on the Vancouver Labour Temple caused some damage and a few bloodied faces, but within a day the strike was over. A further "general" strike came in June 1919, as an expression of sympathy for workers in Winnipeg, who at that time were engaged in a major confrontation with the authorities. Like its counterpart ten months earlier, the Vancouver "general" strike of June 1919 was a disorganized, fragmented one which sputtered on for a month but lacked the profound ramifications of Seattle's postwar strike.[21]

Although the two cities had significantly different experiences during and immediately after World War I, the basic uniformity in their development reappeared in the 1920s. Except for a brief but intense postwar re-

cession, the decade was a prosperous one. Both cities experienced substantial increases in population, home construction, lumber output, and
general economic activity. Seattle's population rose by 50,000 and Vancouver's by 75,000 to reach 365,000 and 240,000, respectively, by 1930.
Realtor Henry Broderick's rhetorical query "When Seattle has a million,
what will you have?" captured the optimism of the era. But the gains,
though impressive, represented a much slower rate of growth than that experienced in the prewar years. The prosperity of the 1920s can best be
seen as a more modest, less consequential version of the dramatic surge
between 1900 and 1912. Population, employment, and output all increased,
but growth rates slowed down, and the general economic characteristics
of the cities remained remarkably constant.

Precise comparisons of occupations in Seattle and Vancouver are difficult, for not only do occupational categories differ between the United
States and the Canadian censuses, but also in the individual censuses
within each nation. Some ideas of the basic economic similarity of the two
cities in the 1920s and of the continued preponderance of white-collar
workers can be gained from Table 12.

Table 12 has some distortions. Seattle's manufacturing employment in

Table 12 Percentage of Work Force by Occupational Category

	Seattle		Vancouver	
	1920	1930	1921	1931
Agriculture, fishing, mining, forestry	4	3	5	6
Manufacturing	31	16	20	20
Hand trades, construction	6	14	13	15
Transportation	10	9	10	12
Trade	16	20	19	17
Public & professional service	10	12	8	7
Domestic & personal service	11	13	13	14
Clerical occupations	11	13	12	9

Source: U.S. Census, 1920, vol. 4, Population, Occupations, pp. 222–38, *U.S. Census, 1930,
vol. 4, Population, Occupations by State*, pp. 1693–1700. *Census of Canada, 1931, Occupation and Industry*, vol. 7, pp. 238–48. The "Manufacturers and Mechanical Industry" in
the *U.S. Census* was separated into "Manufacturers," and "Hand Trade, Construction," on
the basis of employment in Seattle's manufacturing plants. *The Census of Canada, 1911*
did not have a "Clerical Occupations" category. The "Trade, Finance and Insurance" and
"Other Services" listed in the *Census of Canada, 1921, 1931* were combined as "Trade" and
reallocated on a 50/50 basis between "Manufacturers," and "Hand Trades, Construction."

1920, for example, was abnormally high due to the temporary continuation of wartime activities. The number in hand trades and construction in 1920 was abnormally low for the same reason. But with these reservations, the table captures the basic similarity in the kinds of occupation followed by Seattleites and Vancouverites, and shows that there were no drastic changes in the 1920s from what had existed in the prewar decade. In both cities about 35 to 40 percent were in blue-collar occupations and 60 to 65 percent in white-collar occupations. One significant development in the 1920s not demonstrated in the table was the growing proportion of women in the labor force. In Seattle the number of women rose from 21 percent of the labor force in 1920 to 26 percent by 1930. The same pattern evolved in the Canadian city but at a lower level. By 1930 women accounted for 19 percent of Vancouver's work force.

A more detailed look at British Columbia's growth in the 1920s gives an idea of how and why the city developed in that era.[22] During the decade British Columbia's growth exceeded that of any other Canadian province. The province's population increased by about a third, and value of production, capital invested, and per capita income all rose significantly. The opening of the Panama Canal in 1914 led to a significant drop in transportation costs and the expansion of markets for Pacific Coast lumber. Before World War I about a fifth of the province's lumber had been exported, mainly by rail to Prairie markets. By the late 1920s over 60 percent of it was exported, with most of it shipped via Panama to eastern markets in the United States and Canada. Freight rate reductions on the Canadian Pacific and the Canadian National railways also benefited British Columbia, as they extended the area in Alberta and Saskatchewan from which wheat could be shipped to West Coast terminals. Finally, increased national and international demand for pulp, paper, coal, and minerals also benefited the province.

These developments had a magnified impact on Vancouver, for not only was it British Columbia's main shipping and railroad terminus, but its banks, supply houses, sales agencies, and legal firms all catered to the province's export-oriented industries. While British Columbia's population rose by a third between 1920 and 1930, Vancouver's, aided by the annexation of South Vancouver and Point Grey, increased by a half. The dollar value of the era's building boom exceeded even the great surge of 1900–12.[23]

Again it was the single family home that accounted for the largest slice of this construction, mostly in residential areas in Point Grey, Dunbar, Kerrisdale, South Vancouver, Hastings, and Burnaby, all about 4 or more miles from the city's downtown core.[24] The heightened activity on Vancouver's waterfront led to the construction of additional grain elevators, piers, and wharves. In the central business district the Hudson's Bay Company, Spencer's, and Woodward's all carried out extensive building programs. A great variety of workshops, warehouses, garages, and schools were also constructed.

An indication of the accelerated expansion of the 1920s can be seen in a comparison of the activities of the Port of Vancouver in 1920 with that in 1929.[25] In the earlier year, for example, an average of 29 deep-sea ships per month entered the port. By 1929 it was 107 per month. Whereas 84 million feet of lumber were exported in 1920, it was five times that in 1929. Grain shipments had been nonexistent in 1920, and flour shipments negligible. By 1929 Vancouver exported some 70 million bushels of grain and 2 million barrels of flour. In the latter year a total of some 23,000 vessels of all sizes, shapes, and descriptions entered the harbor. Few Vancouverites would challenge Mayor L. D. Taylor's assertion, "The future is ours . . . there is no limit to the possibilities of the city."[26]

Throughout the 1920s publicists in both Seattle and Vancouver never tired of providing detailed statistics to establish the current growth and future promise of their community. But changes during this era went far beyond the pattern of more population, more housing, more lumber, more manufactured goods. During the decade a variety of technological changes had a major impact on the nature and development of these cities. The impact of the Panama Canal on ocean freight rates has already been mentioned. It was also during this era that a variety of electrical motors and kitchen appliances made their appearance. Whether seen in the more efficient drill press, lathe, or planer—or in the vacuum cleaner, toaster, or washing machine—thousands of industrial workers and housewives were influenced. The development of the radio and the appearance of more and more movie theaters also shaped the lives of city dwellers.[27]

But if one single technological change shaped these cities in the 1920s it was the automobile. Before World War I automobiles were still something of a rarity, but in the postwar years, especially the 1920s, they increased dramatically. In 1916, for example, Seattle had some 16,000 cars, by 1921— 48,000, 1924—88,000, 1928—129,000.[28] Vancouver showed much the same pattern, but with its lower per capita income and higher costs car ownership was not as widespread. In 1922 the Canadian city had about 15,000 cars, in 1924—21,000, and 1928—36,000.[29] By 1928 there was approximately one car for every three persons in Seattle, and about one for every seven in Vancouver. The ramifications were almost endless: new gas stations, roads, repair shops, and shopping facilities appeared, and with the intensification of advertising and sales techniques, more and more people moved to the suburbs. One of the most direct consequences was on the streetcar systems of the two cities. This issue would torment city officials for years and is worthy of detailed examination as an excellent example of the impact of technological change on a city's development.

On March 31, 1919, in a wave of enthusiasm and in a conviction that municipal ownership was the only solution to the city's transportation ills, the City of Seattle purchased the street railway property of the privately owned Puget Sound Traction Light and Power Company. The price was $15 million and the system was promptly renamed the Seattle Municipal Street Railway.[30]

The proponents of municipal ownership were soon disillusioned for within the first year a number of distressing events occurred. Traffic fell off sharply with the curtailment of wartime shipbuilding, employees struck for higher wages, jitneys siphoned off business, and an epidemic of runaways and wrecks occurred. A host of questions were raised about the wisdom of the original purchase. Many suggested that city officials had paid too much, others insisted there had been deliberate fraud.[31] The most authoritative answer came from a grand jury that investigated the entire controversy in 1921.[32] They found that the original agreement had been concluded in a frenzy of wartime enthusiasm and that the purchase price had been arrived at with no thorough investigation of the company's assets. No evidence of corruption was uncovered but the grand jury considered the purchase price of $15 million to be grossly inflated, and estimated that the value of the property at the time of acquisition was approximately $5 million.

From its founding in 1919 to its demise in 1939, the lot of the Seattle Municipal Railway was not a happy one. With the benefit of hindsight it is now clear that the golden years of the street railway system in Seattle were from 1900 to about 1912. By the time the city assumed control, the system had begun a long and steady decline. Had the municipal operation not been burdened with heavy debt payments ($750,000 per year interest, plus $833,000 per year on principal) it is possible that repairs, upgrading of facilities, and purchase of new equipment could have significantly prolonged its life.[33] But throughout the 1920s and 1930s, for example, not a single new streetcar was added to the basic fleet that the city had acquired in 1919.[34] Ultimately the increasing automobile competition, rising costs, and declining revenues proved too much. Although a number of hardworking superintendents did their utmost to remedy the situation, and although they were able to show periodic profits in the 1920s, the overall pattern was one of deterioration and decline.

The problems faced by the Seattle Municipal Street Railway were similar to those faced by virtually every street railway in North America.[35] Scholars are in agreement that the burgeoning automobile ownership and use was of primary importance.[36] For whether owners used their car for the drive to work or for an evening or weekend outing, it automatically entailed a decline in patronage and revenues for the street railway concern.[37] But a host of other factors also contributed. The growth of suburbs, for example, siphoned off "downtown" customers, and led to an expansion of suburban lines which seldom proved profitable. Moreover, the development of the motorbus and its adaptability to changing passenger demands also led to a decline in streetcar patronage. And at the very time that revenues were declining, wage rates and maintenance costs were increasing, especially where repair work required the removal of asphalt pavement. Hostile public opinion also played a part. Not only were city dwellers aware that trolleys were crowded and uncomfortable, but they were also convinced that street railway companies were inherently corrupt and monopolistic, indifferent to their needs, and interested only in maximizing profits. Neighborhood groups, businessmen, and city officials all had their ideas and opinions, but with no consensus on what should be done.

The suggestions, recommendations, and reports on "how to solve the street railway problem in Seattle" were almost endless.[38] The more sophisticated usually suggested ways to reduce costs or make the system more efficient, whether by eliminating unprofitable lines, improving equipment, or reducing staff. Some suggested trackless trollies, elevated lines, or subways. Others argued that the unionization of railway workers should be prohibited. Still others, convinced that any competent manager should be able to remedy the situation, saw the solution in very simple terms— "Fire the Superintendent."

The Seattle Municipal Railway turned its last profit in 1929, and by the early 1930s was unable to make the annual payment toward the retirement of its bonds.[39] A special committee of the city council pointed out that "the bonded debt . . . expanding territory . . . decreasing revenues . . . and divided responsibility" had virtually ruled out the possibility of any real progress.[40] Throughout the Depression the company practiced the kind of frantic economy that was typical of businesses throughout the nation. Staff was reduced, wages lowered, overtime eliminated, and retirees not replaced.[41]

In 1935 the city council arranged for a comprehensive investigation of the entire street railway system. The report that it received from the Beeler Organization of New York exceeded all earlier reports in length, coverage, thoroughness, and range of suggestions.[42] In 102 pages it surveyed the entire transportation system and advocated a massive rehabilitation program. This entailed financial reorganization, the purchase of a fleet of trackless trolleys and gasoline buses, major route changes, and the development of an efficient electrical distribution system. The estimated cost was some $7 million. Seattle was unsuccessful in its attempts to get the necessary financial backing but did not abandon the suggestions. In a follow-up report of 1937 the Beeler Organization elaborated its original proposals, but by this time the estimated cost had risen to $12 million.[43] In March of that year, after a long and intensive campaign, city voters decisively rejected the proposed refinancing plan.[44]

Not until September 1938, after prolonged negotiations, did the city obtain the necessary financing to carry out the oft-proposed rehabilitation program. At that time Seattle obtained a $10 million loan from the Reconstruction Finance Corporation. Puget Sound Light and Power agreed on a $3,250,000 cash settlement, and the city began to implement the Beeler recommendation. A major conversion of facilities took place in 1940 as one after another of the streetcar lines were phased out, with new trackless trolleys and buses taking their place.[45] The final streetcar run in Seattle occurred on April 13, 1940.[46] Just one year later the Seattle transit system showed a profit of $1 million.[47] Clearly a new era had dawned.

When we turn to Vancouver's transportation developments we see much that is familiar. The rapid expansion of facilities, the surge in utilization during wartime, the consideration of municipal ownership, the problems entailed in jitney and automobile competition, and the impact of the Depression were all quite like Seattle. But as with many processes north of the forty-ninth parallel there was a decided lag between the transportation developments of the American city and the comparable developments in the Canadian one. While the evolution shared much in common, it unfolded in distinctive ways. As mentioned earlier, in the 1920s automobile ownership in Vancouver was much less widespread. Street railway operations were more viable, and much less was heard about "the streetcar problem." A more favorable perception of the city's transportation facilities evolved, and over the years this would lead to a system with greater reliance on buses, less emphasis on freeways, and a more sympathetic attitude to the construction of a rapid transit system.

The long-term role of the British Columbia Electric Railway (BCER) was especially significant.[48] This London-based organization had assumed control of a number of firms in Vancouver, Victoria, and New Westminster in 1897. Until 1928 when it sold out to a Canadian firm it completely dominated street railway developments in Vancouver. Local managers continually argued for more aggressive expansion of facilities. But the British board was much more concerned with the financial viability of their organization and the confidence of bond holders than they were with the possibility of quick profits. These differences caused considerable irritation on both sides of the Atlantic. Yet over the years its conservative financial policies and the cautious approach to expansion stood the BCER in good stead.

As in Seattle, major growth occurred in the years before World War I when trackage in Vancouver jumped from 13 miles in 1900 to 106 miles in 1912. During the war the BCER faced a number of difficulties.[49] Labor unrest, strikes, and jitney competition were constant headaches. A major blow came in 1917 when the provincial legislature granted Vancouver the right to engage in the light and power business. This step especially distressed the BCER for light and power operations always returned a steady profit and helped compensate for the periodic deficits in street railway operations. For a while it seemed possible that the company might sell their entire system to municipal authorities. But Vancouver lacked the necessary financial resources and unlike Seattle did not take such a step. In addition a one-man royal commission under Dr. Adam Shortt provided a very sympathetic analysis of the company's stance on wage rates and fare structure. The net result of these developments was that the BCER not only survived the war years but consolidated its position.

The 1920s were generally prosperous and untroubled for the BCER.[50] Increased automobile ownership caused difficulties, but the company's introduction of motorbuses helped reduce such losses. For the decade as a whole, labor was relatively quiet and earnings steady. When the Nesbitt Thomson interests of Montreal assumed control in 1928 the company was still in sound financial condition.

The 1930s, on the other hand, were very difficult years for the BCER. Wages were cut, employees laid off, services reduced, and more and more streetcars replaced by buses. Throughout the decade, city authorities insisted that streetcar fares should be reduced and periodically argued for a municipally owned system.[51] A detailed investigation in 1935 by Allan J. Smith, a city-appointed transportation expert, left no doubt about the city's basic position.[52] He considered many of the company's facilities "obsolete," its service "indifferent," and its profits "excessive." He found few public benefits from the privately owned company, and saw no need for any fare increases. All of these charges were heatedly challenged by E. H. Adams, vice-president of the BCER, who considered many of them "utterly without foundation." According to Adams the BCER was an efficiently managed organization, with operating costs well below those of most North American cities. Such charges and countercharges continued throughout the late 1930s. In 1938 the city again considered purchasing all power, gas, and transportation facilities of the BCER, while the company insisted that it would sell the entire system before accepting the fare reduction requested by the city.[53] As in the past little came of either threat, and with the coming of World War II the BCER was still a well-patronized, viable, functioning system.

In the same way that transportation developments in Vancouver lagged behind those in Seattle, and ultimately evolved in a distinctive way, city planning showed much the same pattern. Vancouver did not have a city plan of comparable range and depth as Bogue's *1911 Plan of Seattle* until 1929. But when such a plan ultimately materialized it had a much greater impact on subsequent development than did the earlier plan for the American city.

Like many processes and institutions in Canada, city planning was a complex amalgam of diverse American, British, and Canadian components. During the late nineteenth and early twentieth century the dominant thread in Canadian city planning followed the "City Beautiful" and later "City Functional" patterns that had earlier evolved in the United States.[54] At the same time most planning legislation was based on British precedents, and it was on the basis of such precedents that the British Columbia legislature passed the Town Planning Act of 1925.[55] This act met with hearty approval from a host of Vancouver's businessmen and professionals for it provided the explicit authority for the implementation of city planning that they had long sought.[56] In due course a Vancouver Town Planning Commission was established, which in turn hired Harland Bartholomew and Associates of St. Louis, Missouri, to prepare a comprehensive plan for Vancouver.

At the time of this appointment, Bartholomew was recognized as one of America's foremost city planners. He had already supervised a vast number of city planning projects, and over the years followed a basic operating procedure that varied little from city to city. A key man from the St. Louis office supervised the project and took up residence in the host city for about three years.[57] He and his staff obtained office space in city hall and from that command post gathered data and statistics, drew maps, and prepared preliminary reports. Every city also had a citizens' advisory committee of about 100 members that assisted the technical staff in every way possible. The citizens' committee received the final report, and also played a prominent role in publicizing its content and supporting its adoption. The style and coverage of the final report varied little from city to city. Since an ideal long-range plan could seldom be implemented, a series of immediate steps, plus intermediate moves, were usually suggested. As a rule six major areas were dealt with in each comprehensive plan: streets, local transit systems, railroads and harbor facilities, public recreation, zoning, and civic art.

Bartholomew's *Plan for the City of Vancouver,* 388 pages in all, was available for general study by 1929, and followed a fairly standard model.[58] A detailed street plan entailed the widening and improvement of existing streets to facilitate movement in and out of the central business district. Transit proposals were also extensive, but did not entail any drastic revision of existing systems.[59] Bartholomew estimated that metropolitan Vancouver would have a population of a million by 1960, but the plan assumed that the city's transit needs would be met primarily by streetcars and buses. Considerable attention was also devoted to the harbor and to its railroad support system.[60] The False Creek Basin was to be upgraded as an industrial area and both shores of Burrard Inlet were to be devoted to shipping facilities and industrial sites. New bridges were suggested for Second Narrows and for False Creek.

Public recreational facilities also received attention. Stanley Park's overall quality was recognized, but Bartholomew stressed the need to develop a whole system of parks and recreation grounds. The report emphasized a "systematic and determined campaign of waterfront acquisition." At that time, of the 5.4 miles of English Bay waterfrontage only 1.6 miles were publicly owned and, Bartholomew added, "the entire shoreline should be a public possession."[61] Over the years such guidelines and suggestions would be substantially implemented.

A major component of the overall plan that got much attention at the time was the construction of a major civic center. It would bring together a large number of public buildings and act as a focal point for the entire city.[62] Bartholomew suggested that it be placed on the bluff at the northern end of the yet-to-be-constructed Burrard Street Bridge over False Creek, and that it involve an area of six city blocks. Although the proposal was well thought out, promising, and potentially elegant, little came of it.

When one attempts to assess the significance and impact of Bartholomew's *Plan for Vancouver* it is easy to dismiss it as of minor importance. His suggestions for improving the transit system, for replatting large sections of Hastings and Point Grey, for redeveloping the False Creek area, and for constructing a major civic center were all largely ignored. One can also argue that the increase in automobile ownership and use would have inevitably led to the widening and realignment of streets proposed by Bartholomew.

Yet such dismissal of Bartholomew's *Plan* ignores the very real influence it had on Vancouver's development. In a submission to the Town Planning Commission in 1944, fifteen years after his original report, Bartholomew pointed out, "many cities . . . have officially approved and adopted their Plan, yet made only partial progress in carrying it out. Vancouver is unique in that its Plan has not been officially approved nor adopted by the City Council, but it has been faithfully followed with but very few exceptions."[63] No doubt he was exaggerating the degree of implementation, but the 1929 plan did identify existing conditions and laid out a blueprint for the future. The impact on streets, parks, recreational facilities, and zoning development was significant. The later construction of the Burrard Bridge, the CPR tunnel, Crystal Pool, Fraserview Golf Course, Glen Drive railway yards, as well as the acquisition of 1,250 acres in South Vancouver and improvement to the Spanish Banks, all reflect Bartholomew's plans.

City council's allocation of funds in 1944 for a series of follow-up studies by Bartholomew is also indicative of the recognition of the earlier plan.[64] The nine different studies done between 1945 and 1947, like the earlier study, were mostly a codification of existing population, streets, transit, traffic flows, airports, parks, and suburbs, together with some suggestions for the future.[65] Like the predecessor of 1929, many of the recommendations of the 1945–47 studies were ignored and forgotten. But again, substantial portions were implemented. The continued acquisition of waterfront property for public use, the later development of English Bay, Marine Drive, Spanish Banks, and Queen Elizabeth Park all follow the recommendations and plans of the postwar study. And it is no coincidence that today's Queen Elizabeth Theatre and Playhouse, Canadian Broadcasting Corporation facilities, and the city's main post office are all clustered within the civic center area proposed by Bartholomew in 1946.

When one asks why so many of Bartholomew's proposals were followed, there is little doubt that the sustained domination of Vancouver's municipal politics by the Non-Partisan Association is of primary importance. From its inception in 1937 until the late 1960s, the political power of this propertied, business-oriented, conservative administration was never significantly challenged. This made for a remarkable continuity not only in city council, but in membership and ideas of the Town Planning

Commission and the Parks Board. Over the years the planning commissioners and the park commissioners followed the basic guidelines provided by Bartholomew.

One might conclude that both Seattle and Vancouver are essentially unplanned cities, where community needs and central planning have always been subordinate to private rights and private decisions. From the rejection of the Bogue Plan in 1912 Seattle especially showed little support for such centralized planning. It is true that many zoning and planning commissions have functioned over the years, and that various city officials and professional bodies have periodically insisted that a comprehensive city plan was essential. But whether argued in 1920, 1924, 1930, 1935, 1941, or 1946, such proposals had remarkably little effect on Seattle's actual development.[66] A variety of distinctive conditions and attitudes in Vancouver, on the other hand, made that city more amenable to planning. Government land reserves and the Canadian Pacific Railway are basic to the Vancouver story, but Bartholomew's 1929 *Plan for the City of Vancouver* is also a major contributor.

7

The Response to the Depression

In their classic analysis of "Middletown" the Lynds had this to say about the 1930s. "The great knife of the depression has cut down impartially through the entire population cleaving open lives of rich as well as poor. The experience has been more nearly universal than any prolonged recent emotional experience in the city's history; it has approached in its elemental shock the primary experiences of birth and death."[1] Such a statement is applicable to both Seattle and Vancouver. But as in so many aspects of the history of these cities, when we examine the 1930s at length it is clear that while both shared much they also had a variety of distinctive problems and responses, which once again showed that each city was unique.

The Wall Street stock market crash of October and November 1929, which supposedly precipitated the Depression throughout the United States and Canada, had little immediate effect on the Pacific Northwest or British Columbia. It is true that both Seattle and Vancouver faced a number of worrisome issues at this time, but they were all fairly standard ones. The Vancouver business community, for example, was distressed by the provincial government's expenditures on highway projects.[2] Similarly, Mayor Frank Edwards in Seattle worried over the need for new schools, parks, and water lines.[3] But on most counts 1929 was a banner year for both cities. Construction activity was at an all-time high, the lumber industry prospered, port activity was vigorous, and the real estate markets active and rising.

Even during much of 1930 Seattle and Vancouver remained largely untouched by business depression. The local construction industry, though down somewhat from 1929, continued prosperous. Indeed, the spring and summer of 1930 had much of the quality of the 1920s. People were not worried about unemployment, but excited by the apparently endless prosperity that they were enjoying. In the fall and early winter of 1930 unemployment rose sharply, and the number on relief soared. But even this caused little distress since it was a fairly normal pattern that recurred every year, as loggers, fishermen, and construction workers were laid off with the onset of bad weather. There was little doubt that spring would bring the normal upsurge in seasonal economic activity.[4]

Rather than recovery, however, the spring of 1931 saw a further slump in employment as national economic trends became more and more evident on the West Coast. By the summer and fall there was no doubt whatever that the Depression had hit. Seattle's construction industry plunged from a value of $30 million in 1930 to $9 million in 1931, while in Vancouver it dropped from $22 million to $10 million. Loggers, wood workers, and freight handlers lost their jobs and were soon joined by carpenters, plumbers, electricians, store clerks, garage mechanics, and real estate agents.

While thousands of Seattleites and Vancouverites immediately felt the impact of these layoffs, both cities showed sharp class disparities in unemployment patterns. At a time when bread was about five cents a loaf, hamburger ten cents a pound, and a comfortable home cost under $5,000, a family of four whose head was steadily employed at $100–$150 per month could get through these years without undue difficulty.[5] But maintaining one's job was critical, and here there were marked differences depending on one's occupation, education, and skills. One early study of unemployment in Seattle showed that in middle-class residential districts north of the Lake Washington ship canal, unemployment averaged 12 percent of the labor force, whereas it reached 25 percent in the Duwamish Valley industrial district.[6] Similarly, a 1938 analysis of Vancouver showed that of the age group from sixteen to thirty, 15 percent were unemployed in middle-class Dunbar, while 40 percent were unemployed in working-class Collingwood.[7]

A U.S. Department of Labor study of municipal employment in Seattle for the years 1929–38, gives a vivid picture of class disparities in income and employment patterns.[8] It shows that while pay cuts and layoffs hit all types of municipal employees, there were great variations. As a general rule, middle-class employees with advanced education or specialized skills tended to retain their jobs. And although pay declined, it recovered with the improvement in the general economy. Thus in 1929, Seattle had 2,664 persons employed in education who averaged $156 per month. By 1933 average pay had dropped to $130, but the number in education had risen slightly to 2,694. In 1937 the 2,864 people in education averaged $154 per month. Much the same pattern was evident among those engaged in legal services. The 29 people engaged in that field averaged $235 in 1929. By 1933 only 3 had lost their jobs, and in 1937 the 24 people in the field averaged $228.00 per month. Skilled workers in the lighting and water departments, finance, and city libraries followed the same pattern.

For those without specialized skills it was a vastly different story. If one was fortunate enough to retain a job the pay remained fairly constant, but the probability of losing it was high. City agencies in 1929 employed 122 persons in building maintenance, who averaged $155 a month. By 1933 53 of these janitors and cleaners (42 percent) had lost their jobs, but the fortunate 69 who were still working earned $140 per month. By 1937 the 79 employees in building maintenance averaged $160 per month. People who worked in the maintenance of streets and sewers suffered much the same fate, with a third of them losing their jobs between 1929 and 1934. Like their counterparts throughout the United States and Canada it was Seattle's unskilled and poorly educated who bore the brunt of unemployment in the 1930s.

An early indication of the severity of conditions by 1931 was the appearance of various shantytowns of unemployed, destitute men. Seattle's "Hooverville" on the site of the old Skinner and Eddy Shipyards, and the "jungles" in Vancouver under the Georgia Street Viaduct and on the old Hastings mill site, all created anxiety. Watchman Frank Waters reported to the Vancouver Harbour Commission that there were some 180 to 200 men living on waterfront property. He considered them "reasonable" and "cooperative" and did not find much sign of the "red element" among them.[9] By the fall of the year officials in both cities ordered the shacks burned. This settled the immediate issue, but the pervasive problem of unemployment continued.

By the winter of 1931–32 both cities were in severe straits. In Vancouver, for example, the city's relief committee was overwhelmed with appeals. S. E. Pope, a father of two children, had been out of work for a year, and relied on $12 a month rent from a farm he owned. His request for work was turned down since "there were other cases more pressing."[10] D. W. Gimmett, tenant, asked for $3 a week from the committee. He had paid only two months rent in the previous two years.[11] James Pike needed "a supply of fuel." When his appeal was turned down, "Pike appeared to lose control . . . committed an assault on Alderman Lembke, and was seized and ejected from the meeting.[12] The Vancouver Hebrew Aid Society was compelled to refer their cases to the city for help.[13] The Chinese Benevolent Association pointed out that there were 260 Chinese in the city who were "absolutely destitute."[14] Regardless of the source of the request, or whether it was for money, clothes, transportation or child care, they seemed endless. In a desperate effort to economize the city's relief committee considered discontinuing the ten cents per day allowance to unemployed men without dependents. They ultimately continued it, but reduced the daily allowance for meals from thirty to twenty-five cents, and for beds from twenty to fifteen cents.

The early response of city officials to the Depression was very similar. In both Seattle and Vancouver officials saw the drastic surge in unemployment as temporary, and believed that private resources, charitable organizations, and some public assistance would be sufficient to meet the crises. There was also little doubt that in due course a normal economic recovery would occur.

In Vancouver, officials were quite familiar with the provision and funding of basic relief services, for as early as 1894 council had established a relief committee for the city's destitute and its unemployed transients.[15] In 1915 a permanent Relief and Employment Committee was established, and in the early1920s cost-sharing agreements with senior governments were worked out. Under these agreements, federal, provincial, and municipal authorities each paid a third of the cost of city work projects.[16] "Regular" relief cases remained the responsibility of the city.

Relief expenditures had risen steadily throughout the 1920s, but the monumental unemployment now overshadowed anything that had happened in the past and quickly overwhelmed Vancouver's resources. Some idea of the magnitude and abruptness of the change can be gathered from a comparison of the cases on relief cited by the Relief and Employment Committee. In February 1920, for example, there were 129 cases on relief, in 1928—502, 1930—1,216, and by February 1931—7,298 cases.[17] By this time an annual appropriation of $550,000 could not begin to cover the costs of the multitude who needed help.[18]

From 1930 onward the question continually debated was, "Who is responsible for caring for the unemployed?" Is it the worker himself? charitable agencies? the city? the province? the federal government? or some combination of all of these? As early as 1930 Vancouver spokesmen pointed out that the numbers of unemployed had completely swamped local resources and that a drastic increase in federal and provincial aid was essential. Federal authorities expressed sympathy, but insisted that unemployment was a local problem to be handled by local authorities. They stressed

that the British North America Act placed "charity" under provincial jurisdiction. Provincial spokesmen also expressed concern, but were quick to
cite the Municipalities Act that focused responsibility on local agencies.
The city in turn argued that their revenues were chiefly dependent on
property taxes, that these were both inadequate and declining, and that
additional taxation authority was essential. But all to no avail. Throughout
the Depression this complex issue was analyzed by hundreds of experts
and a host of formulas devised. But the basic arguments presented in 1930
remained remarkably consistent. After ten exhausting years no agreement
was reached and no solution found.

Any group of officials would have had a hard time devising policies
and programs for the 1930s. In Seattle the difficulties of mounting unemployment and slumping revenues were magnified by the existence of basic
social tensions in the city, and a lack of confidence in city officials. The
long tradition of radical labor activity in the region's logging camps and
lumber mills, the intense labor struggles of 1916–19, and the general opposition to union activities in the 1920s had all left a bitter heritage. To the
unemployed worker the city council was but one more organization dominated by the city's business community, and little could be expected from
it. Businessmen and professionals, on the other hand, shared this distrust,
but saw the council as an inefficient, inept group that squandered the tax-
payers' dollars on unnecessary expenditures.[19]

The first organized response to the Depression in Seattle came from a
group of unemployed workers under the leadership of Hulet Wells and Carl
Brannin. Both were socialists, well known in local labor circles. Wells had
been a Socialist candidate for mayor, the head of the Seattle Central Labor
Council, and during World War I had been jailed for distributing antidraft
literature. Brannin headed the Seattle Labor College and was considered
"definitely Marxian." Under their guidance, twenty different groups of unemployed workers came together in September 1931 to form the Unemployed Citizens League (UCL).[20] From the beginning the league left no
doubt about its political beliefs. It condemned all private charity, and argued that the state was obliged to help its unemployed workers, whether
through a massive public works program, a system of unemployment insurance, or a direct relief program.

The UCL grew rapidly, and during the fall and winter of 1931–32 carried out a great variety of self-help activities. Its members sawed and split
firewood, picked unwanted fruits and vegetables in the Yakima Valley, and
obtained unsold fish from local fishermen. These in turn were distributed
to Seattle's unemployed through a system of commissaries set up in vacant

houses. The program quickly received public support and became a major factor in local relief efforts.

On the heels of this UCL activity Mayor Robert Harlin appointed a special commission to coordinate all relief activities in the city, and to develop both public and private employment. This Commission for Improved Employment was headed by Mr. I. F. Fox, president of the Seattle Chamber of Commerce. But in the first three months of operation the commission could find temporary work for less than a third of the 10,349 unemployed who had registered. These in turn earned an average of only $36.84, which was expected to sustain a married man and family for three months.[21]

It soon became apparent that neither the mayor's commission, nor the UCL had the resources to meet the relief needs of the city, and in February 1932 they came together to form the District Relief Organization.[22] By this time many Seattleites were vaguely uneasy about the activities of the worker-led UCL. Commissioner Fox arranged that the city's relief depots and the league's commissaries be amalgamated, and that the unemployed themselves administer all relief funds. Fox saw the arrangement as a buffer, which by coopting the UCL into the public organization diminished the possibility of radical action. The new organization received most of its financing from council appropriations. But the fact that a husband and wife with two children did not qualify for relief if they had an income of over $6 per week, showed once again that relief went only to the most desperate cases.

Many groups found such efforts grossly inadequate and offered more radical proposals. The Seattle Campaign Committee for Unemployment Insurance and Relief, for example, proposed that all existing bond obligations be canceled, that salaries of city officials be cut, that the police force be reduced, and that taxes on high-income groups be sharply raised. But its assertion that in the Soviet Union "the conditions of the masses are constantly getting better" and that the socialist system was "unquestionably superior to the bankrupt capitalist system" aroused little attention or enthusiasm. For with remarkably few exceptions Seattleites retained their conviction that the crisis was a temporary one and that all difficulties would inevitably be overcome. In one of his final presentations to city council in January 1932 Mayor Harlin was gratified that "peace and tranquility have reigned in our midst." In the mayor's opinion this was largely the result of the activities of the Commission for Improved Employment which had "inspired confidence in all" and had done "everything humanly possible."[23]

In Vancouver, as we have seen, a system of public relief services administered and financed by the city itself had been in operation long before the onset of the Depression. Throughout the early 1930s the Relief and Employment Committee steadily expanded its activities. Although such municipal services were more advanced than those in Seattle, they met only the basic needs of the most desperate cases. Mayor Louis D. Taylor, an experienced, popular leader with strong working-class support, could also do little. During his younger years he had advocated a variety of socialist measures. But by the 1930s he was a tired, sickly man with few ideas, capable only of meeting the hundreds of visitors to his office where he could offer compassion and encouragement, but little more. In one of many appeals to the federal government he was reminded that relief had "always been a municipal responsibility . . . federal authorities are still of the opinion that responsibility must revert to the city." The editor of the *Province* provided an apt summary, "and this, it would seem is as far as we have got in three weary years of passing the buck from Vancouver to Victoria and from Victoria to Ottawa and back round and round the sorry circle. What is the matter with our governments? Are they stupid, or blind, or callous, or merely helpless?"[24]

The municipal elections of 1932 received little attention in Vancouver, with Mayor Taylor duly reelected. In Seattle, however, it was quite a different story, with four candidates struggling for the mayoralty. The incumbent Robert Harlan's slogan was "a safe pilot in a troubled sea." Former Mayor Edwards centered his campaign around the need to reorganize Seattle City Light. John F. Dore, lawyer and former reporter with the *Post Intelligencer* and the *Times,* claimed that he would eliminate inefficiency from city hall and again bring city government "back to the people." The final candidate was Victor Meyers, danceband leader and man-about-town. His candidacy was created and sustained by the Seattle *Times,* apparently in an attempt to bring a touch of humor to the proceedings and to highlight the inadequacies of all candidates.

The campaign was a colorful, flamboyant one, with most of the attention focused on the efforts of Dore and Meyers to upstage each other.[25] Dore's critics considered him a reckless demagogue, but few challenged his showmanship or vote-getting ability. Years later Dore's son recalled some of the tactics of that campaign.

> Dad hired sound trucks to go out about four o'clock in the morning of the primary election to play dance-band music and announce 'Vote for Vic Meyers'. . . . He hired a room in the Smith Tower and secretly published a flyer saying, 'Vic Meyers has the endorsement of the Commu-

nist Party.' They were distributed at churches on Sunday morning. But the one that really hurt Vic was when Dad hired Cadillacs and installed Negro drivers in fancy suits. They went all over town with signs on the side saying 'We're for Meyers.'[26]

In the run-off election Dore won decisively.

Although one winces at the steps by which he achieved success, Mayor Dore brought to his office an awareness of the crisis facing Seattle. He set aside Friday of each week to receive the visits of countless citizens. Although he could do little more than offer the occasional basket of food or clothing, he gave thousands the sense that there was someone in city hall who appreciated their desperate straits.[27] He also left no ambiguity about his opinion of state and federal politicians. "President Hoover is a menace to this nation and Governor Hartley is a menace to this state because neither has an understanding of what is confronting us."[28]

But although Dore's personal activities and pronouncements were unorthodox, his policies for combating the Depression were traditional. One of his first steps was an across-the-board salary cut. In a terse note to the city comptroller he rejected a proposed salary of $7,500 a year, and accepted $5,000.[29] The pay cut for all other city employees ranged from 10 percent to 25 percent.[30] But more direct steps to improve the situation remained pathetically inadequate. For example, $5,000 was appropriated to enable workers to pick strawberries and raspberries and transport the fruit to the city. No pay could be provided, but Dore emphasized it would occupy 500 men for a week.[31] The staunchly respectable, business-oriented *Seattle Municipal News* congratulated the mayor for "lopping off more than $2,000,000" from the city budget, and saw the action as a significant step "on the road to recovery."[32]

For the Unemployed Citizens League, on the other hand, Dore's policies were a bitter disappointment.[33] The UCL had strongly supported his candidacy in 1932, helped elect two laborites to the city council, and saw these achievements as the beginning of a new era for Seattle's workers. But as the mayor's orthodox policies unfolded, keen divisions developed within the League over its future direction. By late 1932 a more radical leadership had assumed control of the UCL. They emphasized the need for public ownership of all business and industry, the overthrow of the capitalistic system, and an end to "intolerable exploitation of millions of workers."

The response to these developments left no doubt that the UCL was considered a dangerous political organization. More and more accusations were leveled at the "graft" and "mismanagement" of public relief funds under its jurisdiction. Businessmen withdrew their support from the UCL's self-help program, and Mayor Dore declared that it was of no further use in the city's relief activities. The election of Franklin D. Roosevelt and a Democratic Congress in November 1932 also contributed to the disintegration of the UCL. With the implementation of a variety of New Deal programs, the Seattle and the King County relief organizations were abolished, and by the spring of 1933 the Unemployed Citizens League had virtually disappeared.

During the eighteen months of its existence the UCL distinguished Seattle not only from other American cities but from Vancouver as well.[34] Although the jobless had organized in many cities, in Seattle they obtained the support of public authorities and for a year actually administered the city's relief program. There is little doubt that the UCL was rooted in the city's radical labor tradition. Leaders such as Hulet Wells and James Duncan, for example, had also been active during World War I and in the General Strike of 1919. The league's success in the municipal election of March 1932, when it elected two councillors, supported the winning mayor, and claimed 50,000 members had apparently marked it as a political force. But it quickly aroused fear and lost support when it adopted a more radical stance. The great majority of Seattleites, like their counterparts in the nation at large, never lost faith in the "American system." With FDR's New Deal program, the UCL was delivered a final and fatal blow.

While city officials experienced much anxiety, Seattle remained remarkably free of outright violence during these years. Occasionally the police were called on to control demonstrations or remove protesters from the mayor's office or public buildings; this was usually accomplished with a minimum of friction and no loss of life resulted. But there were some ugly incidents. In April 1933, for example, a group of men in the Rainier Valley fought to prevent the eviction of a family from their home. With fists, rocks, and iron pipes they held off a sheriff and his deputies until further reinforcements were called. Sheriff Claude G. Bannick pointed out, "it was decidedly the worst of several similar outbreaks recently. . . . My men and I were merely doing our duty." Sixteen men were later arrested.[35]

By 1933 state authorities had assumed responsibility for relief payments but many citizens still looked on city hall as the agency that could provide jobs. Seattle's accomplishments in this realm proved to be even more limited than in the provision of relief. The only significant source of revenue available to the city was from property taxes. By the time the city paid for police and fire protection, as well as schools, libraries, and bond interest there was almost nothing left. The emergency fund, for instance, was seldom over $50,000 and would have been exhausted in a day if all the city's unemployed had been hired. If the state had granted additional taxing power, or if the city had been able to borrow additional funds, it might have been able to play a bigger role in creating jobs. But both of these channels were closed.

By the spring of 1933 Mayor Dore insisted that "each community must do something to relieve its own distress," and insisted "much can be done by Seattle to relieve Seattle's distress." Yet actual conditions did not support this conviction. In 1933 and 1934, for example, total construction in the city amounted to $2 million annually, the lowest level in thirty-five years. As the months dragged on with no significant improvement, the mayor came under stronger and stronger attack. His clashes and conflicts with the city council were well publicized. Workers were unhappy with his wage cuts and cautious expenditures, while many in the business community considered him "too radical." The state treasurer expressed "no confidence whatever" in him and found his statements "utterly misleading."[36]

By 1934 the buoyancy and self-confidence that was supposedly the very essence of Seattle had long since disappeared, and a somber, discouraged mood permeated the city. Older residents still had fond memories of an earlier Seattle, but for the generation of the 1930s, the "Old Seattle Spirit" was hopelessly antiquated and a mockery. The *Seattle Municipal News* captured the prevailing outlook when it pointed out "we have slumped spiritually, the old spark of achievement and the dominating leadership of hardy individuals which Seattle had a generation ago have seemingly been lost. . . . There can never be any recurrence of conditions under which Seattle forged so rapidly ahead. Life has become far more complex socially and economically."[37]

In the municipal elections in the spring of 1934 Mayor Dore was decisively defeated by Charles E. Smith, who pledged that his administration would stand for strict law enforcement and a balanced budget. An early presentation to the city council indicated the depth of his understanding of Seattle's problems.

> The Puget Sound area is blessed by providence with things few parts of the world, if any, enjoy. Let us not be too modest in bragging about them. If I've said it once, I've said it fifty times since last March the southern Pacific coast state has a greater population due to its climate and its boosting spirit, call it ballyhoo if you wish, but they have it. They've always had their climate so their growth in recent years must be due to their boosting spirit. Let's emulate it for Puget Sound. Let us

continue to boost for other parts of our great state when we go south, east or west. But above all, let us do some boosting for Seattle. We have the climate, the Sound, the lakes, the mountains, the rivers, and the scenery. Let us tell the world about them. . . . Let us put our shoulders to the wheel and make Seattle a bigger and better city.[38]

At a time when some 40,000 persons were on direct relief in the city, Mayor Smith's analysis of the community's needs did not bode well for the future. During his two-year term, Smith held to his conviction that the essence of good government was to keep all city expenditures to an absolute minimum. "Many things we would like to do and should do for the good of the city," he pointed out, "simply cannot be done."[39] After a year in office he stressed that his administration had spent less money for governmental purposes than any other recent administration. He also claimed that among twenty-five American cities of 300,000 or more, Seattle had the lowest per capita tax for city purposes.[40]

The kind of stringent economy practiced in city hall was duplicated by residents throughout the city. Indeed, by the mid-1930s, "getting by" had become a way of life. Whether by poorer food, cheaper clothing, or reduced medical care, each adapted in his or her own way to the situation. The decline in housing standards was representative. Young couples lived with parents, vacant rooms were rented, apartments were divided and subdivided. Houses designed for one family now housed four or more. As the superintendent of buildings pointed out in his 1936 report, "It is doubtful if we can any longer say that Seattle is a city without slums."[41] While housing conditions deteriorated, construction of new homes and apartment buildings fell off sharply. Not a single apartment building was constructed in Seattle in 1933 or 1934. In 1935 one was built, in 1936 two, in 1937, one. All were very small.

The unfulfilled expectations of Mayor John Dore and his later replacement by the "stand pat" Charles Smith had a striking parallel in Vancouver. The Seattle electorate had opted for the colorful, dynamic Dore as early as 1932; it was not until 1934 that Vancouver turned to Gerald G. McGeer. At the time of his election "Gerry" McGeer was serving as a Liberal MLA in Victoria. From his first day as mayor he left no doubt that he had a definite set of ideas and approaches for grappling with the Depression. According to the *Vancouver Province* his inaugural address was "spectacular." He presented "more of a programme for immediate consideration than the City Hall has heard in the last five years."[42] He proposed to cut the cost of the city debt in half by a flat reduction in the interest rate paid. He argued that public services should take priority over all else, and that debt payments should be secondary. He also proposed a balanced budget, a reorganization of the city's tax system and public services, and a redefinition of the powers of municipal government. And there was no ambiguity in his statements. When he pointed out that the city paid 5 percent on all bank borrowings, but received only 2 percent interest on all deposits, he added "that kind of constitutional thievery will not continue." [43]

It is not surprising that McGeer's proposals aroused immediate controversy and opposition. Thomas Bradshaw, spokesman for city bond holders, and the author of a detailed report on Vancouver's financial position, quite predictably disapproved. He saw Vancouver's financial problems as "temporary" and argued that overdue taxes, then amounting to some $11 million should be "more effectively collected." [44] Similarly, Premier T. Dufferin Pattullo in Victoria, as well as a number of national commentators, all condemned McGeer's position. [45] But the mayor was not taken aback. He pointed out that in the previous five years, Vancouver had paid $10 million in interest when payments on relief and social services came to $6 million. [46] As he added later, "humanity is going to come first and usury is going to take second place as far as I'm concerned." [47] McGeer maintained his position at the Calgary Conference of Western Mayors in January 1935, and the Conference of Canadian Mayors in Montreal two months later. At both conferences speakers maintained that Canadian cities could not meet their financial and social obligations, and that the federal government had to assume primary responsibility. But again little resulted.

As frustration followed frustration McGeer became convinced that he might achieve greater results as a Member of Parliament in Ottawa than as mayor of Vancouver, and in the Liberal landslide of late 1935 won a seat as Liberal MP. In that capacity he proposed a massive public works program to alleviate unemployment, but again achieved little. On a visit to Vancouver he pointed out "there's a strong reactionary element in Ottawa . . . balanced budgets by orthodox methods is something that G. G. McGeer M.P. simply cannot understand anymore." [48]

The fact that McGeer held a seat in the provincial legislature at the time he was elected mayor of Vancouver, and that while mayor he was elected a Liberal MP in Ottawa, gave a kind of publicity and stature to municipal affairs in Vancouver that was not available to Seattle's John Dore. One might assume that since the Canadian mayor could hold municipal and federal office simultaneously he automatically had greater leverage with the federal government than did his American counterpart. Yet such a potential advantage bore few positive results for Vancouver, or for Gerry

McGeer. Canadian governments, whether Conservative or Liberal, failed to implement anything comparable to President Roosevelt's New Deal program. Throughout the Depression Canadian cities had to get by with niggardly federal aid, of the type that the Hoover administration doled out to American cities prior to 1933.

By the winter of 1936 McGeer was roundly condemned both by the right and the left. To the business community he was a demagogue who aroused class tensions and threatened the city's entire financial structure. To the political left and the unemployed he was the foe who saw "Communist agitators" behind every protest action and was quick to utilize the police. In the mayoralty election of December 1936 he was defeated by George C. Miller, an established businessman. After two years of frenzied activity that achieved almost nothing, McGeer was an exhausted, embittered man, who like thousands of others was destroyed by the Depression.

Though it gained little attention at that time, a significant political change that unfolded during McGeer's term as mayor was the abolition of the ward system for election of city aldermen and its replacement by an at-large system. Such a change had been suggested many times, but in the stressful years of the mid-1930s the condemnation of wards intensified. Critics insisted that such a system led inevitably to inefficiency, graft, and corruption, with aldermen interested only in the issues of their own ward and not those of the city as a whole.[49] Most Vancouverites showed little interest in the issue, and only 19 percent of the city's eligible voters actually voted in the plebiscite of December 1935.[50] But the results were unambiguous. Every single ward in the city supported the change to an at-large system of elections with support ranging from 58 percent in east side wards, to 80 percent in wards in the west side.

The consequences of this change did not begin to reveal themselves until the regular municipal election of December 1936. Up to this time the Socialist Cooperative Commonwealth Federation (CCF) had been weak and disorganized at the civic level, winning only the occasional seat on the Parks Board or School Board. But in this first "at-large" election they ran a full slate of candidates and succeeded in winning three of the eight seats on city council.

The sudden appearance of CCF representatives on council caused immediate concern among the city's more conservative elements. While pleased by the victory of the "sound" George Miller as mayor, they were distressed by the role of the new Socialist aldermen, as the latter both acted and voted as a political party. In November 1937, following a series of meetings and discussions, a group of "prominent citizens" established the

Vancouver Non-Partisan Association (NPA). Their goal was "to develop a proper sense of civic consciousness and a due sense of civic pride . . . and to oppose the introduction of party politics into Vancouver's city administration.[51] The new organization was enthusiastically supported by the *Sun* and the *Province,* and just one month later in the regular civic election, seven NPA candidates won council seats. The CCF elected but one alderman. This early and striking success by the Non-Partisan Association established a domination of Vancouver's municipal politics that would not be significantly challenged for a full thirty years.

During the years that Vancouverites were frantically but unsuccessfully attempting to bring about significant change, a fundamentally different process unfolded in Seattle. This had little to do with the efforts of John Dore, or Seattle's city council, but rather resulted from a whole series of policies and programs implemented by President Franklin D. Roosevelt's Democratic administration. From 1933 on, it was federal programs, federal agencies, federal relief, and federal employment that put Seattle on the road to recovery and helped restore the morale of thousands. Such a process had no counterpart in weary, exhausted Vancouver.

In the early 1930s a smattering of Seattleites had been employed in projects supported by the federal Reconstruction Finance Corporation.[52] But such Republican efforts were dwarfed by the multitude of developments that began in 1933 with Roosevelt's New Deal. Whether it was the direct relief payments initiated by the Federal Emergency Relief Administration (FERA), or a work relief project supported by the Works Progress Administration (WPA), both provided badly needed help.[53] The Civil Works Administration (CWA) initiated a significant federal commitment to a public works program, which in turn would be expanded by the Public Works Administration (PWA). And although the efforts of the Civilian Conservation Corps (CCC) focused on nonurban areas it provided employment for thousands of young men, urban and rural dwellers alike. Similarly, federal agencies supported private home construction under the Federal Housing Authority (FHA), were geared to slum clearance under the National Recovery Administration (NRA), and provided public housing under the United States Housing Authority (USHA). Municipal officials had traditionally frowned on such federal involvement in city affairs; now they not only welcomed such involvement, but vigorously pursued it.[54]

The Public Works Administration was especially active. Though Secretary of the Interior Harold Ickes operated the agency with extreme caution, it nevertheless led to the construction of roads, public buildings, airports, water systems, and a host of other urban facilities.[55] Local authorities provided plans, technical staff, and materials for the job.[56] Federal funds accounted for up to 45 percent of the cost of a project, with the condition that all such funds had to be used to pay workers listed on the welfare rolls. Under these arrangements in 1935, Seattle carried out PWA projects valued at some $2 million.[57]

As was true throughout the county, the activities of the Works Progress Administration were more loosely structured, had fewer conditions attached, and covered a much broader range than the projects under Ickes. But in Seattle as elsewhere, WPA Director Harry Hopkins's conviction that people had to be given work, regardless of the immediate value of such activity, led to a great variety of specialized reports, surveys, and studies. Whether it involved the compilation of property assessments, the codification of city ordinances, the analysis of automobile movements, or the cataloguing of library holdings, hundreds of clerks and technicians were employed.[58] Projects at the University of Washington indicate the range of activities. The WPA workers erected both the Penthouse and the Showboat theaters. They enlarged the football stadium, improved the Arboretum, landscaped a golf course, laid out practice fields. A variety of buildings on campus were renovated, enlarged, remodeled, or restored. In addition a whole series of research projects were funded, which employed both faculty, students, and staff. Much the same kind of pattern unfolded in Seattle's high schools and grade schools.

In four and one-half years of such activity the WPA built or improved more than 500 miles of secondary roads in King County and some 300 miles of streets and alleys, with much of this in Seattle itself. Extensive construction was also carried out at Fort Lawton, Sandpoint Naval Air Station, and Boeing Field, with new runways, hangars, and residences. Extensive work was done on the city's parks, water mains, landfills, and dock facilities. It is not at all surprising that city authorities granted office space in the County City Building to the WPA to handle their diverse operations.

Another agency played a major role in the city: the United States Housing Authority. Established in 1936 to provide decent low-cost housing, the USHA loaned up to 90 percent of the cost of a project, with the actual planning and implementation supervised by a local housing authority. Under the direction of Jesse Epstein, the Seattle Housing Authority began work on the Yesler Terrace project in 1939. The opposition of scattered critics was prophetic of future developments, but hundreds looked forward to good housing at moderate rents.[59]

Even with the infusion of federal funds and programs unemployment remained high. In March 1936 voters expressed their dissatisfaction with

Charles Smith's performance and returned John Dore to the mayor's office. Dore showed the same vitality that he had in his earlier term, but abandoned his commitment to a balanced budget and spent heavily. Yet on the whole 1936 and 1937 were difficult, disappointing years with prolonged strikes on the waterfront and bitter disputes between Dave Beck's teamsters (AFL), and Harry Bridge's longshoremen (CIO), for control of the Seattle labor scene. Since Mayor Dore had welcomed Beck's support in 1936, these conflicts became an integral part of the local political scene.

By 1937 federal authorities were convinced that national economic recovery was well under way, and that heavy public expenditures were no longer necessary to sustain the economy. Cutbacks were carried out on a whole variety of works projects.[60] The move proved premature as unemployment soared in cities throughout the nation. The later reinstatement and enlargement of WPA grants and the recovery in Seattle's employment pattern by 1938 once again revealed the city's dependence on such federal grants.[61]

Seattle would not achieve full employment until the 1940s. Yet the election of Arthur Langlie as mayor in 1938 can be taken as the end of an era. Langlie had entered municipal politics in 1935 as a candidate of a local reform group, and had rapidly gained prominence. His mayoralty campaign in 1938 appealed to a variety of middle-class groups, and after a spirited campaign he overwhelmed Lieutenant Governor Victor Meyers. Langlie's approach and support in city council, combined with general economic recovery, all contributed to his later success, and marked a fundamental change in Seattle's municipal politics. Prior to 1938, mayoralty elections had been bitterly fought with significant class consciousness. Incumbents usually lost. Though the elections were ostensibly nonpartisan, both Democrats and Republicans exploited party contacts. Following 1938, on the other hand, elections were low-keyed and sedate. Issues were muted, class tensions less obvious, and the incumbent mayor and councillors tended to be reelected.[62] In Seattle's municipal politics at least, a new era was underway.

Whereas the reinvigoration of federal programs in the late 1930s led to partial recovery in Seattle, these years were especially painful for Vancouver, which experienced a whole series of riots and clashes with the police. Many of these events in the Canadian city were orchestrated by the Communist-led Workers Unity League (WUL). In its emphasis on class struggle, condemnation of capitalism, and appeal to the young and unemployed, the WUL shared much in common with Seattle's Unemployed Citizens League. The early public sympathy it aroused, as well as the anxiety it gradually created, was much like that of its Seattle counterpart. Yet the timing, tactics, and longevity of the two groups were distinctive. The UCL was essentially a phenomenon of the early 1930s, especially 1931 and 1932. It cooperated with public agencies in the delivery of relief services, was ultimately coopted by those agencies, and quickly faded into obscurity as New Deal programs unfolded. The WUL did not become prominent in Vancouver until some five years after the onset of hard times. The subsequent demonstrations and turmoil went on for four years and were but one further indication of the frustration of thousands of unemployed Canadians, and of the failure of their federal government to grapple with the Depression.

The first coordinated move occurred during the spring of 1935 when some 1,500 men left federal relief camps scattered throughout British Columbia and headed for Vancouver. As members of the Relief Camp Workers Union (chartered by the WUL), they sought to publicize the isolation, low pay, and dismal conditions of those camps. They also sought to pressure the federal government to develop some form of reasonably paid work program. Recurring marches and demonstrations, and temporary occupation of floors of the Hudson's Bay department store and the Vancouver Public Library led to clashes with the police, some damage, but few significant results. Many of these men were subsequently involved in the "On to Ottawa Trek" but after a major confrontation where one policeman was killed, returned to Vancouver.

Other affiliates of the WUL were engaged in a series of waterfront strikes. A major disturbance on June 18, 1935, labeled by the *Vancouver Province* as "the bloodiest hours in our waterfront history" involved a clash of 1,000 longshoremen with local and federal police. In the melee on Ballantyne Pier 28 persons were injured.

In the summer and fall of 1937 numerous clashes occurred after police arrested unemployed men soliciting funds on city streets. The "tin canners" insisted they would continue their appeals until the provincial government established a works program.[63] A further crisis developed the following spring when the provincial government closed the relief camps and declared that the cities themselves were responsible for all relief costs. Demonstrations, clashes, and arrests followed with the Georgia Hotel, the Vancouver Art Gallery, and the main post office all occupied on May 31, 1938. After "sitting on a keg of dynamite" for two days, city council voted that $500 be used to secure withdrawal of the men from the Georgia Hotel. Harold Winch, CCF leader in the provincial legislature, later negotiated a withdrawal from the Art Gallery, but the 600 men in the post office refused to budge. After six weeks of deadlock, a full-scale assault by the Royal Canadian Mounted Police with tear gas and clubs cleared the building. Damage amounted to $30,000. There were thirty-nine injuries and twenty-two arrests.

There it little doubt that Communist-led organizations were highly prominent in these clashes of 1935, 1937, and 1938, and that both local and federal authorities in Vancouver were determined to maintain control. Though there were many bloodied faces and broken bones, no fatalities occurred. Yet it is difficult to assess the total impact of such developments. S. Jamieson, a labor historian and economist who observed many of these events, has concluded that on balance they tended "to generate an image of government as oppressor." They also encouraged a "widespread contempt for the law" as an entity designed "to protect property rather than human rights." Such conclusions are both persuasive and sobering.[64]

The Post Office Riot of June 20, 1938, became a symbol of Vancouver's difficulties during the Depression. In December Dr. Lyle Telford, president of the provincial CCF and the MLA from Vancouver East, was elected mayor. Elite Shaughnessy opposed the Socialist Telford by a 9 to 1 margin but strength throughout the city, especially on the east side, brought Telford victory.[65] In his inaugural address Telford emphasized the need for an appropriate division of taxes and for help for the "forgotten man." But like his predecessors he could do little to increase employment or improve conditions. Within a few months aldermen were accusing him of providing little more than "vague statements."[66]

A number of major themes stand out when one surveys the response of Seattle and Vancouver to the Depression. The first is that municipal officials in both lacked the resources to change conditions in any significant way. It is true that the very worst of the relief needs were met, but the sheer magnitude of unemployment entailed costs far beyond the capacity of the city alone, and appeals had to be made to higher levels of government.

A second major conclusion is that with the exception of McGeer's administration in Vancouver and Dore's 1936–38 term in Seattle all city leaders were convinced that the only sensible strategy was to cut expenses drastically to balance the budget and to maintain fiscal solvency. Over and over again city officials emphasized that only vigorous cost cutting could lead to economic recovery. Such ideas combined with modest and declining tax revenues automatically precluded any significant job creation programs.

Moreover, while Seattle's residents endured many privations during these grim years the representative Vancouverite suffered even more intensely. Class divisions were more pronounced in the Canadian city, clashes between the authorities and the unemployed more frequent, and the mood of hopelessness and helplessness more pervasive. With both municipal and provincial governments unable, and the federal government unwilling, to implement significant programs Vancouverites could do little more than tighten their belts and hope that things would get better. And unlike their Seattle counterparts Vancouverites could not look to their nation's capital with confidence and gratitude that something was being done to remedy the situation. As one Canadian spokesman with a touch of envy and some exaggeration pointed out:

> In Canada we had no New Deal, no A.A.A. or other measures designed to give agriculture a parity with urban industry, no Wagner Act for trade unions, no great public housing schemes, no C.C.C. camps for employed youth, no T.V.A. to reconstruct vast blighted areas, no Federal Writers or Federal Artists Projects, no new parkways about our big cities and no new recreation camps among our lakes and forests, and, last but not least, no fireside chats.[67]

In December 1939, three months after Canada's declaration of war on Germany, and for the first time in nine years, Vancouver's relief costs dropped sharply.[68] As in the United States it was the war and wartime demands that ultimately brought an end to the Depression.

8

World War II and the Postwar Decades

The death of Rolland H. Denny, at age eighty-eight, in June 1939, can be taken as the end of an era in Seattle's history. He was the last survivor of the group of twelve adults and twelve children who had come ashore at Alki Point in West Seattle in November 1851. An infant of two months at that time, he had spent his entire life in Seattle, and had seen it expand from a small village to a city that covered 70 square miles and had a population of nearly half a million. But while major growth had occurred during his lifetime the city's commercial and service activities still relied primarily on the region's diverse raw materials, and its manufacturers still catered to the demands of a local market. The size and scope of such activities had expanded prodigiously but still shared much in common with the city of the 1870s.

The year 1939 also marked the beginning of World War II. In the next six years a series of changes that had begun during Denny's later years would all intensify and in time substantially reshape the entire community. The Boeing Airplane Company, for example, had been established in Seattle in 1917. But the war would lead to massive expansion of its facilities, establish aircraft manufacture as the city's dominant industry, and permanently reshape Seattle's economic life. When one speaks of the "military-industrial complex," or of the "martial metropolis," such terms capture a fundamental characteristic that evolved in Seattle during and after World War II. The city's racial makeup also underwent significant change. A trickle of black migrants had been arriving in the city since the early years of the century. This process would intensify during the war and postwar years, and as was true of cities throughout the North and West, would modify Seattle's racial composition. Along with these changes, the distribution of Seattle's population also changed, as residents and new-comers alike opted to live in suburban communities rather than in the city proper. Finally, the federal presence in the city, first begun during the De-pression years, became steadily more evident during wartime. This pro-cess too would be elaborated and extended in the postwar decades. The city would continue to evolve after the war, as well as experience the spurts and the slumps that it had encountered so often in the past. But the Seattle of the 1950s and 1960s would have a significantly different economic struc-ture, racial composition, population distribution, and political orientation than the Seattle of Rolland Denny's era.

Such changes were not unique to Seattle alone, for cities throughout the United States were significantly reshaped by World War II. Historians are in substantial agreement that the war not only restored economic pros-perity and national confidence but that the United States became a more urbanized, industrialized technological society.[1] "For most Americans," one scholar has written, "World War II spelled neither hardship nor suffer-ing, but a better way of life."[2] Historians also agree that wartime demands led to a massive extension of federal agencies and activities, and that busi-ness corporations increased in size and power. The close interrelationship of big government and big business, in turn, when combined with vora-cious demands of the armed services, led to the rise of a military-industrial complex with profound ramifications for the nation. A further point of basic agreement is that employment opportunities for women and blacks increased dramatically, but that long-standing convictions about such ac-tivities changed hardly at all.

While there is general agreement on domestic developments during World War II, scholars differ as to whether these represented distinctive change in American society or merely continued existing patterns. Some stress that the military-industrial complex, for example, represented a new and radical departure from previous American history.[3] Others argue that the mutual interdependence of big business and the military was under way long before World War II, and that the war simply intensified a basic fact of life about American society.[4] Some point out that the migra-tion of blacks from the South was well established by World War I and the 1920s, while others emphasize the magnitude of the change occasioned by World War II. It would be foolhardy to argue that either "change" or "conti-nuity" completely dominated the United States during World War II and the postwar years. But when we focus on Seattle it is clear that developments in that city more strongly support the "change" model than the "continuity" one.

Vancouver too was shaped by World War II. Directly involved in the war two years before Seattle, with enlistments and casualties coming much earlier, it too experienced significant change.[5] Employment soared in the city's shipyards, a host of foundries and machine shops were kept busy, and an infant aircraft industry mushroomed. Yet this surge in manufacturing activity was a wartime phenomenon only. With the end of the war shipyard employment quickly declined, aircraft manufacture disappeared, and the city returned to its long-established role of transportation, supply, and service center. As in Seattle suburban growth was dramatic during the postwar years. North Vancouver, Surrey, Richmond, and Delta all expanded rapidly. At the same time a significantly new stream of immigrants began to arrive in the city. English-speaking migrants from the United Kingdom made up a part of this stream but the influx of Germans, Italians, Chinese, Greeks, Hungarians, and Yugoslavs was unprecedented. This stream would continue for years and gradually transform the Anglo-Canadian city into a much more diverse, cosmopolitan community. In the history of the two cities, World War II was unquestionably a pivotal event that reshaped many of their basic characteristics. They would continue to show a variety of parallel developments in the postwar years, but the divergent trends in their economy and in their population mix would become more and more evident.

The immediate impact of World War II on Vancouver in many ways resembled that of World War I. As in 1914, the Canadian city was involved almost at once, and as before a flock of volunteers rushed to enlist. But the exodus was not as dramatic nor the mood as excited and bellicose as twenty-five years earlier. For hundreds of enlistees, service in the armed forces was a welcome escape from the recurring unemployment and frustrations of a decade-long depression. But few doubted that the war would be long and difficult.

Vancouver's economy thrived during the war years with much of the early work concentrated in the shipyards of the long-established Burrard Dry Dock Company in North Vancouver. At the outbreak of war, it had only 200 workers, but within a year it was deeply involved in wartime activity with orders for four corvettes and six mine sweepers. This main "North Yard" expanded quickly and at its peak employed about 6,500 workers, most of whom were involved in the construction of 10,000-ton cargo vessels. In addition, a new "South Yard" was constructed on False Creek and employed about 4,500 workers. It concentrated on the construction of hulls which were then delivered to the North Yard for outfitting and testing. A further facility at Lapointe Pier did repair and maintenance work and employed 2,000.

All together, these diverse facilities of the Burrard Dry Dock Company produced 109 of the 10,000-ton cargo vessels. Like shipyards everywhere it entailed rough, dirty, and dangerous work. Here is riveter Bill White:

> Well, just picture all this—you can't see the guy next to you because of the smoke from the goddamn pots, there's red-hot rivets raining through the air on all sides of you, there's three ton plates swinging around overhead, its so goddamn noisy from the guns you couldn't hear a warning even if the guy was shouting in your goddamn ear you've got all those people swarming around, most of whom don't know the sharp end from the blunt end. You can't imagine the disorganization there was. I don't know how they got anything done at all.[6]

In the spring of 1941, work began on the construction of an additional shipyard on False Creek, and by mid-1942, this West Coast Shipbuilders had some 4,000 employees. The overwhelming majority of these workers were from British Columbia and the Prairies. But it is noteworthy that the "key men" in the managerial and technical staff were almost all from the United Kingdom.[7] Thus General Manager W. D. McLaren was "born, educated, and worked" in Scotland; A. J. Squire, assistant manager was "born, educated, and worked" in England. The same general background also applied to the engineering superintendent, the assistant engineering superintendent, the hull superintendent, and the plant engineer. Together they provide an additional example of the pervasive and significant role played by the British immigrant in Vancouver's life.

West Coast Shipbuilders launched its first vessel in March 1942.[8] Between then and December 1944, it launched fifty 10,000-tonners, an average of one every twenty-one days. With its work force of 4,000, productivity was comparable to the fifteen Liberty ships per month turned out by Henry Kaiser's 45,000 workers in his Richmond, California, yards. In total, Vancouver shipyards accounted for over half of Canada's total wartime output of major cargo vessels.

These achievements were impressive, but it is noteworthy that Vancouver's wartime shipbuilding began its decline as early as December 1943. Activity would remain vigorous for another year and a half, but within six months of the end of hostilities all shipbuilding on False Creek had stopped.

A flurry of postwar orders sustained activity in the North Yard, but with the completion of these in 1948, shipbuilding employment dropped to less than a tenth of the wartime peak of 17,000.

During the war years, Vancouver also experienced a boom in aircraft manufacture. This grew largely out of decisions made in Seattle, and was sustained largely by orders from the U.S. Navy. Aircraft manufacture in Vancouver had its origin in 1929 when William E. Boeing of Seattle purchased the plant and equipment of the Hoffar-Beeching Company, a local boatbuilder.[9] Renamed the Boeing Aircraft Company of Canada, this small plant on Coal Harbour turned out eight aircraft over the next few years.[10] With the Depression, employment slumped to a staff of about a dozen that concentrated mainly on maintenance and repair work. In 1937–38, employment jumped when orders were received for seventeen Blackburn "Sharks," a two-winged pontoon-type torpedo bomber for the Royal Navy. But with the completion of that order, employment again dropped.

It was not until October 1940 when the Canadian government announced that it would finance the construction of a large new plant at Sea Island, that major expansion of Boeing-Canada occurred. Construction took over a year, cost one and a half million dollars, and in July 1942 the first Consolidated Catalina Flying Boat built in Vancouver was completed.[11] Just why Boeing officials chose to have these American aircraft built in Vancouver for the U.S. Navy is unknown. But the small demand for these specialized aircraft and the decision to concentrate Seattle's facilities on the production of the B-17 Flying Fortress undoubtedly contributed. The Canadian government's provision of a modern plant, the availability of skilled workers, and the slightly lower wage rates in British Columbia probably also played a part in the decision to build the PBYs in Vancouver.

The construction of these two-engined, long-range amphibian aircraft, continued for about two years, though by late 1944 the Vancouver plant concentrated on components for the B-29 Superfortress, as well as diverse parts for the De Haviland Mosquito bomber.[12] According to a report submitted to the city council in September 1945, Boeing Aircraft of Canada had manufactured 362 PBYs and 1,000 bomb bays for the B-29. Its peak employment was 7,552 and it paid a total of $40 million in wages and salaries.[13] Within two months of V-J Day, however, Boeing-Canada operations were completely shut down, and aircraft manufacture in Vancouver came to an end.[14]

Although the United States did not become directly involved in World War II until December 1941, the twenty-six months that elapsed between the outbreak of war in Europe and the Japanese attack on Pearl Harbor was a period of immense change for Seattle. Like other American cities that were directly involved in the defense effort its population rose dramatically.[15] A detailed survey carried out by the Works Progress Administration showed that in the period from October 1940 to November 1941 Seattle received about 42,000 migrants.[16] For a city that had stagnated throughout the 1930s, rising only from 365,000 to 368,000, this influx was especially sudden. Of the thirty-nine major cities covered in this survey only Los Angeles, San Diego, and Washington, D.C., received a larger absolute number of migrants while Seattle's relative growth topped the list.

Like their counterparts throughout the nation, most of these newcomers to Seattle did not travel far. About 45 percent were from Washington State itself, and of these more than half were former residents of Seattle. As a group they were overwhelmingly white (99.5 percent) and predominantly young men. Women were underrepresented and blacks made up only a tiny minority. As the months unfolded the proportion of women and blacks among incoming migrants would increase. The massive defense appropriations of 1940 left no doubt about the future demand for workers, but it took time for Seattle's machine shops, shipyards, and manufacturing plants to "gear up." Throughout the year the grasp of the Depression proved tenacious, for while employment rose, about 13 percent of the city's labor force remained unemployed.[17]

As in Vancouver, it was the shipbuilding industry that most quickly reflected wartime demands. In September 1939, the Seattle-Tacoma Shipbuilding Corporation received an order for five large cargo carriers.[18] This contract for $10 million marked the beginning of a whole series of orders and led to rapid expansion of shipyard facilities throughout the Puget Sound region whether at Seattle's Harbor Island, the East Waterway of the Duwamish or in Tacoma, Bremerton, Bainbridge Island, Kirkland, or Everett. In the early months British and French orders for cargo vessels were especially important, but as the United States intensified its rearmament program, orders for a variety of military vessels also accumulated. In the first year of the war, for example, Seattle yards received contracts for twenty destroyers, while the Puget Sound Navy Yard at Bremerton had orders for six more at a price of about $6 million each.[19]

While shipbuilding led the way, the vast expansion of aircraft manufacture ultimately had the greatest impact on Seattle. Employment at Boeing had been moving up steadily in the late 1930s from 1,500 in 1937, to about 5,000 at the outbreak of war in 1939.[20] Much of the work was concentrated on a four-engined, heavy-duty bomber, the B-17 Flying Fortress. The basic design and development work had been done in the mid-1930s and the first B-17 rolled out of the shops in January 1937. A series of orders were received in the succeeding months, but it was not until September 1940 when the Defense Department placed an order for seventy-seven B-17s at a cost of $70 million, that orders began to accumulate.[21] This huge order confirmed that the Flying Fortress would be one of the nation's primary bombers and that many additional orders would be forthcoming.

The city's war-related buildup was sustained throughout 1941, with ramifications not only for aircraft manufacture and shipbuilding, but for aluminum and steel fabricating plants as well as for the lumber industry.[22] In March, the first of twenty-two B-17s bound for Britain left McChord Field, handled by "eight mild-mannered English youths."[23] The U.S. Army revealed plans for the expenditure of nearly $5 million for piers, transit sheds, and warehouses on South Alaskan Way. In April, the Lake Union plant of Associated Shipbuilders received an order for ten wooden mine sweepers at $340,000 each, to add to the order of four navy seaplane tenders at $5 million each.[24] By mid-year Boeing employed 12,000 workers in Seattle and had back orders for 400 planes. Defense officials announced in June that identical B-17s, with interchangeable parts, would be built at Boeing plants in Seattle and Wichita, Kansas, and by Douglas Aircraft and Lockheed Aircraft in Southern California.[25] In its annual Christmas edition, the *Argus* saw 1941 as a year of change which had transformed Seattle "in a thousand big and little ways" into the defense headquarters of the Pacific Northwest and Alaska. It had received one and a half billion dollars in military-related contracts, and was the city with "America's highest per capita share in the job of rearmament."[26]

There is no doubt that Seattle's manufacturing activities were substantially geared to military production well before the Japanese attack on Pearl Harbor in December 1941. With the declaration of war, the entire city quickly made the adaptation to wartime. Aircraft warning services, volunteer wardens, and auxiliary police were soon organized in the awareness that Japan might launch bombing raids. Precise details on troop movements and aircraft production were censored, the rationing of gasoline, tires, foods, and liquors instituted, and drafting of men into the services begun. As the demand for workers rose, women moved into a variety of jobs traditionally handled by men.[27] The stream of workers to shipyards, manufacturing plants, Boeing, and downtown offices strained the transit system and caused severe traffic jams. Staggered hours, "share a ride" programs, and improved equipment all helped, but did not eliminate the problem. Some critics argued that there was still far too much slackness and indifference, and suggested that only a Japanese bomb on a downtown street would snap Seattle out of its supposed lethargy. Yet the response of local citizens to a whole series of drives—for bonds, household fats, or waste aluminum—was enthusiastic.

By 1943, Seattle had settled into a pattern of activity that would not change significantly until after the war. Boeing plants in Seattle and Renton were on the round-the-clock basis. Most of the "bugs" in the production of the B-17 had been eliminated and the Seattle plant alone averaged one Flying Fortress every two hours—peak production would occur in 1944 with one every ninety minutes.[28] The development and testing of the larger, heavier, B-29 Superfortress was well under way.[29] The Puget Sound Navy Yard and seven private yards were also busy. Demands for workers seemed insatiable with women accounting for 16 percent of the workers in the city's shipyards, and 47 percent of the Boeing labor force.[30] With more and more persons in the armed forces, local restaurants, offices, hospitals, and shops faced many problems getting the help they needed. Total wartime employment in the Seattle-Tacoma area peaked in November 1943 at 385,000.[31] It declined slightly thereafter, though Boeing employment would not peak until January 1945 at 45,000.[32]

Regardless of the yardstick applied, the entire Puget Sound region underwent prodigious expansion during the war years. Between 1940 and 1944 the population of the Seattle-Tacoma-Bremerton region (that is, King, Pierce, and Kitsap counties) went up by about 25 percent. Seattle increased by 40 percent, whereas Bremerton quadrupled from 15,000 to 60,000.[33] Whereas 14,000 persons were employed in regional shipbuilding and aircraft manufacture in 1940, by 1944 such employment had soared to 132,000.[34] Diverse military installations, whether at Fort Lewis outside Tacoma, Seattle's Sand Point Naval Air Station, or the Seattle Port of Embarkation, all created jobs for civilians. Such employment in the region went from 1,500 in 1940 to over 25,000 four years later.[35] Finally, a focus on Seattle itself is revealing. In 1939 the value of the city's total manufacturing output was $70 million. By 1944 Boeing's output alone was valued at $600 million.[36]

Basic to this expansion, of course, were the massive defense expenditures occasioned by the war effort. From June 1940 to November 1944 federally funded war plant expansion in the region amounted to $315 million while contracts for war supplies (exclusive of Bremerton) amounted to $3.45 billion.[37] About 75 percent of these contracts were awarded to Seattle firms, with most of it destined for aircraft manufacture. The magnitude of such expenditures was unparalleled and would leave a permanent imprint not only on Boeing Aircraft but on Seattle itself.

The wartime stream of defense workers to Seattle and Vancouver proved an immense strain to the housing facilities of both cities. But while the adaptation was made with a minimum of difficulty in the Canadian city, it caused considerable anxiety in Seattle, where residents were not unaware that many of the newcomers were black. The city had a small, long-established black community in the vicinity of East Madison Street, but it accounted for only 1 percent of the city's total population at the outbreak of war.[38] With the inrush of job seekers in the early 1940s, blacks began to assume a much more important role in Seattle's population makeup. The editor of *Argus* left no doubt about his opinion when he wrote "undesirables by the thousands are moving into our city."[39] He went on to insist that southern jails had been emptied of "undesirable Negroes," who were then encouraged to seek jobs in the Pacific Northwest. But his contempt was not aimed solely at blacks, since "equally objectionable white itinerants have settled down here."

The blacks' struggle for employment, housing, and social acceptance was long and bitter in Seattle, as it was throughout the nation.[40] The move into menial jobs as dishwashers, casual laborers, and janitors was made with a minimum of difficulty, but the move into semiskilled and skilled occupations in the city's war plants was an entirely different story.[41] The struggle for jobs at Boeing, for example, was tied up with a complex labor dispute that focused on Local 751 of the Aeronautical Mechanics Union, an AFL affiliate.[42] Boeing insisted that it was powerless in the matter of black employment, because Local 751 prohibited black membership and it was labor's sole bargaining agent with the company. Although the union voted to accept blacks in July 1940, it was badly split, with both internal and external critics charging that it was "the victim of Communist strategy." In April 1941, the AFL suspended Local 751. After months of tension and some violence, Local 751 was reinstated. Communist members were expelled, and black members no longer admitted.

Not until April 1942, after pressure had been applied by the nation's Fair Employment Practices Commission (FEPC), did blacks begin to obtain employment in substantial numbers.[43] One AFL official spoke for many whites when he pointed out, "We rather resent that the war situation has been used to alter an old-established custom."[44] By 1944, when employment was near its wartime peak, Boeing had some 1,600 black workers, or about 3 percent of its total work force. At the same time, Seattle area shipyards employed another 2,000 blacks.[45]

The blacks' struggle for satisfactory housing was another major problem. White hostility, restrictive covenants, and threatened violence effectively excluded them from all facilities outside existing black neighborhoods and led to severe overcrowding. One authority estimated in 1944 that at least 7,000 blacks were "living in the same areas and for the most part in the same buildings housing 3,789 negroes in 1940."[46] Although single blacks could usually get some type of accommodation with relatives or friends, the difficulties faced by black families were acute. By all odds the best available housing was provided by the Seattle Housing Authority, the local agency for the nation's Federal Housing Administration. Under the direction of Jesse Epstein, a mild-mannered but deeply committed leader, it made good use of federal funds to construct Yesler Terrace, the city's first permanent public housing project.[47] This was followed by additional facilities at Rainier Vista, Beacon Hill, West Seattle, and Sand Point on Lake Washington. All were racially integrated, clean, and comfortable with affordable rents. Although tensions occurred in previously all-white neighborhoods, integration went smoothly in the older downtown projects. Public housing throughout the United States has usually been a distinct cut below generally accepted middle-class standards, and regarded as appropriate for temporary accommodation only.[48] Permanent residence in such facilities seemed to indicate that the occupant "had not made it" and had to "rely on the government." This traditional pattern quickly unfolded in Seattle. As superior private housing became available, white residents tended to leave, and the proportion of blacks in public housing rose steadily.

In Vancouver, too, federal agencies played a significant role in providing housing to meet wartime demands.[49] Under the existing constitutional arrangements responsibility for the provision of housing rested with provincial and municipal authorities. But with wartime shortages regional officials were pleased to accept federal intervention, a federal Crown corporation, Wartime Housing Limited, ultimately constructed 750 units for shipyard workers in North Vancouver, and an additional 300 units in Richmond for employees of Boeing Aircraft of Canada. Unlike Seattle, however, there was little organized support for the continuation of such facilities. Municipal officials, financial institutions, local builders, and real estate agents, as well as the federal housing bureaucracy itself remained convinced that such federal activity was both socialistic and dangerous and that the private sector could do a better job. The Socialist CCF, on the other hand, condemned the housing as both shoddy and inadequate. With such criticism from both the right and the left the Wartime Housing Limited was not reconstituted as a permanent federal agency. By 1947 it was dissolved, with the houses sold to the occupants.

As Vancouver's wartime immigrants were primarily from western Canada and almost exclusively white, it did not face the racial tensions experienced in Seattle. But in the wartime treatment of their Japanese residents a basically similar pattern unfolded.[50] Decisions of their respective federal governments shaped the events in both cities. But there is no doubt that Vancouverites and Seattleites played a large part in generating the conviction that the Japanese had to be removed. There is also no doubt that while both nations ran roughshod over the rights of their Japanese citizens, such treatment was even more blatant and more sustained in the Canadian setting than in the American one.

In the twenty-seven months that elapsed between the outbreak of war in Europe and the Japanese attack on Pearl Harbor, the long-standing hostility that British Columbians held for all Orientals became focused more and more on the Japanese. With most of Canada's 23,000 Japanese living in British Columbia, many of them concentrated in or near Vancouver, and with the increasing anxiety over Japan's military moves in the Pacific, the city was ridden with rumors of supposed sabotage by this minority element. A local unit of the Royal Canadian Mounted Police could report to federal authorities that their investigations showed that the Japanese community was loyal, and posed no threat to the nation. But Alderman Halford Wilson's insistence in city council that diverse restrictions were essential, and that all Japanese-owned fishing vessels should be confiscated, was much more typical of the mood that permeated the city.[51]

The outbreak of war with Japan in December 1941 precipitated a series of direct actions. Thirty-eight Japanese nationals deemed dangerous to national security were quickly arrested, and much of the Japanese fishing fleet was immobilized. Hotels and mills discharged their Japanese employees, Japanese language newspapers and schools closed voluntarily. Along with these steps came a host of suggestions to local and federal authorities that all Japanese be evacuated. As an editor of the *Vancouver Sun* pointed out, "We told the people to be calm. Their reply was a bombardment of letters that the Japs all be interned."[52] No single leader or pressure group dominated this process. Politicians, labor unions, service clubs, and neighborhood groups were united in their conviction that the Japanese posed a threat to national security and had to be removed. Spokesmen in Vancouver and Victoria were especially active, and their ideas were picked up and reinforced. The Japanese community itself could do nothing to establish its loyalty. Tears, a hopeless shrug, and "Shikata-ga-nai" (It can't be helped) summed it all up.[53]

On February 24, 1942, the Mackenzie King government passed an order-in-council that empowered the minister of justice to remove "any and all persons" from any designated "protected area" in Canada. This decision for evacuation of the Japanese was taken in response to the public clamor in British Columbia with cabinet member Ian McKenzie (Liberal MP of Vancouver Center) playing an especially important role, but there is no doubt that the Canadian government was aware of the developments in the United States. Just five days earlier, President Roosevelt had granted comparable authority to his secretary of war. Indeed, the Canadian order-in-council was almost identical to the American order.[54] The public announcement three days later that all persons of Japanese ancestry were to leave Canada's Pacific Coast began a process that would last for nine months. By November 1942, some 21,000 Japanese (a fifth of whom were from Vancouver) were removed from their homes. Whether they wound up in isolated camps in eastern British Columbia, in the beet fields of Alberta and Manitoba, or in prisoner of war camps in northern Ontario, all were deeply scarred by the experience.

The developments in West Coast American cities did not differ significantly from what occurred in British Columbia. In Seattle, Portland, San Francisco, and Los Angeles, a standard pattern unfolded. There too the concentration of Japanese residents was high, with about 9 out of 10 of the nation's 127,000 Japanese living in California, Oregon, or Washington. There too the deep-seated and long-standing distrust of all Japanese residents quickly surfaced. There too it would be later realized that the Japanese community was loyal, and that there was not a single demonstrable case of sabotage or espionage by that community. There too newspapers and public spokesmen emphasized the need for constant vigilance.

But whereas British Columbia's private and public spokesmen played a major role in molding the decisions of their federal government—with military authorities generally in opposition—in the United States military authorities dominated the decision-making process.[55] Within seventy-two hours after the attack on Pearl Harbor, a military proposal for mass evacuation was developed, and by December 19, General J. L. DeWitt, Western Defense Command, San Francisco, officially recommended that "action be initiated at the earliest practicable date to collect all alien subjects fourteen years and older and remove them to the interior of the U.S."[56] Although no immediate action was taken, such statements intensified public fears and led to a host of petitions to "do something" about "all of the Japs running loose." Justice Department officials, however, resisted the proposals that the Japanese be removed from coastal areas. They argued that although such an approach could be applied to Japanese aliens, it would violate the rights of U.S. citizens who were of Japanese descent. But this opposition disappeared after February 19, 1942, when President Roosevelt authorized the War Department to carry out any evacuation plan that it considered appropriate.

Conflicting testimony given to a congressional committee hearing in Seattle in early March 1942 captures the profound division of opinion. According to Mayor Earl Millikin,

> the sentiment of the people of Seattle is overwhelmingly in favor of evacuation. . . . It is the element that may have come in say in the last three or four years . . . or individuals sent here for espionage purposes by the Japanese government . . . that should be regarded as dangerous. We can't afford to take chances. . . . We have about seven thousand to eight thousand Japanese in Seattle. . . . There is no doubt . . . that seven thousand nine hundred probably are above question, but the other hundred would burn this town down and let the Japanese planes come in and bring on something that would dwarf Pearl Harbor.[57]

To James Y. Sakamoto, editor of the *Japanese American Courier,* on the other hand,

> We are Americans. We want to do our duty where we can serve best. We make these statements, not because we fear evacuation, but because we believe to the bottom of our hearts that the best interests of the United States, our nation, are to be served by being permitted to stay, work, fight, and die for our country if necessary, here where we belong.[58]

On March 24, 1942, the first significant evacuation occurred when fifty-four Japanese families were removed from Brainbridge Island, 10 miles west of Seattle and home of the Bremerton Navy Yard. It was a dress rehearsal that would be repeated many times in the following months throughout Washington, Oregon, and California. Seattle's Japanese community of 6,900, the city's largest minority element, was eliminated.[59] In all, some 112,000 men, women, and children were ultimately relocated in hastily built camps in the Mountain States as well as in California and Arkansas.

There is little doubt that the removal of the Japanese met with emphatic public approval both in the United States and Canada. The long-standing hostility directed toward all Orientals, combined with the conviction that the Japanese were a threat to national security during wartime, overwhelmed any potential opposition. A plaintive note from Kimiko Mitsui to Mayor Millikin in April 1942 captured the reality of the situation for thousands of native-born Japanese. "If I am here to graduate," she wrote, "do you suppose that I could obtain permission to stay out after eight o'clock to graduate at our high school auditorium."[60] But the editor of the Seattle *Argus* spoke for most city residents when he asserted that "the government's pampering of these people is something we find difficult to understand . . . there are few if any loyal Americans among them."[61] The overreaction of public authorities in British Columbia and the Pacific Coast states can best be appreciated when it is realized that in Hawaii, where 150,000 persons of Japanese ancestry made up 37 percent of the population (as opposed to 2 percent in Washington, and 3 percent in British Columbia), only a tiny minority of 1,875 were relocated to the mainland. Officials in Washington D.C. were unhappy, but had to agree that a mass evacuation was "not feasible."[62]

Throughout the war years the authority of the British Columbia Security Commission, Department of Labour, and the Department of Justice to keep the Japanese interned went unchallenged, and the entire issue was largely ignored. In the United States, on the other hand, the legality of the decision was challenged on a number of occasions by citizens of Japanese descent.[63] A major case involved Gordon Hirabayashi, a senior at the University of Washington. In 1942, he challenged the constitutionality of the original curfew and evacuation order on the grounds that it violated his rights as an American citizen. The Supreme Court ultimately rejected the argument, and ruled in 1943 that the government's action was appropriate "in the crisis of war."

The decision by the U.S. Army in September 1943 to use Japanese-Americans as combat troops signaled a significant change in governmental policy. Up to that time, both public opinion and governmental policy had been essentially repressive. After September 1943 a general liberalization occurred, and though there would be much opposition and many setbacks the new approach was sustained. The outstanding performance of these infantry units in Italy, their heavy casualties, and the wide publicity given these events undoubtedly changed public opinion about the loyalty and the rights of Japanese-Americans. All of these developments in turn facilitated postwar reconciliation.

In Canada a significantly different process unfolded with both public opinion and federal policy remaining dogmatic and inflexible. A sprinkling of nisei (second-generation Japanese-Canadian) were allowed to attend Canadian universities, but the Department of National Defense was adamant in its refusal to enlist Japanese-Canadians.[64] When change occurred, it was an indirect, highly secretive manner. In the summer of 1944, the British Army approached the Canadian Government to obtain nisei volunteers for a variety of intelligence and translation work in the Asian theater of war. Originally these men were to be attached to the British Army, but in February 1945 Ottawa quietly changed its policy and admitted a small group of nisei to the Canadian Army. But even this modest step was not publicly acknowledged until after the war. As Ken Adachi points out in his perceptive *The Enemy That Never Was*, the impact of this nisei contribution on later race relations in Canada was "almost negligible."[65]

Postwar developments showed that traditional racist convictions still prevailed in Canada. Though the prime minister could point out that no Canadian-born Japanese had been charged either with subversion or disloyalty during the war, the government nevertheless felt obliged to disperse the Japanese community across the nation and prevent their return to coastal British Columbia. In August 1945, all Japanese internees—citizen and alien alike—were informed that they must choose either to return to Japan, or else settle somewhere "east of the Rockies." The legality of the deportation order was challenged, but before the policy was abandoned in 1947, some 4,000 Japanese, over half of whom were Canadian-born, were transported to Japan.[66] They discovered that they were as much "the outsider" in that nation as they were in the one they had left. Some returned to Canada, but not until March 1949, almost four years after the war, were Japanese finally allowed to vote in federal elections anywhere in Canada.

The American treatment of the Japanese community during wartime was a harsh, vindictive one. But when we consider the willingness to accept legal challenges, the approach to voting rights, the acceptance of the nisei for combat service, the freedom of choice in the location decision, the willingness to set aside "repatriation requests," or the compensation paid for seized property, the treatment was much superior to the Canadian performance. Some Japanese-Canadians could look back on their wartime experience as being "all for the better," but for the great majority it was a searing experience that left them permanently embittered.

With the end of World War II, both Seattleites and Vancouverites were aware that much had changed in the previous six years. Seattle had suffered 1,100 war-related deaths, or about one death for every ninety families in the city.[67] This was somewhat higher proportion than in Vancouver, but although it brought grief to the immediate families, such casualties were modest when compared with those suffered by countless European communities. Virtually every family in Seattle or Vancouver had its fearful moments during wartime, but for most people, the years from 1939 to 1945 meant steady employment, good wages, and increased savings which pushed the despair of the Depression years far into the background. With the exuberance of V-E Day and V-J Day behind them, many could look forward to the new appliances, cars, or houses that they had long sought and now could obtain.

Along with this basic optimism were definite fears of postwar depression. Shipyard employment in both cities had plummeted, aircraft employment in Vancouver had disappeared, and the Boeing work force in Seattle had dropped to 9,200 by 1946, about one-fifth its wartime peak.[68] Yet, the feared depression did not materialize. Purchases with wartime savings helped sustain employment and recovery was rapid, especially in Seattle. Contracts for a variety of military aircraft were obtained, and the Boeing Stratocruiser, a modified version of the B-29 bomber, found purchasers at Pan-Am, United, Northwest, and American Airlines.[69] By 1948, Boeing employment had recovered to 18,000 and five years later reached 31,000.[70]

No single process can be said to have dominated the postwar era in Seattle and Vancouver, but it is certain that the sharp rise in population was of primary importance. Between 1940 and 1950, Washington State grew by 37 percent and British Columbia by 43 percent or twice the growth rate of their respective nations. The influx of war workers, the decisions of thousands of former servicemen to relocate on the West Coast, and the rise in the number of marriages and births all contributed. But while the rise in absolute numbers was impressive, the rate of growth of both cities fell far below the rates that had been achieved in the late nineteenth and early part of the twentieth century. Table 13 traces these patterns over the years.

Almost all cities in Washington and British Columbia shared in this postwar growth, but the development of suburban communities outside the major cities was especially significant. Lake City, Burien, Bellevue outside Seattle, and West Vancouver, Burnaby, Richmond near Vancouver, all grew dramatically and tilted the balance of metropolitan population more and more to the suburban side. In 1940 about 20 percent of the metropolitan population of both cities lived in the suburbs; by 1950, it had jumped to 40 percent. Decentralization continued in the following decades and by 1980 two-thirds of the population of Seattle and Vancouver lived outside the core city.

Table 13   Population Growth in Seattle and Vancouver 1860/61 to 1980/81

	Seattle	Vancouver
1860/61	302	—
1870/71	1,107	—
1880/81	3,553	300
1890/91	42,837	13,709
1900/01	80,671	27,010
1910/11	237,194	100,401
1920/21	315,312	163,220
1930/31	365,583	246,593
1940/41	368,302	275,353
1950/51	467,591	344,833
1960/61	557,087	384,522
1970/71	530,831	426,256
1980/81	493,846	414,281

Source: (U.S. Census, Population, 1860 to 1980; Census of Canada, Population, 1881 to 1981. The population figure for Seattle in 1860 includes all of King County. The Vancouver population for 1921 includes South Vancouver and Point Grey which did not officially join the city until 1929; the 1881 population figure for Vancouver is based on R. T. Williams, ed., *British Columbia Directory*, 1882/83.

Beyond the population growth and dispersion evident in Table 14, the ethnic makeup of the two cities also transformed in the postwar decades. Such changes were in large part a reflection of the differences in the immigration policies of the two nations. Seattle's foreign-born groups continued their long-term decline from the peak of 1920 when the Immigration Acts of 1921, 1924, and 1929 effectively ended America's traditional policy of unrestricted immigration. By 1970 Seattle's total foreign-born residents made up 9 percent of the city's total population and as in the past were mainly from Scandinavia, Canada, Great Britain, and Germany.

While these gradual declines were occurring in Seattle's foreign-born element, the makeup of the city's native-born Americans was also changing. The wartime exodus of thousands of blacks out of the South to jobs and opportunities in the North and West did not cease with the conclusion of the war, rather it continued throughout the 1950s and 1960s. Seattle, like every other major city in the nation, shared in this massive redistribution of population. Between 1940 and 1970 its black population went up tenfold, reaching 38,000 or 7 percent of the city's population by 1970.

Table 14 Central City and Suburban Population in Metropolitan
Seattle and Vancouver, 1900/01 to 1980/81

Metropolitan Area		Central City		Suburbs	
Year	No.	No.	%	No.	%
SEATTLE					
1900	80,885	80,671	99.7	214	0.3
1910	255,622	237,194	92.6	18,428	7.4
1920	357,950	315,312	88.1	42,637	11.9
1930	420,663	365,583	85.9	55,080	13.1
1940	452,639	368,302	81.4	84,337	18.6
1950	844,572	467,591	55.4	376,981	44.6
1960	1,107,213	557,087	50.3	550,126	49.7
1970	1,421,869	530,831	37.3	891,038	62.7
1980	1,607,469	493,846	30.7	1,113,623	69.3
VANCOUVER					
1901	28,985	27,010	93.5	1,885	6.5
1911	123,902	100,401	81.1	23,501	18.9
1921	198,468	163,220	82.3	35,248	17.7
1931	304,854	246,593	80.9	58,261	19.1
1941	374,665	275,353	79.2	72,312	20.8
1951	561,961	344,833	61.4	217,127	38.6
1961	790,165	384,522	48.5	405,643	51.5
1971	1,082,352	426,256	39.4	656,093	60.6
1981	1,268,183	414,281	32.7	853,902	67.3

Source: U.S. Census, 1910, vol. 1, pp. 73–74; *U.S. Census, 1920*, vol. 1, pp. 62–64; *U.S. Census, 1930*, vol. 2, p. 19; *U.S. Census, 1940*, vol. 1, p. 1135; *U.S. Census, 1950*, vol. 2, Pt. 47, p. 16; *U.S. Census, 1960*, vol. 1, Pt. 49, p. 18; *U.S. Census, 1970*, vol. 1, Pt. 49; *U.S. Census, 1980*, vol. 1, Pt. 49, p. 24; *Census of Canada, 1911*, vol. 1, p. 39; *Census of Canada, 1931*, vol. 2, p. 104; *Census of Canada, 1941*, vol. 2, p. 143; *Census of Canada, 1951*, vol. 1, Table 6, p. 85, Table 12, p. 2; *Census of Canada, 1961*, vol. 1, Pt. 1, Bull. 5, Table 7, p. 54, Bull. 6, Table 10, p. 3; *Census of Canada, 1971*, Pt. 1, Bull. 8, Table 8, p. 4; *Census of Canada, 1981, Population*, vol. 2, Provincial Series, *British Columbia*, Table 5, p. 5.

In Vancouver, the number of non-Canadian-born residents showed a sharp increase in the postwar period, reaching 146,705 (35 percent) by 1970. About a third came from the United Kingdom and the United States, yet it is significant that immigrants from those nations showed both an absolute and a relative decline after 1940. The distinctly new feature in Vancouver's makeup was the great increase in the number of persons from Europe and Asia. In 1970, for example, Vancouver had over 10,000 foreign-born Italians, 8,000 Germans, 6,000 Scandinavians, 5,000 Russians, 4,000 Poles, as well as 25,000 persons of unspecified European origin. In addition there were 15,000 foreign-born Chinese, mainly from Hong Kong and Taiwan, as well as 4,000 migrants from India and Pakistan. By 1970 approximately 1 Vancouverite in 5 was from a non-English speaking country. The abundance of Chinese, Italian, and Greek restaurants, the intense ethnic rivalries in local soccer matches, the range of accents and complexions in downtown department stores, and the high enrollments in "English Conversation for New Canadians" classes, all reflected the increasingly diversified nature of the city.

This postwar migration entailed a significant change in Vancouver's traditional Anglo-Canadian makeup, and to a large degree reversed the role of the two cities. Seattle, reflecting the more restrictive immigration policies of its federal government, became more and more a native-born city in the years after World War II. The immigration policies of the Canadian government, on the other hand, had indirectly softened the strongly British features of Vancouver's population profile, and made it a much more diverse, cosmopolitan city than formerly. Canadian visitors to Seattle were often surprised by the number of American blacks they encountered; the American tourist was equally surprised by the number of Chinese in Vancouver.

During the postwar decades one of the most dramatic developments in Seattle occurred in 1962 with the presentation of Century 21—the city's world fair. On the basis of a substantial bond issue by city voters, along with corporate donations as well as state and federal appropriations, the six-month-long exposition had an attendance of some 10 million persons. Many of the commercial and foreign exhibits were less than memorable. But the United States Science Pavilion, designed by Seattle-born Minoru Yamasaki, captivated all, with its delicately soaring Gothic arches, and complex interplay of light, water, and stone. Contrary to all expectations, Century 21 did not entail further debt. A complex of buildings, as well as the Monorail link to downtown, was maintained, while the 600-foot Space Needle became a prominent landmark and symbol for the entire city.[71]

A much more significant long-range development during these years was the construction of a massive freeway system in the city and its environs. This development is worthy of detailed consideration for not only does it provide an example of the enormous role of the federal government in the American city, but it simultaneously highlights a different pattern than what evolved in Vancouver.

In the late 1940s and early 50s as population rose and as more and more suburbanites drove to work in the city, increasingly severe traffic congestion became a constant headache for Seattle's planners and transportation experts. One-way traffic, wider roads, and improvement to bridges and intersections brought some relief, as did the construction of the Alaskan Way Viaduct along the waterfront and the Battery Street Tunnel under the central business district. Over time, however, more comprehensive solutions were demanded and from the early 1950s onward the issue of freeway construction was never far from the minds of city officials. A variety of plans for regional transportation systems were proposed but expected costs far exceeded local resources and little actual construction took place.[72]

The enactment of the Federal-Aid Highway Act of 1956 drastically altered the local situation. The federal government had long provided subsidies for the construction of roads throughout the nation, and this role had been expanded as a relief measure during the 1930s and as a national defense measure in the 1940s. Yet the size of the program and the degree of federal sponsorship in the 1956 legislation outstripped these past programs. It outlined a massive interstate highway network of some 41,000 miles, which would link all of the nation's major cities. As in the past, state authorities would carry out the planning and construction, and would follow a set of federal guidelines and standards. Most significant of all, 90 percent of the costs would be borne by the federal government, the remaining 10 percent by the states.[73]

Within a year of this critical federal legislation, the Washington State Department of Highways had a fully developed proposal for a Tacoma-Seattle-Everett freeway. There was little questioning of the route beyond Seattle's boundaries. But the heavy north-south traffic, the elongated shape of the city between Puget Sound and Lake Washington, and the narrow waist near the central business district made the choice of a route through the city a difficult one. Ultimately, the City Planning Commission approved the state-proposed route.[74] It essentially bisected the city from north to south. But while it facilitated through traffic and the movement of cars and trucks to and from the core district, it pinched the city's already narrow waist to a band of about seven blocks wedged between the Alaskan Viaduct on the waterfront and the freeway itself. According to Seattle's Planning Commission, the Central Freeway was consistent with "sound principles of city planning." Construction of this new Interstate-5 began in 1960, and it was opened to traffic in 1965.

During the years of the planning and construction of I-5, plans were also unveiled for the construction of two additional north-south freeways.

One, the Empire Freeway, later renamed the R. H. Thomson, would be to the east, while the Bay Freeway to the west would tie in with the existing Alaskan Viaduct.[75] In addition, a new bridge across Lake Washington was proposed with major interchanges planned in the city, so as to link the major east-west route with the north-south routes. The interchanges would be in the heart of the city's black community and would require considerable demolition and relocation of families. All of these projects received original approval but as more and more persons became aware of the impact of four, six, and eight-laned concrete roadways on residential neighborhoods opposition mounted steadily.

The opposition to the R. H. Thomson Freeway was especially intense and in many ways representative of the "freeway revolt" that occurred in numerous American cities.[76] The proposed route from the north would cut through portions of the Ravenna, University, and Montlake districts, all prosperous, white, middle-class neighborhoods. As it proceeded south, it would enter Capital Hill, an ethnically and racially mixed community, and further south, would cut into the Central Area, a low-income neighborhood of modest bungalows which housed the great majority of Seattle's black population. In the early years, much of the opposition centered on the ecological impact of the proposed freeway on the university's renowned Arboretum. But as neighborhood groups, university faculty, and black spokesmen became more vocal, the issue focused more and more on the displacement of low-income groups, and the destruction of established neighborhoods for the benefit of car-driving commuters. With court challenges, protest meetings, and numerous modifications to the original plans, the issue would not be finally settled until February 1972, when Seattle voters unambiguously turned down both the R. H. Thomson Freeway and the Bay Freeway.

Throughout the decades after World War II the overwhelming majority of Seattleites saw the automobile and the freeway as the primary answer to the city's transportation needs. For a brief interlude between 1966 and 1968, it seemed possible that a significant commitment might be made to rapid transit. Under the leadership of James R. Ellis, and through the activities of an organization called Forward Thrust, an extensive capital improvement program was submitted to city voters in February 1968.[77] Diverse bond issues for a stadium, highways, parks, sewers, and fire protection were approved, but $385 million earmarked for a metropolitan transit system did not get the required majority. The defeat was doubly painful since for every dollar provided by local authorities, the federal government guaranteed two. Some Seattleites continued to advocate a rapid transit system, but as of the early 1980s it was not forthcoming. Bus patronage had increased, but the automobile still reigned supreme.

Vancouver too confronted a gamut of transportation issues in the postwar decades, with rising incomes, more cars, and increased suburbanization all contributing to the demand for additional roads, bridges, and freeways. As in Seattle, the responsibility for the planning and financing of these facilities was divided among municipal, provincial, and federal authorities. But whereas the jurisdiction of such authorities was defined with reasonable precision in the American setting, it was much more ambiguous in Canada. There was nothing as clear-cut as the Federal-Aid Highway Act of 1956, with its 90/10 split. In Canada, each issue tended to be a special case. A 50/50 federal/provincial split was typical, but much depended on the size, location, and function of a particular facility, as well as on the role of particular public officials in Ottawa and in Victoria. Such conditions ultimately led to a much smaller commitment to urban freeways in Vancouver than in Seattle.

A brief summary of the extended discussion over a proposed third crossing of Burrard Inlet gives an idea of the way in which the process unfolded.[78] By the early 1950s, it was obvious that the rapid population growth of North Vancouver and West Vancouver was straining the facilities provided by the Lion's Gate (First Narrows) Bridge, and the Second Narrows Bridge. In 1952, the private company that had constructed the Lion's Gate Bridge in the 1930s announced that it was prepared to build a parallel bridge, with private capital, at a cost of $12 million. Little came of this original offer. Between 1955 and 1965, a series of suggestions and proposals were made by British Columbia's Social Credit Premier W. A. C. Bennett and his Minister of Highways P. Gaglardi. But whether the proposal was for a parallel bridge, a tunnel, or a bridge-tunnel system, whether it was to have tolls or be toll-free, whether it was to be four, six, or more lanes wide, whether the province would make a lump sum payment, or have some provincial-municipal cost-sharing plan, or whether the premier supported or rejected his minister's statements, little was achieved. There is no doubt that the expected costs of the project intimidated even the most enthusiastic booster. They rose from $25 million in 1955, to over $100 million by 1965.

By the late 1960s, both municipal and provincial politicians suggested that federal financing might be available, especially if the proposed crossing was considered part of the Trans-Canada Highway system. As a result of these suggestions, and with much wheeling and dealing on all sides, federal authorities offered a number of proposals and financial packages between 1968 and 1972. Under one of these in 1969, the federal government was to provide $100 million for a tunnel system, with the provincial government adding $27 million and the various municipalities $33 million. Debated vigorously, it underwent a number of modifications, but got preliminary approval from all three levels of government. Particularly heated opposition from a number of Vancouver's professional groups and concerned citizens forced a reconsideration of the entire project. The death blow came in September 1972 when British Columbia's recently elected New Democratic government announced that the $41 million committed by the previous Social Credit government would no longer be available for a third crossing. It marked the end of an era.

Numerous transportation facilities were constructed in Vancouver in the postwar decades; however, the third crossing controversy suggests the nature of much of the debate and the critical issue of financial responsibility. As a general rule the financing of such facilities tended to be divided between two or more levels of government, though sometimes one level of government dominated. Thus the Georgia Street Viaduct was mainly a municipal undertaking, the Port Mann Bridge and Freeway was a federal-provincial project, and the bridge across the Fraser River to Vancouver's International Airport was a federal project with some municipal support. At the time this latter agreement was hammered out the municipal government refused to allocate funds for entry and exit ramps for the bridge. As a result, commuter traffic from nearby Richmond to downtown Vancouver was virtually sealed off from this predominately federal undertaking.

The evolution of Vancouver's transportation network demonstrates that Bartholemew's 1929 *Plan for the City of Vancouver,* with its subsequent revisions, long dominated the thinking of Vancouver's officials, traffic engineers, and planners.[79] G. Sutton-Brown, formerly planner of the county council of Lancashire, became Vancouver's director of planning in 1954. In that capacity, and later as city commissioner until 1972, he played a significant role. On the basis of a series of joint municipal-provincial studies, a further updating of Bartholemew was carried out. This *Freeways with Rapid Transit* or "The Sutton Brown Plan of 1959" suggested "a radial freeway system, with an additional Burrard Inlet Crossing." For the next dozen years, this basic Bartholemew/Sutton-Brown approach was upheld. One detailed investigation has shown that between 1952 and 1972, some forty-five major studies were done on the highway needs of metropolitan Vancouver. In addition, there were fifteen confidential studies by provincial and by federal teams, and twenty-five staff reports related to these studies. The total cost of these investigations came to about $10 million. Except for the occasional reference to the need for rapid transit, all of these studies—whether done by private consultants, municipal, provincial, or federal agencies—consistently advocated the development of some form of downtown-oriented freeway network, along with a third crossing of Burrard Inlet.[80]

With such a consistent chorus, one might well ask why Vancouver has no freeways. The immediate answer would lie in the intense public opposition to such facilities that developed in late 1967 and early 1968. In October 1967 the city council had approved the construction of a major connector route through Chinatown. This decision was widely publicized and bitterly opposed, with the Chinese community, concerned professionals, and a number of University of British Columbia faculty members being especially active. After much debate and a series of public meetings which roundly condemned council's action, the original decision was rescinded.[81] These developments stimulated the creation of TEAM, a civic reform party which both challenged and changed the policies of the long-established Non-Partisan Association.

In the long run however, heavy financial costs were probably the critical item that curbed freeway development in Vancouver. Many analysts have pointed out that Canada's larger area and smaller population have led to a less intensive use of transportation facilities and a higher per capita cost than in the United States. The same concept applies when comparing British Columbia with Washington State, or Vancouver with Seattle. During the 1950s and early 1960s, virtually every planner, politician, and spokesman saw freeways as a logical and appropriate facility for Vancouver. But while everybody apparently wanted freeways, nobody was prepared to assume the costs entailed. Each level of government believed that the others should account for a larger slice of the financial pie. Though endless negotiations were carried out, no mutually acceptable agreement was found. The proposed third crossing of Burrard Inlet again provides the classic example.

It is also significant that Vancouver's involvement with freeway issues lagged some half-dozen years behind comparable developments in the United States. Such a lag has been noted many times in the history of Seattle and Vancouver, whether in the construction of transcontinental railroads in the 1880s, the pursuit of the Klondike trade in the 1890s, the commitment to the automobile in the 1920s, or the production of merchant ships in the early 1940s. The lag in freeway development at least was a beneficial one. By the mid-1960s a vast number of urban freeways had been completed in the United States, and many American cities (as well as Toronto) were fully aware of the consequences of such facilities. While the "freeway revolt" in the United States resisted further construction, Vancouver's "freeway debate" of 1967 focused only on a proposed facility. In the same way that the planning and construction of U.S. freeways provided an example, it seems likely that the organization and tactics of freeway opponents were also noted. In the early 1960s Seattle residents were constantly reminded of the problems of a freeway-choked Los Angeles. By the late 1960s Vancouver had Seattle as a model to be avoided.

9
Thirty Years of Municipal Politics

Municipal politics in Seattle and Vancouver were strikingly similar in the post–World War II era. Mayors enjoyed long terms, there were few closely contested elections, council members were returned year after year, and citizens were apathetic. Seattleites and Vancouverites were pleased with the growth and prosperity of those years and were in general agreement that their city enjoyed "good government." Whether one considers the politics of the 1940s, 1950s, and early 1960s as stable, unexciting, or downright dull, there is little disagreement about their basic nature. In the late 1960s, however, both cities underwent significant political change. The old guard was challenged and new issues, new styles, and new leaders came to the fore. The reform tide associated with TEAM (The Electors' Action Movement) was sustained in Vancouver for six years, but by the mid-1970s, politics in the Canadian city had returned to a more traditional pattern. In Seattle, the Wesley Uhlman administration gave a distinctively new thrust to the city's politics between 1970 and 1978, and it was continued by his successor. This chapter will focus on municipal politics in the two cities from the mid-1940s to the mid-1970s. As a case study of a specific time span it shows that while the politics of Seattle and Vancouver were independent of each other, the basic similarity in their political evolution was unmistakable.

The organization of city government in Seattle and Vancouver had much in common during the postwar decades.[1] Both had a "weak" mayor, council form of government with the mayor elected independently in both cities. In Seattle, with the city council's approval the mayor appointed the heads of various city departments and administrative boards. In Vancouver only the city council had the power to appoint. Neither the Seattle nor the Vancouver mayor had independent authority to develop or control the city budget. Consistent with British parliamentary practice, the Vancouver mayor participated in city council's deliberation and had the right to vote in the council. The Seattle mayor, on the other hand, under the American principle of the separation of executive from legislative powers, had greater independence and could veto city council's bills—but this in turn could be overridden.

Council members in both cities were elected at large. Since 1966, all ten aldermen in Vancouver were elected every two years. Seattle's nine council members served four-year terms, with four positions contested in one election, and five in the next election two years later. Much of the day-by-day work in both cities was done by committee, with considerable consultation between committee members and city staff. In due course, committee chairpersons reported to council, and if the proposals were approved by that body and signed by the mayor, they became an "ordinance" in Seattle, and a "by-law" in Vancouver. Both cities also had a variety of administrative boards and commissions that supervised specific municipal activities and had varying degrees of authority. The School Board, for example, was elected in both cities. Seattle's mayor appointed the members of the Transit Commission, the Library Board, Civil Service Commission, and the Planning Commission. In Vancouver, it was either the provincial government, city council, or both, that appointed the Library Board, Planning Commission, Traffic Commission, Board of Police Commission, and the Board of Variance.

Though the qualifications for voting in civil elections were minimal, Americans and Canadians alike showed little interest in municipal politics. Between 1944 and 1952, for example, approximately 32 percent of Seattle's eligible voters actually voted in the municipal primary elections and about 52 percent in the general municipal elections.[2] Voter turnout in Vancouver was also low.[3] Between 1938 and 1975 an average of only 38 percent of the eligible voters actually voted in mayoralty elections, and in off-year elections for city council voter turnout dropped to 30 percent.

The decision by Vancouver voters in 1935 to abolish the ward system and institute an at-large system of voting for aldermen set in motion a variety of changes that had a significant long-range impact on local politics. One year later, the socialist CCF entered a full slate of candidates and succeeded in electing three aldermen to council. The CCF's move, in turn, was quickly met by a countermove on the right when a group of businessmen, professionals, and propertied interests established the Non-Partisan Association.

The new organization achieved success almost immediately. In 1937, the NPA won three out of four contested seats, and by 1938, had seven out of eight seats on city council.[4] Its strength tended to be concentrated in the west-side, middle-class districts of Vancouver, but within a few years, it received substantial support throughout the entire city. By 1940, for example, the west side voted some 68 percent for NPA candidates, and even the working-class east side gave 45 percent of its vote to the NPA candidates.[5]

This early success continued, and for some thirty years the Non-Partisan Association dominated Vancouver's municipal politics. It was active only during election campaigns, and functional primarily as a slate-making body, but its organizational strength and the financial support of commercial and industrial concerns gave it a distinct boost.[6] Public indifference toward municipal politics, at-large elections, and name familiarity of NPA candidates also helped. Finally, the general acceptance of NPA arguments that "politics should be kept out of City Hall," that city officials should provide "honest," "efficient," "economical" government, and that everything possible should be done to promote Vancouver's economic development, also stood it in good stead. It is true that the occasional anti-NPA candidate or anti-NPA faction appeared over the years. Thus, the CCF as well as the Civic Voters Association, the Civic Reform party, and the Vancouver District Labour Council had some success.[7] But the fact that both the School Board and Parks Board were controlled by NPA candidates for over thirty years, and that the NPA seldom lost either the mayorality or a majority on the city council, suggests that such opposition efforts were only minor eddies in the broad current of NPA domination.[8]

The election of Arthur Langlie to Seattle's city council in 1936, and his later victory as mayor in 1938, would seem to have little in common with developments associated with the rise of the NPA in Vancouver. Yet, as mentioned in Chapter 7, Langlie's victory in 1938 marked a significant departure from the prevailing system of government and set in motion a new style of politics that would be sustained for years. One detailed study of Seattle's municipal politics from 1928 to 1953 sees these twenty-five years falling into two distinct periods, with 1938 marking the dividing line. "Before 1938 . . . elections were sharply fought, often on class lines. Incumbent mayor and councilmen lost more often than they won. . . . In the post-1938 period, the political complexion of the nonpartisan city elections seemed to change noticeably. Incumbents won most elections. Issues were generally not so sharply defined and there were fewer cases of open partisan activity during non-partisan elections. Class appeals became less marked."[9]

The reasons for the change are quite clear. Seattle had followed a non-partisan, at-large electoral system since 1910.[10] But in the troubled 1930s the city council reflected the growing rifts within the community itself. A prolabor element, which gained most of its support from working-class groups in the central and southern districts of the city, pushed for increased expenditures and greater relief activities, and was generally indifferent to the charge that Seattle was a "wide open town" of gambling joints and brothels that needed "cleaning up." From 1934 on the campaign for "good government" came to be identified with a new municipal party called the Order of Cincinnatus.[11] It stood for "absolute cleanliness and honesty" and stressed the need to reduce taxes and cut governmental expenditures. With the support of diverse middle-class elements, the Order of Cincinnatus had three representatives on city council by 1935. Rhetorically labeled "a Fascist triumverate" by the left, they would play an increasingly important role in the city's political life. One of these councilmen, Arthur Langlie, ran for mayor in 1936. He did not win at that time, but ran again in 1938, this time successfully.

Langlie's election as mayor in 1938, his vigorous reform administration, and his overwhelming reelection in 1940, established a tide of "good government" that would dominate Seattle's political life for the next thirty years. The Order of Cincinnatus itself had largely disintegrated by 1940, but the long-established Seattle Municipal League provided the kind of direction at election time offered by the Non-Partisan Association in Vancouver.[12] When one compares the political evolution of the two cities, one can see that their postwar politics grew out of similar political situations, had similar leadership, similar sources of support, similar goals, similar electoral systems, and similar longevity. More precisely, in both Seattle and Vancouver the fear of the left in the 1930s, the leadership and finances provided by the business community, the support from middle-class elements, the desire for prudent, efficient economical government, the at-large nonpartisan electoral system, and the thirty years of basic political continuity were all strikingly alike.

Municipal politics aroused little interest or concern during the war years. As Seattle's *Argus* quipped in January 1942, "Whether Earl Millikin or your Chinese laundryman sits in the mayor's office next year, the course of the war will not be affected one way or another." Wartime demands pushed concern over schools, roads, and city planning well into the background and few changes were made in leadership.

Within a year of V-J Day, Seattle and Vancouver were largely back to normal as their overseas servicemen had returned, wartime rationing was gone, and military uniforms had virtually disappeared from city streets. Prices had jumped with the removal of wage and price controls, but people were buying the houses, cars, clothes, and steaks that they wanted. Shipyard employment had plummeted in both cities, and Boeing's work force was down sharply, but the depression that many feared did not materialize. Rather, wartime population growth continued with suburban districts showing especially dramatic increases. This growth and expansion was welcome, but it heightened the need to upgrade and rebuild physical plants. The years of neglect in the 1930s and the priority given national defense needs during wartime meant that the transit systems, roads, schools, sewers, and fire halls were all badly run down.[13] On top of these public needs, thousands of persons sought better housing, while the business community clamored for office space, warehouses, and industrial plants.

This pent-up demand for a host of facilities and services, and the subsequent provision of them dominated the municipal life of Seattle and Vancouver for the next twenty years. There was heated questioning of the merit of specific development projects, the location of public facilities and freeways, and the level of expenditures on bus systems, police force, or parks. Yet such critics were in the minority. Most city officials, as well as the general public, saw these developments as sensible and desirable. Supporters of Vancouver Mayor Frederick Hume (1951–58) boasted in 1958 that during his administration the Granville Bridge, Empire Stadium, public library, General Hospital, art gallery, and airport terminal had all been constructed.[14] Eight years later Mayor William Rathie could point to activities on Block 42–52, Project 200, and the MacMillan Bloedel Building and announce, "The big projects are just starting."[15] Similarly, when the *Argus* surveyed William Devin's ten years as Seattle's mayor, it characterized the period from 1942–52 as an era of "sound municipal financing . . . balanced budgets . . . domestic tranquility . . . [and] co-operation."[16] This general satisfaction with local development goes a long way to explain the political stability and continuity of these years.

When one asks, "How did city government really work in Seattle and Vancouver?" the issue becomes much cloudier and more debatable. Much depended upon the time, the specific issue, and the particular individual involved. But as a general rule, power was more centralized in Vancouver than in Seattle. From World War II until the late 1960s, Vancouver's civic bureaucracy grew steadily. Through a combination of public apathy, NPA ideas on how a city should be run, and a number of able, conscientious civic bureaucrats, leadership moved into the hands of senior administrators.[17] Theoretically, Vancouver's city council established policy and various civic officials carried it out, but during the 1950s and 1960s, the council largely rubber-stamped the programs sent to them by city staff. These arrangements were formalized in 1956 with the establishment of a Board of Administration. Originally it consisted of the mayor plus two appointed commissioners, but by 1959 it consisted solely of the two appointed officials. From 1956 until its modification in 1973, this appointed executive agency administered civic affairs, and in all but name, Vancouver had a city manager form of government.[18]

During much of this time, the NPA-dominated council was sympathetic to a whole series of projects sought by developers, real estate firms, and the general business community.[19] Issues concerning building codes in the West End, proposals for the waterfront, an Oakridge shopping center, and urban redevelopment in Chinatown were all first evaluated by the Board of Administration, submitted to the city council by Commissioner Gerald Sutton-Brown, and in due course usually became city policy. Prior to 1968, the procedure went smoothly and aroused little public attention or concern.

Power was much more decentralized in Seattle. In *Big City Politics,* political scientist Edward C. Banfield entitled one of his chapters "Seattle: Anybody in Charge?" and ultimately labeled the existing system as "Seattle's do-it-by citizen-committee style of government."[20] According to one local official, Seattle was "governed by a network of little administrative hierarchies, each with a council committee at its apex.[21] Mayor William Devin pointed out, "What we have is not one mayor, but ten mayors, each of them with his own empire and each jealous of the others' power."[22]

Regardless of the descriptions applied, Seattle's "weak" mayor system, and a city council concerned primarily with balancing the budget and preserving its prerogatives, meant that little was done by public officials.[23] City voters were also reluctant to spend much money. Between 1952 and 1958, they turned down eight of the eleven bond issues proposed by their government.[24] In this situation, leadership fell largely to a variety of citizens' associations and interest groups. "If you want to get anything done in Seattle," Ross Cunningham of the *Times* pointed out, "you get about six members of the Big Ten together and tell them it's a good project. If you convince them, you're in."[25]

But it was not only downtown merchants, real estate agents, and business leaders who were active. The driving force behind the development of METRO, which handled the district's sewage disposal, was the long-established Seattle Municipal League. Occasionally, Boeing made its weight felt, and less frequently, the Teamster's Union. The Central Association, an organization of downtown businessmen, vigorously promoted a redevelopment scheme for the Pike Place Market area, and were just as vigorously opposed by the Friends of the Market under the leadership of Victor Steinbrueck, a professor of architecture at the University of Washington. Hotelman Eddie Carlson, "The single most important guy in town . . . if you want to get a big civic project off the ground," and Ford dealer Joe Gandy provided leadership for the Seattle World Fair of 1962. A variety of neighborhood groups, including Citizens Against Freeways, successfully opposed the construction of an additional north-south freeway through the east side of the city. Forward Thrust, an enormous capital improvement project for parks, highways, sewers, stadium, and neighborhood improvements, which ultimately got voter approval for $334 million, was substantially credited to the sustained efforts of James R. Ellis.

Most of these organizations were temporary ones. They had good leadership, were well organized and publicized, had plenty of volunteer workers, and were directed toward a specific goal. Once that goal was achieved, they disbanded. Depending upon the specific issue involved, they can be seen as either "democracy in action" or "another move by the Establishment." But in either case, the range and impact of such groups, especially when contrasted with the lack of major city-generated projects, leave little doubt about the decentralization of authority in Seattle and the modest role played by mayor and council in the 1950s and 1960s.[26]

Both Seattle and Vancouver reveal notable similarities in the nature and consequences of nonpartisanship on city politics.[27] First of all, both cities show that persons who served in nonpartisan municipal office seldom used it as a stepping stone to political activity at the regional or national level. Between 1938 and 1968, for example, sixteen different mayors served these cities, but only Seattle's Arthur Langlie later achieved partisan prominence when he served three terms as Republican governor of Washington. Gerry McGeer served briefly as a Liberal MP in Ottawa, before returning to the Vancouver mayoralty. The movement from partisan politics to nonpartisan municipal office was also infrequent in Seattle, especially before 1968.[28] In Vancouver, on the other hand, movement from the provincial legislature to municipal office was a fairly common occurrence. Mayors McGeer, George Miller, Telford, and J. W. Cornett all served as MLAs in Victoria before their election to city office.[29]

Nonpartisanship and at-large elections favored incumbents in both cities. In Seattle, for example, in sixty-five contests for council positions between 1940 and 1964, incumbents were defeated only five times.[30] Incumbents also did well in Vancouver. Of a total of 145 aldermanic contests from 1938 to 1968, incumbents were returned in 93 cases, and "new-comers" won in 52.[31] The recommendation of the Seattle Municipal League or the endorsement of Vancouver's Non-Partisan Association virtually guaranteed success, and year after year the same faces appeared in council chambers. The representative alderman in Vancouver served about six years or three terms, but service of ten or more years was not exceptional.[32] Length of service in Seattle was even more impressive. Between 1938 and 1968, a group of twelve councillors averaged sixteen years of service each.[33]

The proposition that minority group candidates are disadvantaged by nonpartisanship also had considerable validity. After World War II, Vancouver's Chinese population rose from about 2 percent of the city's population to over 7 percent, but before the 1980s, no Chinese ever sat on city council. Europeans, especially Germans, Italians, Greeks, Hungarians, and Yugoslavs, made up about a fifth of the population in 1970, but few won political office.[34] Mayor Jack Volrich (1977) was only the second Vancouver mayor not of Anglo-Saxon origin. The first, David Oppenheimer, was elected in 1887. Seattle has done somewhat better in this regard. Two Chinese, Wing Luke and Liem Tuai, served on city council during the late 1960s and early 1970s. Sam Smith, Seattle's first black councilman, was elected in 1967 and still served some twenty years later.

There is no doubt that nonpartisanship favored candidates who lived in "the better parts of town." Main Street in Vancouver has long been considered the dividing line between working-class east and middle-class west. Since the late 1930s, most city aldermen have lived in the more affluent districts west of Main. This disparity was not especially notable in the early years. The 1940 council, for example, had six aldermen who lived west of Main, and three who lived east of Main. Both the 1945 and 1950 councils showed five from the west and five from the east. Since then, the preponderance of west-side aldermen has been overwhelming. The 1955 council showed a 7/2 breakdown, 1960– 11/0, 1965—9/2, 1971– 10/1.[35] During these years, about half of Vancouver's population lived east and half west of Main. In Seattle, there is no convenient demarcation of "the better parts of town." Though generally located in the northern sector of the city, such districts tend to be scattered: Queen Anne, Montlake, Laurelhurst, Ravenna, and Green Lake, as well as the handsome residential areas in Mount Baker would all qualify as "better" districts. Nine of the twelve persons who dominated city council for some thirty years lived in these districts.[36]

Finally, like nonpartisan governments in many cities, those in Seattle and Vancouver considered their basic task to be promotion of the commercial and industrial growth of the city. They were business-oriented, conservative in their spending on welfare, and aggressive in their desire to promote a favorable business climate. The occasional petty scandal erupted, but there were few patronage jobs and a decided absence of flagrant graft or corruption. As Edward Devine, Mayor Dorm Braman's assistant, pointed out, "When I first moved into Seattle's city hall in 1964, I took a look around to find out who the crooks were. You've got to have crooks in city hall, right? . . . I was terribly chagrined when I didn't find any."[37] For the middle-class Seattleite or Vancouverite such government was "good government." It was honest, efficient, and kept the taxes down.[38]

The 1960s were turbulent, difficult years for Seattle, and the changes that occurred in municipal politics after 1969 can best be seen as a response to problems that had gradually accumulated. For a city that had long enjoyed a stable, tolerant social environment, the racial tensions of the 1960s, clashes with the police, vandalism, and the general rise in crime all indicated that much had changed. Seattle prospered economically during these years, but the bitter controversy over American involvement in Vietnam was an ever-present issue that steadily intensified as the decade unfolded. Freeway construction, housing projects, and urban redevelopment schemes that had been supported in the 1950s faced strong opposition in the 1960s. Campus demonstrations, charges of police brutality, the contempt for federal authorities, or the burgeoning drug culture—all reflected the disillusionment, cynicism, and anger that beset the era.[39]

Tensions and violence peaked in 1968. On July 30, the Seattle *Times* reported, "Seven police officers and two civilians were injured and several police cars damaged in disturbances marked by gunfire, rock throwing and fire bombs in the central area last night."[40] With minor variations, such reports recurred throughout the summer months. In October, Mayor Dorm Braman pointed out that "racial disorder and growth of crime" took nearly all of his time and energy. He noted his many consultations with black leaders, his appointment of a black judge, and the fact that his administration had utilized a series of federally funded programs—Model Cities, Neighborhood Youth, Office of Economic Opportunity—to remedy local conditions.[41] But his conviction that the recent disturbances were "part of a conspiracy," backed mainly by the Black Panthers and the Students for Democratic Society, revealed a rather simplistic analysis of the situation.

A report by the Seattle Urban League, a moderate civil rights organization, provides a substantially different insight into conditions in 1968.[42] It pointed out that 81 percent of Seattle's 40,000 blacks lived in the Central

Area, and that between 1960 and 1967, the black population of that Garfield/Madrona district had jumped from 20,800 to 32,400. With the district's population up by 60 percent, housing units had increased by a mere 4 percent. Two-thirds of the Central Area's black families had annual incomes under $7,000, and of these, about one-half were in poverty or marginal poverty, that is, in the $3,000–$4,000 range. Legal separation in schools had long since been outlawed; nevertheless, the concentration of blacks in this district meant that eight elementary schools in the area averaged 75 percent black students, with Mann and Leschi schools being 94 percent black. All of these conditions contributed to a mood of hostility and distrust and a recognition that "the problems of the ghetto rest in white racism."[43]

The election of Mayor Wesley Uhlman of 1969 did not bring about any immediate changes in Seattle's fortunes. Indeed a precipitous drop in Boeing employment between 1968 and 1971 intensified the city's problems. During that three-year period, aircraft industry employment in the Seattle-Everett area slumped from 105,700 in 1968 to 38,100 in 1971, with a subsequent jump in unemployment from 4.9 percent to 13.6 percent of the labor force.[44] Yet, over the eight years of his administration, Uhlman expanded, speeded up, and dramatized a series of changes that significantly altered municipal politics, and in the process, made city hall much more responsive to the needs of the total community.

One of his primary steps was the aggressive pursuit of federal funds. Such a process was well under way before Uhlman came to office, but in the 1970s, it was intensified. As one indication of this, the mayor established a Division of Grant Programs. It was meant to uncover areas in which federal funds were available, as well as to develop and monitor all applications to federal agencies. Regardless of the particular agency that provided the funds, or whether they were channeled into special programs for children, blacks, the handicapped, or the elderly, they were of profound importance to the city. In 1977, Uhlman claimed that if all local monies were withdrawn, 95 percent of Seattle's primary programs would continue to operate because of that federal support.[45]

Uhlman also carried out a series of organizational changes that transformed the mayor's office into an efficient, powerful executive agency. Again, this process was under way before he assumed office. The state legislature had granted budget-making authority to the mayor's office in 1967. With the establishment of an Office of Management and Budget, modeled on the presidential office of the same name, Uhlman fully exploited this authority. It gave him control over departmental budgets, staffing levels, and programs. A variety of special purpose agencies were also restructured and made directly responsible to him. The combination of a more powerful mayor and a group of new members on city council also facilitated the re-ordering of city affairs. One of the many symbols of change was the rise in the number of blacks, Asians, and Hispanics employed by city hall. In 1968, for example, Seattle employed ten black firemen and eleven black policemen. By 1974, this had risen to fifty-three firemen, and sixty-three policemen. Total minority employment rose from 7 percent of the city's 8,800 employees in 1968, to 14 percent of the 11,400 employees in 1974.[46]

Uhlman's personal style and skills also played a large part in his suc-cess. "He is no administrator," one of his assistants pointed out, "his style is purely political." In the early years, the *Times* considered him "moddish," and the *Post Intelligencer* said he had "pizzazz." His supporters were not displeased when a national publication likened him to Mayor John Lindsay of New York. His reforms delighted many, they also created enemies. Yet his continued emphasis on citizen participation brought support, and even the local business community became an ally. By the time he left office in 1978, this hard-working, polished, and slightly aloof man—who also found time to boost local theater and art—had become a symbol of a more self-confident, urbane, and tolerant Seattle. It was all a long way from the tensions and anxiety of 1968–69.[47]

Vancouver underwent significant political changes in the late 1960s, but neither the problems encountered nor the public reaction reached the level of intensity experienced in Seattle. Though often exciting and hotly debated, the issues in the Canadian city were more traditional ones that did not create profound anxiety. Rather than a war in Vietnam, a pre-cipitous rise in unemployment, and the fear of urban riots, Vancouverites were concerned about freeway proposals and the approval given a variety of development schemes by a pliant and sympathetic city council. The cities also differed in that while political change in Seattle was prominently associated with Mayor Wes Uhlman, the "new politics" in Vancouver re-flected the activities of organized groups with many of the attributes of civic political parties.

Organized opposition to the Non-Partisan Association appeared in 1966, when, largely through the efforts of Alderman Bob Williams, a city planner and active member of the New Democratic party, a group called Citizens for the Improvement of Vancouver put up a slate of four candi-dates in the regular election for council. None were elected; however, the results indicated that some form of organizational support was a great advantage in an at-large election.[48]

Two years later, the movement toward the development of a policy-oriented, reformist party was confirmed when a diverse group of academics, professionals, and businessmen organized TEAM. The action was precipitated by a major controversy over a proposed freeway, designed to go through Vancouver's Chinatown. It was strongly supported by the Board of Administration and the NPA-dominated council, and bitterly opposed and ultimately defeated by neighborhood groups and concerned professionals. The actions of Mayor Tom Campbell, a colorful, outspoken lawyer and real estate developer, also contributed. Angered by opposition to proposals for an additional crossing of Burrard Inlet, he dismissed his opponents as a group of "Maoists, pinkos, left-wingers and hamburgers."

In a broader sense, TEAM can be seen as the arrival of a new generation, anxious to make its mark on city affairs. By the late 1960s, Vancouver had experienced twenty-five years of virtually uninterrupted growth and prosperity. The grim unemployment, sparse opportunities, and low incomes of the 1930s were only a vague memory. More and more people were beginning to question the traditional conviction that increased population, wider freeways, and more intense downtown development were automatically desirable.[49] It is impossible to pinpoint the precise ways in which developments in the United States during the 1960s influenced events in Vancouver. Yet there can be little doubt that the condemnation of the establishment in the United States, student unrest, women's liberation, black protest movements, urban riots, disillusionment with freeways and urban redevelopment schemes, and the emphasis on citizen participation and the need to return "power to the people"—all filtered into the Canadian psyche in various subtle ways.

In the regular municipal election of December 1968, Vancouver's Non-Partisan Association faced a vigorous fight for the first time in years. Though the NPA maintained control of the city council, Parks Board, and School Board, the intensity of the opposition, especially from TEAM candidates was real. According to Earl Adams, an NPA veteran of sixteen years on city council, "The results show that there are still enough sensible, democratic, free enterprise thinking people in Vancouver who will not let the city be run by left wingers, socialists, fellow travellers and Communists. . . . Thank God for the intelligence of the Vancouver electorate."[50]

In the next four years, a long series of bitter disputes erupted when the civic administration supported a variety of projects proposed by private developers.[51] In each case, the two new TEAM members on council (A. Phillips and W. Hardwick) were joined in opposition by Alderman Harry Rankin, an ardent Socialist, and the single representative of Vancouver's second civic political party, COPE (Committee of Progressive Electors). With its emphasis on the underprivileged and the impoverished, its working-class support and its Marxist interpretation of society, COPE was well to the left of TEAM. With periodic support from other members of council, the two TEAM aldermen and the COPE alderman succeeded in modifying or blocking a number of NPA-backed development projects.

In 1972 TEAM's drive to power culminated when they elected the mayor, eight out of ten aldermen, eight of nine school trustees, and four of seven park commissioners. There is no doubt that the council of 1972–74 was quite unlike the small businessmen, managers, and developers who made up the representative NPA council. Of the eleven persons on the 1972–74 council, most were young professionals, including a social worker, lawyer, engineer, architect, and transportation expert. All eleven were university graduates, eight had done postgraduate study, and four were university professors.[52] In the following year, they implemented a number of TEAM programs. The most significant step was a series of administrative changes by which the power of the civic bureaucracy was reduced and city council's role in policymaking and implementation significantly increased. Neighborhood participation in local planning was encouraged, freeway proposals killed, downtown development brought under greater council control, and the False Creek industrial area reshaped under civic supervision into a diversified residential area.

Yet at the very peak of its apparent success, the TEAM reform coalition gradually disintegrated. Public interest in civic affairs declined, and voter turnouts, which had reached 45 percent in 1968 and 1970, dropped back to 32 percent in 1972 and 1974. The strong pro-ward stance of TEAM declined and even its supporters were confused about the party's position on that critical issue. Internal division became more and more evident. Two aldermen withdrew from the party to run as independents, while another accepted NPA endorsement. Other TEAM aldermen withdrew from municipal politics to return to private life, and the organization did not come up with strong replacements. By 1978, city politics had an old and familiar look with NPA-endorsed candidates once again in control of the mayoralty, council, Parks Board, and School Board.[53]

Did Vancouver's NPA, TEAM, and COPE qualify as parties? One would have to answer "yes," but a qualified "yes." As civic political parties they had no official connection with either the provincial or federal Conservative party, Liberal party, or New Democratic party (NDP). Similarly, they lacked some of the attributes that are normally associated with political parties. Thus, party identification of city voters and party discipline among elected members were not well developed. Rather, crossovers and inconsistencies abounded. On the other hand, and like traditional political parties, both TEAM and COPE operated on a year-round basis with a small staff. The NPA operated primarily in the period preceding elections. Candidates for all civic parties were chosen largely from party members. Election campaigns were financed, organized, and conducted by the organization on behalf of its candidates. Both on official ballots and in public discussions, candidates for office were identified by party label. Finally, these civic parties virtually monopolized access to elected office, and even the independents in municipal politics first achieved office as party candidates.[54]

Municipal politics of the postwar generation in Seattle and Vancouver essentially reflected the comfortable, prosperous nature of those communities. Income inequality and poverty had not been eliminated, and substantial numbers of the elderly, the unemployed, and the poorly educated were just "getting by" on old age pensions, welfare payments, unemployment insurance, and social security payments. But the overwhelming majority of Seattleites and Vancouverites were far removed from such a condition, and when measured by virtually any standard yardstick had achieved middle-class status (see Table 15).

The evidence in the table is fragmentary. It nevertheless indicates the predominance of comfortable, well-educated, white-collar home owners in both cities.[55] Over the years both Seattle and Vancouver had substantial numbers of workers in logging, lumbering, and fishing. Class tensions, radical labor movements, and radical political movements are very much a part of their historical experience. But after World War II the middle-class nature of both cities became steadily more evident. This in turn helped shape a set of values or cluster of beliefs about city government which could be labeled a "middle-class ethos" or an "Anglo-Saxon Protestant ethos."[56]

According to this set of beliefs the city was a community of like-minded people who agreed on what was good and what was needed. There might be variations in income, occupation, and background, and there might be distinctive needs of particular districts or groups, but such disparities were seen as minor ones. The dominant belief was "We're all middle class—have the same kinds of needs—want the same kind of city."

The basic need was for "good government," and this meant honest, efficient, impartial government. Schools, fire stations, parks, or transit systems should be provided in a crisp, economical way with no graft, corruption, or favoritism. The mayor and city council should establish the basic guidelines for furthering the city's commercial and economic develop-

Table 15   Selected Comparative Data on Seattle and Vancouver

	Seattle			Vancouver		
	1950	1960	1970	1951	1961	1971
Population (000's)	467	557	530	344	384	426
% Foreign-born	13	11	9	33	34	34
% White	94	92	87	97	95	90
% Black	3	5	7	0.1*	0.2	0.2
% "Other"	3	3	6	3	5	10
% labor force in white-collar jobs	58	59	65	59	62	63
Median yrs. schooling	12.1	12.2	12.5	9.5*	10*	10.5*
% univ. grad.	7	8	10	3*	4*	5
Median family income	$3,106	$6,942	$11,037	$2,700*	$5,600*	$9,029

% families w/incomes
    below $1,000/
    $2,000/$4,000
	17.6	6.7	10.7	NA	NA	11.2*

% Dwellings, owner- occupied	54	53	50	63	61	47
Median rent/month	$39	$75	$106	$43	$77	$127

Note: NA—Not available; *—Estimated from available census data. All income data for Seattle are in $ U.S., and for Vancouver in $ Canadian.

Source: U.S. Census of Population and Housing, 1950, Census Tract Statistics, Seattle, Wash; U.S. Census of Population and Housing, 1960, Census Tract Seattle, Wash; U.S. Census of Population and Housing, 1970, Census Tract Seattle-Everett, SMSA; Census of Canada, 1951, Population and Housing Characteristics by Census Tracts, Vancouver, Bull. CT-11; Census of Canada, 1961, Population and Housing Characteristics by Census Tracts, Vancouver, Bull. CT-22; Census of Canada 1971, Population and Housing, Characteristics by Census Tracts, Vancouver, CT-28A, and CT-28B.

ment, the civic administration should see that these guidelines were met, and the business community should handle the actual construction and development of these facilities.

Good leadership was essential, and the experienced business leader or professional was clearly the best qualified for such a role. Because traditional city politics were considered graft-ridden and corrupt it was essential to "keep party politics out of City Hall." After all, "there is no Republican or Democratic way to pave a street," you just pave it. All city politics should be nonpartisan, and at-large elections were essential to keep local ward issues from intruding on the needs of the general public.[57] All citizens should exercise their right to vote, but after they had carried out this function they should stand aside and let their elected representatives get on with the business of actually running the city.

Postwar politics in Seattle and Vancouver never reached this "ideal." The party preference of numerous elected officials was well known, and indeed often accounted for their election. Pressure groups such as the Chamber of Commerce or the Board of Trade were active. Local neighborhood groups, whether in Ballard or in Kitsilano, vigorously sought their own special interests. Minor scandals flared up periodically and voter turnout remained low. Yet the "middle-class ethos" was nevertheless real, and the postwar generation in both Seattle and Vancouver steadily pursued it.

10

The 1970s, 1980s, and a Look Backward

The decade of the 1970s did not begin auspiciously for Seattle. Although the United States had begun the long process of disengagement from Vietnam, more than a quarter of a million American troops were still in that quagmire, and local protest marches and demonstrations went on. Memories of the turmoil in the city's Central Area were still fresh, and more and more Seattleites were aware of the frustrations and anger of the city's black citizens. Tensions and incidents at the University of Washington and at Garfield High continued, and in May 1970, a crowd of protesters besieged the Federal Court House at First and Madison. After two and a half hours, $40,000 damage, and seventy-five arrests, the crowd was dispersed. During these difficult years, the economic situation was also grim. Between 1968 and 1971, Boeing employment in the Puget Sound region plummeted from 105,000 to 38,000, and Seattle's level of unemployment soared to 13.6 percent of the labor force. Unemployment among the city's black teenagers was at least twice that level. Newly elected Mayor Wes Uhlman pointed out in 1970 that Seattle had "the dubious distinction of being number two in the nation in the number of bombings." Many hoped that the new mayor might bring about improvement, but there was understandable doubt about the capacity of any single man to bring about significant change.

In Vancouver too, the problems and the controversies of the late 1960s carried over into the 1970s. Though issues were significant and created much excitement, they lacked the searing intensity of the problems that confronted Seattle. Concerned citizens and the civic reform party, TEAM, opposed various development schemes that were supported by an NPA-dominated council. The issues were traditional, however, involving the construction of shopping centers, high-rise apartments, or downtown parking garages, and could be handled through normal political channels.

As the 1970s unfolded, conditions improved in Seattle. The scars left by Vietnam and Watergate would be permanent ones, and the memories of local riots and the collapse of Boeing employment would not be forgotten. Yet as the economy recovered and the grim realities of the late 1960s and early 1970s faded, the city gradually recovered a sense of confidence and optimism. In Vancouver as well, the 1970s were expansive, confident years. But rather than marking any departure from the previous years, they merely sustained the optimism and prosperity that had dominated much of the postwar era. A common factor that accounted for this sense of well-being in both cities was the physical development that took place, especially in the downtown areas.

One striking example was the extensive restoration of Seattle's Pioneer Square and Vancouver's Gastown. Both were the original sites of their respective cities, and both were badly run down from years of neglect. Projects begun by private businesses were aided by municipal and federal expenditures. Over time, a variety of boutiques, shopping malls, restaurants, and art galleries made their appearance. Despite the considerable approval and revitalized decaying areas, the rise in rents automatically pushed many elderly, impoverished tenants to other less-expensive quarters.

Seattle's Pike Street Market was also modified. After years of bitter controversy, the efforts of developers and planners to erect a massive shopping plaza and residential complex that would be "attractive," "modern," and "functional" were fortunately defeated.[1] One could still buy fresh fish, vegetables, and fruit as well as ceramic ware and books at its open stalls, and a vital component of Seattle's downtown was preserved. Vancouver officials meanwhile redeveloped Granville Street. The addition of trees, shrubs, and benches was welcome, as was the prohibition of automobiles. But city council's earlier approval of a series of underground shopping malls largely negated these improvements, as more and more pedestrians opted for the convenience of underground shopping.

An additional development and one repeated in almost every large city in North America was the construction of massive athletic facilities. Seattle was especially proud of its Kingdome, a covered stadium that seated some 60,000 and allowed fans to enjoy baseball, soccer, football, or basketball regardless of the weather. Constructed in the region south of Yesler, and taking up some 35 acres, it was opposed by many as disrupting both the Japanese and Chinese communities in the adjacent "International District." Vancouver was equally pleased with its Pacific Coliseum on the grounds of the Pacific National Exhibition. It enabled the Vancouver Canucks to obtain the long-sought but oft-postponed franchise in the National Hockey League. By the early 1980s, Vancouver also enjoyed a covered stadium for its football and soccer teams.

Two extensive public developments that gained major attention in Vancouver were the redevelopment of the False Creek Basin, and the construction of the Robson Square court house and office complex. The first of these involved the conversion of 100 acres devoted to freight sheds, warehouses and antiquated industrial plants into a handsome, liveable complex of condominiums, townhouses, parks, and schools. Some provision was made for cooperative housing, but most of it catered to affluent, young urbanites. By the 1980s it housed about 5,000 residents on land leased from the city itself. The Robson Square complex also required the acquisition of extensive urban land and the close cooperation of provincial and municipal authorities. Its multileveled combination of court house, government offices, restaurants, and public areas provided a graceful and intriguing addition to the city's downtown. A critic for the *New York Times* considered it "sophisticated" and with its less commercial, more public quality, "different from its American counterparts."[2] In Seattle, the construction of a thirty-seven story Federal Office Building at the corner of First and Madison, the site of Tom Burke's law office in the 1880s and 1890s, also became an immediate focal point.

In addition to these large public and semipublic facilities, both cities also experienced a vast amount of private construction. Apartment houses, business offices, department stores, and shopping centers appeared throughout both. The Bank of California, the Seattle First National Bank, the Toronto Dominion Bank, and the Bank of Nova Scotia each sought to establish their preeminence by building higher and higher. Residents of the cities took a peculiar delight in the revolving restaurants perched atop the Space Needle in Seattle or Sear's Harbour Centre in Vancouver. The view was superb, although serious trenchermen seldom made return visits.

Such development did not go unnoticed and both cities received favorable attention from a variety of national publications. In the mid-1970s a flurry of articles appeared in *Harper's, Christian Science Monitor, Atlantic Monthly, Time,* and *Saturday Review,* and for Seattle's reading public provided some very satisfying information. All of these articles attempted to measure and quantitatively assess the quality of life in various American cities. A prototype was provided by *Harper's* in January 1975 when under the title "What is America's Worst City?" the author attempted to rank fifty of the nations largest cities. With the use of statistical data from the U.S.

census on wage rates, cost of living, income distribution, and number of unionized workers, for example, the author provided a comparative rating of the general economic life of these cities. The same type of procedure was followed to assess a city's political life, its housing, health, education, race relations, and general social amenities. The article showed that America's more highly rated cities tended to be the newer, smaller, less-industrialized ones, whereas the older, larger, more-industrialized cities of the Northeast ranked near the bottom. Seattle only occasionally received the primary ranking in any specific category, but on the basis of its high rating in virtually all categories it was judged "America's Most Liveable City." Jersey City, N.J., on the other hand, was judged "the worst" of all fifty cities. With minor variations all such articles followed the same basic procedure, but whether it was "The Ten Best Cities for Living a Good Life," or "The Best Cities in the West," Seattle consistently rated at or near the top.[3]

As Canada's third largest city, and as the focal point of West Coast activity, Vancouver also received considerable attention from eastern newspapers and publications in the 1970s. The picture that came across was much like that given for Seattle. According to the Toronto-based *Saturday Night,* for example, Vancouver "has passed through adolescence and grown up happy. It doesn't any longer feel inferior in the face of Toronto's vastly superior economic clout. It isn't even much worried by the prospect of Calgary becoming the West's most powerful city. Vancouver which was once described as a setting in search of a city, has blossomed into one of the most attractive places in North America."[4] It was equally satisfying to read detailed and highly complimentary treatments in the *Atlantic Monthly* and in *National Geographic.* The *New Yorker* devoted a major article to Arthur Erickson, a prominent Vancouver architect and designer of Simon Fraser University, the Robson Square complex, and the University of British Columbia's Museum of Anthropology. One of the travel editors for the London *Sunday Times,* after a tour of various West Coast cities, had this to say of Vancouver: "It is a civilized city where people live well. There is crime . . . there are hordes of hookers, but the immediate and lasting impression is of a clean, prosperous and lively city in the most magnificent, natural setting."[5]

Even Seattle-based writers had complimentary things to say. Under the caption "Big City North," Emmett Watson of the Seattle *Post Intelligencer* spelled out in detail why he enjoyed Vancouver.

> It is a city that turns on life's juices. . . . Without seeming to try very hard Vancouver lures people from all over the world because it has

beauty, thrust, vitality. . . . Buildings of remarkable and daring design are sprouting constantly in downtown Vancouver. But what makes the city exciting . . . are the teeming downtown streets. Vancouver proliferates with apartments within five minutes walking distance of downtown—they have discovered long ago what we are just beginning to learn, that so called "in city" living is what gives the downtown core a vitality most cities lack. Many of the apartments to be sure are architectural abominations, but a lot of them are reasonably priced and within reach of young working couples. Restaurants are varied and good . . . ethnic eateries of all types—and they are usually jammed. . . . What I'm really saying is that the reason I keep going back to Vancouver is that it offers that rare combination—all kinds of outdoor pleasure, scenery and sports, within minutes of a truly cosmopolitan city.[6]

An additional insight into the nature of the two cities can be gained from the opinions offered by university students. In the late 1970s I asked students in my third- and fourth-year history classes at the University of British Columbia to write a brief paragraph on their image and impression of Seattle, regardless of whether or not they had actually visited that city. In the same way comparable groups of students at the University of Washington wrote on Vancouver. No claim can be made that this exercise was a controlled experiment, that it contained a representative sample of the two cities, or that the results are statistically verifiable. In addition, it is probably true that a substantial number of the residents of each city have little interest whatever in the other city. But for those Vancouverites who do have an opinion about Seattle it is probably captured in these outspoken comments by University of British Columbia students.

I've been there a number of times. . . . My impression has improved. What bothers me about it is that it's big and I feel a little afraid walking around. This is probably due in part to the fact that I am a stranger there. I'm also aware of the presence of blacks. . . . It isn't really an ugly city, no more so than Vancouver.

My day long visit left me with the impression of overall ugliness. Looking back on my visit the only images I can conjure up are neon signs, car lots, fast-food restaurants and a seedy downtown area.

A hustle and bustle city during the normal working hours . . . deserted in the evening . . . downtown Seattle holds no appeal for people.

Seattle is like the 25th highest scorer in the NHL [National Hockey

League]—easily forgettable. Its major highlight is a ghastly scar of a freeway ripping right through its middle. It's pretentious and dull. . . . If it wasn't for Boeing (and this undoubtedly is a biased generalization) it probably wouldn't even exist.

My image of Seattle is one of a deteriorating business centre, growing old, dirty and drab, yet a city with beautiful lakes, clean parks, and scenic drives. . . . The University district and other suburbs show how beautiful people and places can be.

It seems a nice place to me when I visit, but somehow it lacks a certain feeling of style. It doesn't have much flair. The people seem typically American, that is open, friendly, courteous. . . . The city gives me a jumbled feeling like there is no centre to it. In walking around I have never come across a place where people congregate.

Seattle is a graceless city . . . loud and brash . . . has few redeeming qualities apart from lower prices, more liberal drinking regulations and occasional special events. Seattle is the capital of a depressed region and is itself depressing.

It's in a fantastic setting, unpolluted . . . has a newness to it . . . is a good reflection of what I would call west coast affluence. I know that the city has some undesirable features—racism, the freeways, but I only concentrate on the good aspects . . . when I visit it.

Seattle is a young Pacific Northwest centre trying very hard to be a recognized cultural, economic and sports centre on the west coast. They are striving to become a showpiece in America, as a very ultra modern town.

My image of Seattle is dominated by the overwhelming sense of "American-ness" and "foreign-ness" which I feel as a Canadian when I visit there. The presence of a black community, pornographic movie houses, and slums give the city an ambience quite unlike Vancouver. The mental picture I have of the city is of grey concrete, grey shops and, above all, grey people.

These student comments provide an accurate picture of how many Canadians view Seattle. Whether written or heard in conversations with Vancouverites, the unfavorable image of Seattle is unmistakable.

This pattern contrasts sharply with the generally favorable opinions that Seattleites have of Vancouver. Here are some representative selections from University of Washington students.

It has the feel of a very cosmopolitan city similar possibly to San Francisco more so than Seattle. . . . In my experience in B.C. I have always (this is no glorified exaggeration) been met by very receptive and courteous people except when I got lost in downtown Vancouver. . . . It sure seems like an easy place to get lost in.

Vancouver stands out as being far more European in flavor than Seattle. . . . I could see living in Vancouver without experiencing any major revision in my lifestyle.

The people are most congenial. I lived in Vancouver for one and a half years. . . . As a black man I find more racial pressure in Seattle (which isn't much) than I ever did in Vancouver. To simply state it: I love Vancouver.

City itself seems well-planned and clean. Gastown is unique. . . . People there, and Canadians in general, are total asses. They go out of their way to make Americans feel uncomfortable and unwelcome. Also prices are skyhigh. . . . In sum, keep the city, export the people.

My impression of Vancouver as a city is that it is beautiful and fun. The striking thing to me is how on the streets themselves there is such a diversity of races. Walking along I noticed people of every race *seeming* to be existing in harmony with white Canadians. No one was staring at others who looked different like they do in downtown Seattle. I feel that white Canadians probably have the same prejudices against other races, but since there is so much diversity it isn't seen on the surface as it is here.

I happen to love going to Vancouver. The city has such an international feel to it. It is similar to San Francisco I think. . . . Basically there is such a variety of international type things plus lots of family type, inexpensive things to do. . . . One thing we always exclaim about is the extreme high density and number of apartments in the central area. That is so unlike Seattle where private homes are so prevalent.

For such a large city their highway system is the worst in the world. . . . They have no street signs. A person could drive forever as I have done, and without asking directions could never get home.

A truly cosmopolitan city . . . I love it. A very friendly city with people who are happy to get to know you. Fairly prosperous, good restaurants, great nightlife, and a beautiful downtown area.

Isn't Vancouver where the dumb Canucks live? Seriously though—
I've always pictured Vancouver as a larger, more international and
more cosmopolitan city than Seattle . . . although separated only by an
open border and 100 miles there isn't much open friendliness between Seattle and Vancouver.

At times one forgets that it isn't actually an American city, yet one
meanders down Robson Street with the multitude of European spe-
cialty shops and thoughts of it being another Portland or Seattle are
dismissed.

From the wide range of impressions offered by these Canadian and
American students, one can uncover many contradictions. To some a specific city is rundown and dirty, to others it is modern and clean. To some
the residents are surly and hostile, to others open and friendly. Some say, "I
could live there quite easily," others say "I wouldn't want to live there." Yet
even with these contradictions the predominantly favorable impression of
Vancouver held by American students, and the predominantly unfavorable
opinion of Seattle held by Canadian students is clear and unambiguous.
Canadians have long complained of American ignorance of their nation. At
least as far as these two cities are concerned, the complaint should be re-
directed. When University of British Columbia students learn that Seattle
is rightfully regarded as one of America's most liveable cities, the usual
reaction is one of shocked disbelief.

By the late 1970s both Vancouver and Seattle were reasonably prosperous, self-confident cities. Quebec separatism, inflation, and unemployment were still constant worries in the Canadian setting, but the sense of
pride and self-worth that had been growing throughout the postwar years
continued. Individual Vancouverites still migrated to the United States,
but it was a trickle, not a flood. Since the urban riots of the 1960s, the
disaster of Vietnam, and the turmoil over Watergate, the United States was
no longer seen as a success story nor as a nation to be envied. Somehow
the fact that clothing, food, and housing still cost more in Canada was not
as important as it had been in the past.

For Seattle too, the late 1970s were basically good years, even though
there were still plenty of problems. Measured by income, occupation, or
housing, substantial numbers of Seattle's blacks were clearly middle class.
But at the same time, some 20 percent of black families were still mired in
poverty. Employment at Boeing had stabilized, but there was an uneasy
awareness that it could slump again. Increased inflation took a big bite out

of pay envelopes, yet the basic outlook about the future was guardedly optimistic. A detailed investigation of Seattle's development between the mid-1960s and the mid-1970s led one editor to conclude:

> Seattle today is very simply a very different place from what it was ten years ago. It is unquestionably more accomplished, more sophisticated, more skeptical, more aware. But it is also less optimistic, less certain that growth is its destiny, less confident that every problem has a solution. It has gained theatres and restaurants but lost people; built gleaming office buildings but let neighborhoods and schools decay; attracted young urbanites but lost middle class families to the suburbs. Paradoxically, it is a "bigger" city—more cultured, more international—with fewer people. Perhaps we have lost our innocence. Certainly we have lowered our sights and raised our consciousness.[7]

The victory of the Seattle Super Sonics over the Washington (D.C.) Bullets, and the winning of the National Basketball Association championship in 1979 provided an immense thrill. The final win was greeted by a burst of excitement and celebration that was unparalleled in the city's history. Police estimated that over 100,000 persons flocked to Fifth Avenue to celebrate the Sonics' victory and welcome the players home. Such a frenzied response to an athletic victory can be dismissed as trivial and inconsequential. But in a sports-saturated, television-saturated society, where "winning is everything," the Sonics' victory gave the city a recognition and national prominence that it had sought for a long, long time. The athletic fame might be fleeting, but it was nevertheless very real and very satisfying. A writer for the *Post Intelligencer* possibly explained it all when he wrote, "For the first time ever, Seattle is the world champion of something."[8]

Vancouver had its own moment of athletic glory in 1979 when its Whitecaps defeated the New York Cosmos and the Tampa Bay Rowdies to win the championship of the North American Soccer League. A few Canadians were on the team, but the heart of the Whitecaps consisted of veterans from First and Second Division clubs in Britain. Fans were equally pleased when the Vancouver Canucks reached the National Hockey League finals in 1982, before being defeated in four straight games by the New York Islanders. But although Vancouverites were excited by such events they were minor ripples when compared with the tidal wave brought on by the Seattle Sonics' achievement.

At the very time that Seattle and Vancouver were basking in their achievements and national prominence, the population of both cities was actually declining. It is true that the metropolitan populations continued to grow in the 1970s, reaching about 1,600,000 in Seattle and 1,250,000 in Vancouver by the end of the decade. Yet the population of both central cities showed a definite decline. By 1980, for example, Seattle's population had dropped to 494,000, well below the 530,000 of 1970, and even further below the peak of 557,000 reached in 1960.[9] Vancouver too declined, though about a decade later than Seattle. In 1971 it peaked at some 426,000, but by 1981 had dropped to 414,000. Later analysis showed that moves to the suburbs, a drop in marriages, and a fall in the birth rate had all contributed to the population slump in the central city.[10] Yet contrary to the long-held conviction that growth and expansion were essential for a prosperous city, both Seattle and Vancouver were in basically good health as they entered the 1980s.

The parallel trends in Seattle and Vancouver in the late 1970s and early 1980s once again underline the broadly comparable development of these two cities over the years.[11] Yet whether one scans their entire history or focuses on recent developments there is no doubt that a great variety of distinctive characteristics also exist. One can never capture all of these unique characteristics—for they are virtually endless—but a brief examination of comparable institutions or processes can provide some understanding of this diversity.

The University of Washington (uw) and the University of British Columbia (ubc), for example, are both large tax-supported institutions. They provide a great range of offerings in the traditional academic disciplines, as well as more specialized work in extension programs, professional schools, and research institutes. Tuition fees are modest, and the great majority of some 35,000 students at uw and 25,000 at ubc are from the immediate region, with many driving daily to the campus. Some of the differences are obvious. When the Washington Huskies play the Oregon Ducks in football, crowds of 50,000 are not uncommon. When ubc plays the University of Alberta, a "big" crowd amounts to 1,000. Other differences are deeper. The history departments of both have about forty full-time faculty members and provide comparable offerings. But an undergraduate taking history courses at ubc is likely to have faculty members provide lectures, lead discussion groups, read papers and mark exams, his or her counterpart at uw is more likely to have teaching assistants leading the discussion group and assessing class work. The emphasis on graduate work also differs. The University of British Columbia granted its first Ph.D. in history in 1968; uw by that time had granted ninety. Faculty members have a collective bargaining agreement with the administration at ubc; this is not the case at UW. "Town-gown" relationships also differ. Seattle might be closely identified with its Huskies and Vancouver indifferent to its Thunderbirds, but UBC faculty members are much more likely to pursue and achieve direct political office, especially at the municipal and the provincial level. In the early 1970s, acting president Lem Tuai of Seattle's city council, angered by some queries posed by UW Professor Victor Steinbrueck at a public hearing, retorted, "Why don't you intellectuals stay out at the University— where you belong?"[12] At this same time, four UBC professors were serving on Vancouver city council.

The organization and nature of police activity in the two cities was also distinctive. In Seattle the chief of police was appointed by the mayor. Throughout the city's history a standard first move by a newcomer to the mayor's office was to appoint a new chief of police to "clean up the mess." Police scandals seldom equaled the range and intensity of those experienced during Mayor Hiram Gill's tenure in office, but charges of corruption, fraudulent behavior, favoritism, and inefficiencies were perennial. The police in Vancouver were responsible to a board of police commissioners appointed by the provincial government. Police chiefs generally served long terms, were seldom well known, and seldom became the focal point of public controversy. The scandals that flared up periodically were generally minor. A disproportionately large number of the force, and especially of its supervisory officers, were from England and Scotland with previous military or police experience.[13] The values, traditions, and approach of that experience were undoubtedly reasserted in the Canadian setting.

Statistical data on criminal activity in the two cities are not directly comparable, especially over an extended number of years.[14] Yet a comparison of murder rates reinforces the traditional viewpoint of the higher incidence of violence in the American than in the Canadian setting. Seattle had 9.2 murders/100,000 population in the 1970s, whereas Vancouver had a rate of 6.3/100,000. Although Vancouver had the highest murder rate of any large city in Canada, it was still well below Seattle's average rating for American cities. As was true throughout the industrialized world the incidence of murder was much more common among the impoverished than among the more prosperous. Blacks, for example, made up 7 percent of Seattle's population in the 1970s, but accounted for 42 percent of those arrested for murder. In Vancouver, many of the murders were directly related to the heavy drug traffic in the city.

An examination of housing prices in the two cities in the 1960s and 1970s also offers distinctive insights.[15] One might assume that the price of

Table 16   Housing Prices and Price Indices for Vancouver
and Seattle, 1960–76 (1967 Index is 100)

	Vancouver	Index	Seattle	Index
	$		$	
1960	13,050	73	19,757	87
1961	12,348	69	19,984	88
1962	12,158	68	20,892	92
1963	12,636	71	21,120	93
1964	13,202	74	21,347	94
1965	13,964	78	21,347	94
1966	15,202	85	22,028	97
1967	17,836	100	22,709	100
1968	20,595	115	23,390	103
1969	23,939	134	26,343	116
1970	24,239	136	26,297	116
1971	26,471	148	26,343	116
1972	31,465	176	27,251	120
1973	41,505	232	28,160	124
1974	57,861	324	30,430	134
1975	64,471	370	32,702	144
1976	68,900	386	35,200	155

Source: Goldberg, "Housing and Land Prices in Canada and the U.S." p. 222.

an average house in Seattle or Vancouver would be roughly comparable. But a study by Professor Michael A. Goldberg of the University of British Columbia shows that although house prices in Vancouver were well below those in Seattle during the 1960s, since 1970 this relationship has progressively changed, with Vancouver prices surging far ahead of those in the American city (see Table 16).

How does one account for the more volatile market in Vancouver, especially the sharp differences of the 1970s? The immediate answer would seem to be that Vancouver suffered a shortage of housing in the 1970s, and as a result prices rose. But Goldberg's analysis of the total supply of housing shows that this was not the case. Rather than a supply shortage, it was the rapid increase in demand that fueled the price rise in Vancouver. The more rapid rate of population increase of metropolitan Vancouver than metropolitan Seattle between 1960 and 1976 (49 percent versus 28 percent) would be one contributing factor. Similarly, the sharper rise in per capita income in British Columbia than in Washington (230 percent versus 153 percent) also contributed. Lower unemployment rates in Vancouver and higher property tax rates in Seattle would also play a part.

Beyond these local supply and demand factors, national policies also shaped the real estate market in the two cities. The expansive monetary and mortgage policies of the Canadian government increased the demand for housing and stimulated price increases. At the same time the limited program of freeway construction in Canada tended to discourage outward movement, and maintained a greater relative density in Vancouver. In the United States, on the other hand, the government pursued a policy of vigorous freeway construction. This opened up large areas of suburban land to potential buyers, dispersed the city's population, and kept house prices down.

An additional factor sustaining the high house prices in Vancouver is that the representative Canadian sees that city as a highly desirable environment in which to live and work. The representative American has more doubts about Seattle. Goldberg argues that this difference is largely the result of extensive federal involvement in the American city. Whether this entailed freeway construction, urban renewal programs, or federal housing projects it led to "disruptions," "uncertainties," and loss of "investor confidence." The Canadian city, according to Goldberg, has retained its vitality, liveability, and financial solvency because of the limited, fragmented federal role in urban Canada and the much greater reliance on private initiative and private funds. Such an argument is less than convincing. It downplays the massive problems in U.S. cities created by black-white tensions, urban violence, and ghetto poverty. Goldberg's neglect of any detailed analysis of the racial and ethnic makeup of Seattle and Vancouver automatically ignores a major variable that could help account for the greater vitality and appeal of the Canadian city.

A comparison of the development of transit systems during the 1970s and 1980s is also revealing, for while Seattle relies on a fleet of buses for such service, Vancouver has made a significant commitment to a rail transit system. Public mass transportation was intensively utilized in Seattle during the World War II years, but in the postwar decades went into a long decline. Rising incomes, availability of cars and gasoline, better roads, and freeways encouraged thousands of former transit passengers to purchase automobiles and provide their own transportation. Thus transit passengers declined from a peak of 130 million in 1945 to 30 million twenty years later. After an extensive publicity campaign in the mid-1960s, Seattle voters were asked to approve a bond measure that would have committed the city to a 47-mile rail transit system costing some $1.2 billion.[16] Decisively rejected by city voters in 1966, it reappeared as a modified bus-rail system in 1970 but was again voted down. A proposal for an all-bus system was approved in September 1972.

Since then Seattle's all-bus Metro Transit has grown dramatically. Between 1973 and 1980 transit passengers doubled, from 32 million to 66 million, and the number of buses in service rose from 570 to 1,200. With extension of routes and more frequent service, annual vehicle miles increased from 19 million to 31 million. But like public transit systems throughout North America, Seattle's Metro Transit required major subsidies. In a typical year operating revenues accounted for 30 percent of operating expenses, with sales taxes, excise taxes, and federal grants making up the shortfall.[17]

The postwar evolution of the transit system in Vancouver showed much in common with that in Seattle. There too ridership peaked during World War II. Transit passengers declined sharply from 1945 to 1965 but partially recovered thereafter. By 1975 about 90 million passengers per year were using Vancouver's public transit. Seattleites voted down different rail transit proposals in 1966 and 1970; Vancouverites expressed a decided preference for some kind of transit system in a detailed poll carried out by the City of Vancouver. Subsequent studies of appropriate systems culminated in 1969 when the Greater Vancouver Regional District (GVRD), following up on a mandate given by the provincial government, provided a detailed plan for a conventional rapid transit system. It envisaged a system of rail cars with a driver on every train, sharing a right-of-way with automobile traffic, and including several traffic intersections at grade.

In the spring of 1981, William Vander Zalm, British Columbia's minister of municipal affairs, announced that the province would proceed with an Advanced Light Rapid Transit (ALRT) system, designed and engineered by an Ontario Crown corporation, the Urban Transit and Development Corporation.[18] This unilateral decision provoked immediate concern from city and GVRD officials. The new system differed significantly from the existing proposal in that it was highly automated, required a separate elevated roadbed, and at some $900 million was much more expensive. Conflict was heated, but provincial authorities ultimately determined both the financing and the development of the entire system.

Under a series of agreements the federal government granted $60 million, and the Province of British Columbia made a $275 million grant toward capital costs. Interest on the remaining borrowed capital was to be divided between the province and the municipalities involved. Actual construction of the 21.4-kilometer (13-mile) system linking Vancouver to New Westminster began March 1982 and was opened for service in January 1986. While critics considered it extravagant and unnecessary and argued that it would require massive subsidies, the public saw it as a modern, attractive, and desirable addition to the city.

Vancouver's slightly higher population concentration than Seattle, its fewer automobiles per capita, and its concentration of Europeans familiar with urban transit systems all contributed to the success of the city's new rail transit system. Moreover, city and GVRD planners also played a part. Ultimately, however, it was provincial authorities, provincial decisions, and provincial funds that accounted for the development. Federal subsidies granted in the hope that Vancouver's "Sky Train" would be a showpiece of Canadian technology were also critical to the entire operation.

The development of EXPO 86 to celebrate Vancouver's 100th birthday provides an additional example of the importance of provincial decisions on the city's life. Originally planned as a minor exposition on transportation developments, it was strongly opposed by Mayor Michael Harcourt. But as Premier William Bennett continued his steps, the mayor became a supporter. Over a three-year period, the entire north shore of False Creek was redeveloped under provincial funding, with the federal government simultaneously developing a handsome sail-topped trade center on the main waterfront. At a time when British Columbia's unemployment rate was over 12 percent, critics condemned the provincial expenditure of some $900 million as an extravagant megaproject that would entail heavy future debt.

The official opening of the fair on May 2, by the Prince and Princess of Wales met with enthusiastic public approval. Over its five and a half months, EXPO had an attendance of 22 million. With over 150 international, national, and corporate exhibits only the most devoted fairgoer could hope to visit them all. To Robert Fulford of the Toronto-based *Saturday Night Magazine,* EXPO did not amount to much. He found the exhibits "mundane," the architecture "commonplace," and the entertainment "unremarkable." Most visitors were not disappointed, and enthused about EXPO's setting, holiday mood, and overall professionalism. Premier Van der Zalm, Mayor Harcourt, EXPO chairman James Pattison, and the man on the street all agreed that EXPO had permanently changed Vancouver's image and indisputably established it as a world-class city. Not only had Vancouver profited directly, but it would continue to reap benefits for years to come. EXPO's estimated deficit of some $300 million was seldom mentioned.[19]

Further comparisons might be done on a host of comparable institutions in the two cities. One could profitably compare metropolitan governments, religious organizations, architectural developments, or the support for symphony orchestras. Despite the myriad similarities and differences, it is the dissimilarities that are most intriguing and the reasons for these differences that are most challenging. No all-inclusive hypothesis can account for the many distinctions between the two cities, but a reexamination of their history suggests a number of factors of continuing importance.

If one were to choose a single concept that explains their many differences, it would be the obvious but nevertheless basic fact that they are in separate, independent nations. Whether one compares these cities in the 1860s, the 1930s, or the 1980s, one cannot ignore the fact that Seattle is part of the United States and Vancouver is part of Canada. The ramifications of the political separation are almost endless. It may be as obvious as the variations in freeway systems or as subtle as the difference in the public's perception of the police. But in each case local characteristics and processes reflect the distinctive histories, roles, and values of two separate nations.

The fact that the United States is an immensely bigger, more powerful nation than Canada is revealed in diverse ways in the history of the two cities. Seattle's original settlement and early rise to prominence mirrored the more advanced development of the entire western United States. Not only was there a proliferation of settlement throughout the Puget Sound region in the 1860s and 1870s, for example, but the concentration of population in the San Francisco area provided a market for the lumber and coal of the Pacific Northwest. In much the same way, the larger population base and regional demand enabled Seattle's businessmen to construct local coal lines, shipping facilities, and service activities far beyond the level provided in Vancouver. The completion of the Canadian Pacific Railway in 1887 was an immense stimulus to Vancouver's growth and reduced the gap between the two cities. Yet even in the late twentieth century the bigger local, regional, and national market served by Seattle enabled it to maintain its lead over its Canadian counterpart.

Measured by central city population or by metropolitan population, Seattle has always been substantially larger than Vancouver. Yet, paradoxically, present-day Vancouver is seen both by residents and by visitors as the bigger city. This can be explained in part by Vancouver's greater relative importance in Canada compared to Seattle's position in the United States. After the completion of the CPR, Vancouver assumed immediate importance, and by the time of World War I was firmly established as Canada's third largest city. Seattle, on the other hand, did not enjoy such a role. There was no doubt of its regional importance, for Minneapolis, 1,500 miles to the east, and Portland, 150 miles to the south, were the nearest big cities in the United States. But when one broadened the field to the entire nation, Seattle's stature diminished, and it became merely "the Capital" of the distant Pacific Northwest. By the time Vancouver was the third largest city in Canada, Seattle ranked twenty-first in the United States, and the relative importance of the two cities has remained virtually unchanged. Local boosterism and the endless citation of population statistics differed little between the two cities, but Vancouver's conviction that it was an important national center could be sustained much more easily.

Especially in the late twentieth century, the sense of "big city" Vancouver is also supported by a concentration of facilities in the relatively small, and geographically confined, central business district. The 2-square-mile peninsula defined by Burrard Inlet, False Creek, and Stanley Park contains not only the city's main department stores, business offices, theaters, hotels, restaurants, and art galleries, but also has some 50,000 permanent residents all within easy contact of these facilities. Seattle's central business district is somewhat more diffuse and elongated, defined largely by Elliott Bay in the west, the I-5 freeway to the east, and Yesler Way to the south. It contains similar shopping, business, and entertainment facilities, yet Seattle lacks the concentration of permanent downtown residents enjoyed by Vancouver. Thus its lively daytime vitality largely disappears when its clerks, executives, and office workers head for homes in West Seattle, Northgate, or Bellevue after work.

A further indication of the significance of national separation can be seen in the prominence of military-related employment in Seattle contrasted with its virtual absence in Vancouver. Throughout the 1950s, for example, total defense purchases in Washington State averaged $1.15 billion per year. Such purchases dropped slightly in the 1960s, rose again in the 1970s, and by 1980 had passed the $2 billion per year mark.[20] The vast majority of these awards went to Boeing plants in the Seattle area, with the U.S. Naval Yard in Bremerton also receiving substantial contracts. A study done for the U.S. Arms Control and Disarmament Agency shows that in fiscal year 1963, out of a state total of about $1.1 billion in defense contracts, the Seattle-Tacoma metropolitan area received awards valued at $1,002,559,000.[21] Of this, "aircraft and missiles" accounted for $843,346,000, and "shipbuilding" $108,032,000. The remainder was distributed among a variety of small firms and organizations. The distribution of contracts in fiscal year 1964 was virtually identical.

Economists differ in their assessment of the impact of such defense expenditures on the area's total employment. All agree that besides the direct employment of Boeing workers, for example, one must also consider the indirect employment of subcontractors who provide component parts to the Boeing Company, as well as the induced employment of numerous carpenters, bank tellers, or store clerks, all of whom provide the various goods and services needed by the original Boeing employees. The Arms Control and Disarmament Agency study pointed out that the direct employment in defense-related activity in the Seattle-Tacoma metropolitan area amounted to 47,000, while the indirect and induced employment came to 86,000. These 133,000 workers, in turn, accounted for 23.8 percent of the total civilian employment in the area.[22] Charles M. Tiebout, professor of Economics at the University of Washington, arrived at an even higher estimate. He concluded that defense-generated employment accounted for 42.2 percent of metropolitan Seattle's total employment.[23]

During the postwar era there have been major fluctuations in the military/commercial mix of the Boeing Company's sales.[24] In the early 1960s, for example, military sales to the U.S. government accounted for about 70 percent of that company's total sales. Beginning about 1965, sales to domestic and foreign airlines began to assume a larger and larger share of the company's business, and by the late 1970s U.S. government purchases had dropped to about 28 percent of sales. But over the entire period from 1960 to 1980 U.S. government purchases of aircraft, missiles, and space equipment accounted for 36 percent of Boeing's total sales. One might question the precise impact of defense spending on Seattle's total employment in any given year. But the sustained importance of such spending, whether through the Boeing Company, the Bremerton Naval Yard, the Military Transport Service, Fort Lewis, or the McChord Air Force Base, is unquestionable.

Another significant consequence of national separation can be seen in the different ethnic makeup of the two cities. Throughout much of its history Seattle has been a more ethnically diverse and cosmopolitan city than Vancouver. This reflected the fact that the United States was not only a much more prominent nation, but that its remarkably liberal immigration policy enabled virtually anyone who wanted to settle there to do so. A sprinkling of Scandinavians, Germans, Italians, and Russians also settled in the Canadian city but seldom achieved the significance of their counterparts in Seattle. With the passage of restrictive immigration legislation by the United States in the 1920s, the traditional influx of foreign-born migrants was drastically curbed, and over the years Seattle reflected that change. The Canadian government, on the other hand, especially in the years after 1945, followed an expansive immigration policy. Potential migrants from Europe and the Orient found it easier and quicker to qualify for admission to Canada than to the United States, and the impact on Vancouver's population profile was quickly apparent. By the late twentieth century it was Vancouver that was the cosmopolitan city, while Seattle was essentially a native-born American city.

The major role of the British immigrants in Vancouver, compared with their more limited activity in Seattle, is one more indication of the significance of political separation. A move to Canada was a big step for the Britisher, but it did not mark as sharp a break from friends and traditions as did a move to the United States. Consequently, it is understandable why many more opted for Vancouver than Seattle. The impact of these thousands of English, Scots, Welsh, and Irish on the Canadian city is unmistakable; it is revealed in the political activities of organized labor, the method and approach of the police, the types of houses and gardens, and the style given the city's schools, stores, and offices. Taken for granted by the local resident, it is quickly evident to the outsider. The importance of the British immigrants has declined in the years since World War II, but they still account for a tenth of Vancouver's population, and still have a significant impact on the city's life.

The racial makeup of the two cities also indicates national separation. As part of an overwhelmingly white nation, blacks make up only a small segment of Vancouver's population. Seattle, on the other hand, reflects the fact that about one-tenth of the U.S. population is black. Before World War II, Seattle's small black community was on the periphery of the city's economic and social life, but with the massive migration of the war and postwar years it grew dramatically. By the 1980s, 45,000 blacks accounted for about 9 percent of the city's population. Seattle's adaptation to this dramatic increase was much like that of cities throughout the North and West. While its whites were convinced that Seattle was inherently a tolerant city with no significant racial problems, its blacks were equally aware of the slowness of change, white racism, segregation in housing and education, and the fact that they were usually the "last hired and first fired."

A brief survey of the steps by which Seattle desegregated its public schools provides an insight into the nature of race relations during the postwar decades.[25] The 1954 decision by the U.S. Supreme Court in *Brown* v. *The Board of Education,* that white and black students could no longer be segregated in public schools, received little attention in Seattle. School officials and citizens alike believed that segregation did not exist and that the court's ruling had no direct bearing in Seattle. Yet subsequent studies done in the late 1950s showed that the heavy concentration of blacks in the city's Central Area led to significant segregation in that districts schools with one cluster of six elementary schools having an average of 70 percent black students.

The first tentative step toward desegregation occurred in 1963 when the school board announced a voluntary racial transfer program. Although the plan allowed for 1,600 students to transfer, less than 100 actually took the step and the program was soon forgotten. A slightly more successful plan was initiated in 1967 when a mandatory busing program for students in the fifth to eighth grades was begun. But when attempts were made to extend the program, strong opposition surfaced and the plan gradually petered out in the early 1970s. Not until 1977 when the Urban League, the National Association for the Advancement of Colored People, the American Civil Liberties Union, and the Seattle Council of Churches all pushed for it did Seattle actually meet the intent of the Supreme Court's 1954 ruling. On December 15, 1977, the Seattle School Board voted six to one to desegregate its public schools by mandatory racial assignment of students. Seattleites were understandably proud of the fact that the step had been taken voluntarily, and that it had not required a court order as had been true in many American cities. Yet the fact that such integration took a full twenty-three years after the Supreme Court's ruling indicates both the anxieties and fears it engendered as well as the strong opposition it faced.

Vancouver has a sprinkling of blacks in its population, but the Chinese are the dominant minority element and give a distinctive ambience to the entire city. From their original appearance in the late nineteenth century, Chinese were ever aware of white hostility to their presence, but over the years their numbers grew steadily and by 1920 some 6,000 lived in Vancouver. The passage of the Chinese Immigration Act of 1923 was a critical blow, for it effectively stopped further immigration for some twenty-five years. Not until the Canadian government modified its policies in the postwar years did Chinese immigrants again enter Canada in significant numbers.

The passage of the Immigration Act of 1967 marked a pivotal change. That legislation established a completely new policy under which all potential immigrants were assessed on a merit system based on skills and possible contribution to Canadian society. No racial distinctions were made and Chinese were treated on an equal basis with all other immigrants. The effect of the legislation was dramatic and immediate. Whereas Chinese immigration amounted to 1,500 to 2,000 per year prior to 1967, in the following years it jumped fivefold. By 1980 Vancouver had about

40,000 Chinese or some 10 percent of the city's population. Unlike their predecessors of the early twentieth century, they were usually from an urban background, prosperous, and well educated, with many fluent in both Chinese and English. As they gained influence and power such newcomers transformed Chinatown from an insular, insecure, and seedy district into a shopping and dining focal point for the entire community, Chinese and non-Chinese alike.

There is no doubt that since World War II both cities have progressively lost the bigotry and racial intolerance that marked so much of their early history. A number of factors have contributed to the relative ease of this process in Vancouver. The tenacious family structure in the Chinese community, the respect for authority, and the conviction in "work hard and you will get ahead" have all been helpful. The strong business tradition and the rapidity with which Chinese immigrants moved into a variety of economic activities have also played a part. The strong sense of community, nourished by a host of fraternal and cultural organizations, was significant, as was the Chinese emphasis on education. The stream of able young men and women going on to university bode well for the future.[26]

Despite Seattle's great strides in acceptance of its black citizens, greater tensions and problems were evident. By the 1980s a substantial majority of Seattle's blacks were unquestionably middle class, living in comfortable housing throughout the city and working in a variety of professional, managerial, technical, and service occupations. Yet the prevalence of single-parent households, high unemployment, and the persistence of poverty and criminal activity were conducive to much tension. The 1980 census showed that while only 4.3 percent of Seattle's white families had incomes below the poverty level, 19.4 percent of Seattle's black families fell into that category. The sustained prevalence of this poverty and the resultant social ills among this "black underclass" go a long way in explaining the undercurrent of anxieties.

Differences in the actual federal systems of the United States and Canada also contribute to the uniqueness of Seattle and Vancouver. Political centralization has proceeded much further in the American setting, and average Seattleites are more directly influenced by the activities and programs of their federal government than their counterparts in Vancouver. Such a process was firmly launched in the 1930s by President Roosevelt's New Deal administration. Funding for housing, transit, education, or urban renewal fluctuates, depending on the national administration in power; still there is no denying of the federal presence in Seattle. Mayor Uhlman's claim in 1977 that 95 percent of the special programs for the young, the handicapped, and the elderly would be continued by federal funding even if all local funds were withdrawn, suggests its importance. The construction of the thirty-seven-story Federal Office Building in Seattle was also symbolic. With its 2,600 federal employees it directed the activities of 16,000 other federal workers in the area, and provided services for thousands of local residents in their dealings with the federal government.

Because of Canada's distinctive history such political centralization has not proceeded as far as in the United States. Through judicial interpretation and long-term provincial-federal conflict, Canadian provinces have increased their power and authority, while the federal presence in cities has remained more limited and fragmented. Vancouverites have many direct contacts with their federal government and funds from Ottawa play an important role in the rehabilitation of houses, the construction of bridges and freeways, and the development of transit systems. But the fact that British Columbia's lumber and mineral resources, for example, are primarily under provincial jurisdiction makes for a greater sense of regional control, regional significance, and regional identity than is the case in Seattle. The large and attractive Robson Square complex in downtown Vancouver which houses a variety of provincial courts and provincial agencies is a fitting symbol of this different orientation.

A subtle but nevertheless significant distinction between Seattle and Vancouver, and one that has been continually revealed throughout their history, is that Vancouver's officials and citizens have shown a less-intense form of individualism, and a weaker commitment to private enterprise than is true of their Seattle counterparts. Such an assertion is hard to establish, since in both Seattle and Vancouver it has been private property, private needs, and private rights that have dominated. It is true that both cities reveal a whole range of behavior and values. But whereas Vancouver has shown a definite leftward tilt toward the public-rights side of the spectrum, Seattle clearly tends toward the right with its emphasis on private needs and individual responsibility. There are numerous exceptions and contradictions to this pattern, but the basic distinction holds.

One of the manifestations of this distinction is the much greater tendency in the Canadian city to develop facilities through some type of public or semipublic agency or on the basis of some form of collective activity. The original survey of the English Bay region by the Royal Navy and the setting aside of large amounts of land for military, Indian, and townsite reserves offers an early and significant example. But it was the provincial grant of some 6,000 acres of land to the Canadian Pacific Railway, in the heart of the future city, that provides the classic demonstration of the role of the semipublic agency in Vancouver. The CPR automatically became the city's preeminent landowner, and its plans and activities would shape not only Vancouver's physical layout, but its economic, political and social life as well.

Such a pattern differed significantly from the dominance of private initiative and private enterprise in early Seattle. From the arrival of the original settlers in 1851 the entire area was open for preemption. The plans developed by Denny, Boren, and Maynard for the infant city were substantially followed, and a multitude of individuals pursuing their own goals would create the mills, wharves, rail lines, and shipping facilities needed by the new community. The vigorous activity of Seattle's founding fathers was a far cry from the passiveness of Vancouver's original "Three Greenhorns" and would be revealed many times in the following years, whether in the pursuit of the Klondike Gold Rush trade, the rapid adaptation to wartime shipping demands, or even in the substantially larger estates accumulated by Seattle's cluster of millionaires.

More recent symbols of the divergent approach to development can be seen in the evolution of False Creek in Vancouver as contrasted with Lake Union in Seattle. Both areas were about 2 square miles, ringed by housing, boat yards, machine shops, and storage depots. Over the years both had become run down and dilapidated, with endless suggestions as to how they might be improved. Such concerns became particularly strong in the late 1960s and early 1970s. But while changes to Seattle's Lake Union were limited to a conversion of a municipal gas plant into a children's playground, changes in the False Creek area were much more comprehensive. A handsome urban complex of townhouses, condominiums, parks, and marinas was constructed with appropriate roads, transportation, and schools for 5,000 residents.

One of the basic factors contributing to this difference was the concentration of landownership in the Canadian setting, contrasted with the abundance of owners in the American one. Vancouver began its acquisition of land on the south shore of False Creek during the late 1960s. After a series of major land transactions, the B.C. government wound up with 400 acres on Burnaby Mountain, the subsequent location of Simon Fraser University. Marathon Realty, the real estate wing of the CPR, obtained 190 acres on the north side of the creek that would later become the site of EXPO 86, Vancouver's world fair. The city itself added 85 acres to its existing holdings on the south side of the creek. It was in this latter area where the residential redevelopment occurred.

Differences in the decision-making process were also critical, and again reveal the distinctive political culture of the two cities.[27] In Seattle, the city council played a relatively passive role with the impetus for change coming from private individuals and groups. In response to such requests the council authorized the establishment of an independent nine-membered Lake Union Advisory Committee. But after two years of investigations and hearings that body could not reconcile the multiplicity of private interests and made no significant recommendations to the council. In Vancouver on the other hand, a special three-membered city council committee established in 1972 under Alderman Walter Hardwick provided effective direction. This committee worked closely with the City Planning Department and although citizens were periodically consulted and kept informed of developments, their direct involvement was much more limited than in Seattle. The entire project was also facilitated by the fact that federal authorities were simultaneously carrying out an extensive redevelopment of Granville Island near the mouth of False Creek. Yet the overall control and direction provided by the city was significant and the degree of public, private cooperation impressive.

Over the years Vancouver's officials and citizens have shown a greater awareness of public needs and public rights than have their Seattle counterparts. Just why this characteristic has been sustained in the Canadian setting is not easily answered. It may be through the influence of generations of British immigrants, a more active and influential political left, the long-standing assertion of city rights against the powerful CPR, or possibly just the greater willingness of Vancouverites to accept the decisions of political authorities. Whatever the reason it means that modern-day Vancouver has a greater variety of public facilities and services than does Seattle.

The miles of public bathing beaches in Vancouver contrasted with the isolated acres of such facilities in Seattle provide one of the most striking examples.[28] Comparable touches can be seen in the greater abundance of public tennis courts, playgrounds, sailing facilities, community centers, or even in the number of bus shelters and benches in the Canadian city. Both cities have a variety of medical, dental, hospital, and car insurance plans; these tend to be privately provided in Seattle but are under public agencies in Vancouver. The development of an urban transit system in Vancouver, as opposed to Seattle's greater reliance on automobiles and freeways, is also indicative. Many of these Vancouver facilities are the result of joint city-provincial-federal efforts, and they exemplify an approach that departs from the American model.

From their beginnings in the mid-nineteenth century until well into the twentieth century the two cities were clearly alike in their nature and development. Although Vancouver's population lagged far behind Seattle's, both were predominantly white, English-speaking, Protestant communities that relied on the lumber industry and a diverse supply trade for their livelihood. Not until the Depression years and the World War II era did that basic uniformity change significantly. During that transition era federal programs and funds became much more important for Seattle, the Boeing Company became a major employer, and the city's black population rose significantly. All three developments were permanent, with profound ramifications for the American city.

When one considers Seattle and Vancouver in the 1980s there is no doubt that both continue to reflect the roles, problems, and outlook of their respective nations: Seattle's economic life is still significantly shaped by the activity at Boeing and nearby military installations; Vancouver remains primarily a service center catering to the diverse needs of a resource-based economy. Seattle's adaptation to the needs and demands of its black minority is both enlightened and progressive but it entails numerous frictions and anxieties. Vancouver's acceptance of its Chinese minority is no less tolerant, but it involves few fears and attracts little attention. Seattleites can be largely indifferent to Canadian developments, while Vancouverites remain ever aware of the possible ramifications of American actions. Whether such patterns will be perpetuated is anyone's guess. All one can predict with any confidence is that as in the past, each city will follow its own separate path.

Notes

1 Frontier Villages

1 Richard C. Wade, *The Urban Frontier: The Rise of Western Cities 1790–1830* (Cambridge: Harvard University Press, 1959), pp. 3–34; Blake McKelvey, *The Urbanization of America 1860–1915* (New Brunswick, N.J.: Rutgers University Press, 1963), pp. 20–34; John W. Reps, *Cities of the American West: A History of Frontier Urban Planning* (Princeton, N.J.: Princeton University Press, 1979), pp. 2–33.

2 Arthur A. Denny, *Pioneer Days on Puget Sound* (Seattle: C. B. Bagley, Printer, 1888), pp. 9–22. Denny, one of Seattle's founders, wrote this book some twenty-five years after the events described. It is the source of virtually all accounts of Seattle's early years. See also Frederick J. Grant, *History of Seattle* (New York: American Publishing and Engraving, 1891); Roberta Frye Watt, *Four Wagons West: The Story of Seattle* (Portland, Ore.: Binsford Mort, 1931); Clarence B. Bagley, *History of Seattle,* 3 vols. (Chicago: S. J. Clarke, 1916). The best account is Roger Sale, *Seattle: Past to Present* (Seattle: University of Washington Press, 1976).

3 According to Hubert Howe Bancroft, *History of Washington, Idaho and Montana 1845–89* (San Francisco: A. L. Bancroft, 1890), Low and Terry were convinced "that they had discovered the choicest spot for a great city to be found in the north-west" (p. 22).

4 Denny, *Pioneer Days,* p. 19.

5 Reps, *Cities of the American West,* shows that the gridiron street plan was virtually universal. For his treatment of Seattle, see pp. 362–65. It does not treat the Denny-Boren plat, but focuses on the Maynard plat.

6 This discussion is based primarily on material available in *Plats, King County,* I, available in Special Collections Division, University of Washington Library. See also Bagley, *Seattle,* 2:563–72, and Denny, *Pioneer Days,* pp. 20–21.

7 Myra L. Phelps, *Public Works in Seattle: A Narrative History, the Seattle Engineering Department 1875–1975* (Seattle: Kingsport Press, 1978).

8 An examination of the disposition of portions of C. D. Boren's claim gives some idea of how the process unfolded. The original 320 acres remained substantially intact until

1856 when Boren sold 160 acres in the eastern half of his claim to Charles Terry and E. Lander for $2,500. Terry in turn bought out Lander for $5,500 in 1865. On Terry's death in 1867 his wife Mary assumed control, and in 1869 filed a plat for "Terry's First Addition." Between 1874 and 1875 the Seattle and Walla Walla Railroad bought 100 acres of Terry's First Addition for $10,000, John McNaught bought 20 acres for $2,066, and J. T. Dunn bought 10 acres for $970. Besides these large transactions, some 150 different persons bought land in Terry's First Addition between 1869 and 1872. Most bought only one or two lots, but many purchased four or more. The Fred Sander Collection in the Seattle Museum of History and Industry contains about sixty "Abstracts of Title" to property throughout Seattle. An examination of them provides insight into land transactions and real estate activity.

9 See Bagley, *History of Seattle*, 1:17–52; Watt, *Four Wagons West*, pp. 110–51.

10 F. W. Howay, "Early Settlement on Burrard Inlet," *British Columbia Historical Quarterly* 1 (April 1937): 101; M. A. Ormsby, *British Columbia: A History* (Toronto: Macmillan, 1958), pp. 189, 193.

11 Policies for the disposal of crown lands in British Columbia were developed originally by Governor James Douglas during the late 1850s and early 1860s, in consultation with the Colonial Office. The simultaneous desire to "encourage settlement," "prevent speculation," and "promote adequate income" would lead to many changes in the regulations. The standard work is Robert E. Cail, *Land, Man and the Law: The Disposal of Crown Lands in British Columbia 1871–1913* (Vancouver: University of British Columbia Press, 1974). See esp. chaps. 1, 2, 3.

12 F. W. Laing, "Colonial Farm Settlers on the Mainland of British Columbia 1858–71," typescript, 1939, Vancouver City Archives.

13 The details of John Morton's activities are from an interview with his son Joseph Morton by J. S. Matthews in 1932. The probate of John Morton's will in 1912 showed an estate valued at $769,000. See J. S. Matthews, "The First Settlers on Burrard Inlet," typescript, 1932, Vancouver City Archives, pp. 9, 17.

14 B.C. Department of Lands, Registry Office, Victoria. Their preemption claim was challenged by Robert E. Burnaby who argued that he had previously preempted the same land. But regardless of the legitimacy of the challenge Morton, Brighouse, and Hailstone got official title. Additional MSS no. 5H, vol. 13, File M273, Vancouver City Archives, provides some additional detail.

15 See B.C. Department of Lands, Registry Office; Townley MSS, Vancouver City Archives; Howay, "Early Settlement," pp. 104–5.

16 Cail, *Land, Man and the Law*, p. 14.

17 F. W. Howay, "Early Shipping in Burrard Inlet 1863–70," *British Columbia Historical Quarterly* 1 (Jan. 1937): 4.

18 Ibid., p. 20.

19 These differences are developed at length in James W. Morton, *The Enterprising Mr. Moody, the Bumptious Captain Stamp* (North Vancouver: J. J. Douglas, 1977).

20 "Plan of the Town of Granville," March 10, 1870, British Columbia Archives.

21 Howay, "Early Settlement," p. 114.

22 T. R. Weir, "Early Trails of Burrard Inlet," *British Columbia Historical Quarterly* 9 (Oct. 1945): 273–75.

23 Burrard Inlet had a population of about 900 at this time. But the Voters' List of the Burrard Inlet Polling Division for 1886 suggests it was a highly transient population since

only 177 men met the necessary residential and property requirements. Their addresses indicate the nature of settlement. Burrard Inlet had 73 eligible voters, Moodyville 41, Granville 25, Howe Sound 9, Fraser River 7, Jervis Inlet 6, English Bay 5, Hastings Mill 5, Richmond 3, B.C. Camp 2, False Creek 1. See B.C. Sessional Papers, 1886, pp. 67–70, University of British Columbia Library.

24   R. T. Williams, ed., *British Columbia Directory 1884/85.*

25   Roger Conant, *Mercer's Belles: The Journal of a Reporter,* ed., Lenna A. Deutsch (Seattle: University of Washington Press, 1960).

26   Bancroft, *History of Washington, Idaho and Montana,* pp. 31–33; Edmund S. Meany, Jr., "The History of the Lumber Industry in the Pacific Northwest to 1917" (Ph.D. thesis, Harvard University, 1935), pp. 97–105, 121. See H. T. Coman and H. M. Gibbs, *Time, Tide and Timber: A Century of Pope and Talbot* (Stanford: Stanford University Press, 1949), pp. 31–35, 53–55, for the founding of Port Gamble.

27   Frederick Jackson Turner, *The Frontier in American History* (New York: Holt, 1920), is the classic statement of the nature, development, and impact of the frontier. For the pivotal role of cities see Reps, *Cities of the American West,* pp. ix–xii and passim; Wade, *Urban Frontier,* esp. chaps. 1, 12. Duane A. Smith, *Rocky Mountain Mining Camps: The Urban Frontier* (Bloomington: Indiana University Press, 1967) persuasively argues that these communities, too, were urbanized. Historians of the Canadian West are in basic agreement that urban communities usually preceded rather than followed significant rural settlement. See Harold A. Innis, *Settlement and the Mining Frontier* (Toronto: Macmillan, 1936); Gilbert A. Stelter, "The Urban Frontier in Canadian History," *Canadian Issues* 1 (Spring 1975): 99–114; Alan F. J. Artibise, "The Urban West: The Evolution of Prairie Towns and Cities to 1930," *Prairie Forum* 4 (1979): 130–54; Paul Voisey, "The Urbanization of the Canadian Prairies 1871–1916," *Histoire Sociale-Social History* 8 (May 1975): 77–101.

28   F. E. Melder, "History of the Discovery and Physical Development of the Coal Industry in the State of Washington," *Pacific Northwest Quarterly* 29 (April 1938): 155.

29   Ibid., p. 156.

30   *U.S. Census, 1870,* vol. I, *Population,* p. 283.

31   Senate Executive Document, 33d Congress, 2d Session, no. 78, 1854, *Reports of Explorations and Surveys to Ascertain the Most Practicable and Economical Route for a Railroad from the Mississippi River to the Pacific Ocean,* pp. 46–48.

32   Dorothy O. Johansen, "Capitalism on the Far Western Frontier: The Oregon Steam Navigation Company" (Ph.D. thesis, University of Washington, 1941), and William Trimble, "The Mining Advance into the Inland Empire," *Bulletin of the University of Wisconsin History Series* 3 (1914): 15–45.

33   Grant, *History of Seattle,* p. 147. The Seattle *Weekly Intelligencer* of June 28, 1873, pointed out that a "bountiful offer" had been made, but added "we withhold the exact amounts for reason of local policy."

34   Seattle *Weekly Intelligencer,* July 5, 1873.

35   Ibid., July 19, 1873.

36   Ibid., May 2, 1874.

37   Seattle *Post Intelligencer,* November 19, 1876.

38   Ibid., November 16, 1877.

39   See James B. Hedges, *Henry Villard and the Northwest Railways* (New York: Russell and Russell, 1930), esp. pp. 57–67, for a detailed account of his activities and aims.

40   Seattle *Post Intelligencer* of April 13, 1883, estimated Seattle's population as 6,000, by July 31, 1883, it claimed 8,145, and on January 1, 1884, 9,000.

41   A. A. Denny to Henry Villard, November 18, 1882, microfilm of portions of Villard Papers, Special Collections Division, University of Washington Library.

2   Two Transcontinental Railroads

1   John R. Kellet, *Railways and Victorian Cities* (Toronto: University of Toronto Press, 1979), captures the variety of ways railroads shaped London, Birmingham, Manchester, Liverpool, and Glasgow in the mid-nineteenth century. His repeated emphasis that railways did not act in isolation, and that existing patterns of landownership, population concentration, economic activity, and political organization also played a part, is pertinent for any urban historian dealing with the impact of a railway on a city.

2   Hedges, *Villard,* pp. 110–11. Throughout 1884 and 1885 the Seattle *Post Intelligencer* was critical of a whole series of actions by the Northern Pacific Railroad. See, for example, April 9, 13, 17, 22, 1884; October 2, 4, 1884; October 27, 1885.

3   Vancouver *News Advertiser* and *Victoria Colonist,* May 24, 1887.

4   Vancouver *News Advertiser* and *Vancouver World,* June 13–16, 1887, both give detailed treatment. See also W. Kaye Lamb, "The Pioneer Days of the Trans-Pacific Service," *British Columbia Historical Quarterly* 1 (July 1937): 149–60.

5   The anti-Chinese outbreaks in Seattle have been treated by numerous authors. All rely primarily on newspaper accounts in the Seattle *Post Intelligencer* and the Seattle *Daily Call,* with some additional information from government communiqués or personal reminiscences. Robert Wynne, "Reaction to the Chinese in the Pacific Northwest and British Columbia" (Ph.D. dissertation, University of Washington, 1964), and Jules Karlin, "The Anti-Chinese Outbreaks in Seattle 1885–86," *Pacific Northwest Quarterly* 39 (April 1948): 103–30 are especially valuable. Robert Nesbit, *"He Built Seattle": A Biography of Judge Thomas Burke* (Seattle: University of Washington Press, 1961), focuses on Burke's role. George Kinnear's *Anti-Chinese Riots in Seattle* (Seattle, 1911), available in Special Collections Division, University of Washington Library, was written twenty-five years after the event by one who commanded a troop of soldiers in the riot. See also Grant, *History of Seattle,* pp. 187–212; Bagley, *History of Seattle,* 2: 455–77. Vancouver newspapers carry a great variety of references to the city's Chinese; see especially the weeks before and after the anti-Chinese riot on January 17, 1887. For other representative examples, see *News Advertiser,* July 5, August 14, 1894; January 19, August 15, 1895; July 7, September 19, 1896; March 20, April 1, 1897; January 20, May 28, 1899. For detailed treatments of developments in Vancouver see W. Peter Ward, *White Canada Forever: Popular Attitudes and Public Policy Toward Orientals in British Columbia* (Montreal: McGill-Queens University Press, 1978); Patricia E. Roy, "The Preservation of the Peace in Vancouver: The Aftermath of the Anti-Chinese Riot of 1887," *B.C. Studies* 31 (Autumn 1976): 44–59; Edgar Wickberg et al., *From China to Canada: A History of the Chinese Communities in Canada* (Toronto: McClelland and Stewart, 1982), pp. 13–72.

6   Seattle *Daily Chronicle,* April 21, 1882.

7   Ibid., April 13, 1882. See also Seattle *Post Intelligencer,* April 15, 16, 28, 1882.

8   Seattle *Daily Call,* September 25, 1885, quoting St. Paul *Dispatch.*

9   Robert A. Campbell, "An Added Objection: The Use of Blacks in the Coal Mines of Washington, 1880–96" (M.A. thesis, University of British Columbia, 1978), esp. chap. 1.

10 The Seattle *Post Intelligencer* and *Daily Call* of September, October, and November 1885 provide detailed coverage of the membership, ideas, and approaches of the two rival groups.

11 Seattle *Post Intelligencer,* July 13, 1886.

12 Ibid., July 12, 1887.

13 Vancouver *News Advertiser,* June 2, 1886.

14 Ibid., January 7, 1887.

15 Roy, "The Preservation of Peace in Vancouver," pp. 51–54.

16 Ormsby, *British Columbia,* pp. 247–302, passim. See also Pierre Berton, *The National Dream: The Great Railway 1871–81* (Toronto: McClelland and Stewart, 1970).

17 *Victoria Colonist,* January 14, 1885. Some investors knew of the decision well before the public announcement. See G. W. S. Brooks, "Edgar Crowe Baker: An Entrepreneur in Early British Columbia" (M.A. thesis, University of British Columbia, 1976), esp. pp. 192–204, for the activities of a group of Victoria's businessmen who invested substantial sums in Coal Harbour, Burrard Inlet, lands during 1884.

18 Norbert MacDonald, "The Canadian Pacific Railway and Vancouver's Development to 1900," *B.C. Studies* 35 (Autumn 1977): 3–35.

19 B.C. Sessional Papers, 1885, pp. 129–36, 385–86, Provincial Archives of British Columbia, Victoria B.C. provides the main details of the discussion between premier William Smithe of British Columbia and William Van Horne of the Canadian Pacific Railway (CPR). Both the government and the railway were anxious to have the main line extended to Coal Harbour, and although the CPR originally sought some 11,000 acres, they later accepted the offer of 6,000 acres. See also *Victoria Colonist,* January 14, 1885.

20 B.C. Legislative Assembly Journals, 1888, XL–XLI, Provincial Archives of British Columbia.

21 This estimate was made from an examination of L. A. Hamilton, Map of Vancouver, 1887, and the Vancouver Assessment Roll of 1888, both available in Vancouver City Archives. See also Brooks, "Edgar Crowe Baker," esp. pp. 202–4; and J. S. Matthews, *Early Vancouver: Narratives of Pioneers of Vancouver, B.C.* (Vancouver, 1932–33), 2:91–110, passim.

22 Alan Artibise, *Winnipeg: A Social History of Urban Growth* (Montreal: McGill-Queens University Press, 1975), pp. 70–73; Pierre Berton, *The National Dream: The Last Spike* (Toronto: McClelland and Stewart, 1971), pp. 302–4, 321–22; Max Foran, "Early Calgary, 1875–95: The Controversy Surrounding the Townsite Location and the Direction of Town Expansion," in A. R. McCormack and Ian MacPherson, eds., *Cities in the West: Papers of the Western Canada Urban History Conference* (Ottawa: National Museum of Canada, 1975), pp. 26–45.

23 See Robert M. Fogelson, *The Fragmented Metropolis* (Cambridge: Harvard University Press, 1967), p. 59; Grant, *History of Seattle,* p. 147.

24 A "Plan of the City of Vancouver—1886," by H. B. Smith, predates a better-known 1887 map by L. A. Hamilton. The earlier map is detailed and accurate, showing the precise location of the various CPR facilities. Smith spent most of his career as an engineer and surveyor with the Vancouver Water Works and assisted Cambie in the early CPR surveys. The 1886 map by Smith is in the Vancouver City Archives; Hamilton's 1887 map is in the British Columbia Archives.

25 Early real estate ads clearly indicate the CPR's assessment of their property as well as their long-range plans. See Vancouver *News Advertiser,* June 1, 1886; February 10, 1887; and November 14, 1888. See also Goad's *Fire Insurance Map of Vancouver,* 1897, Vancouver City Archives.

26 The Hamilton material is based primarily on letters he wrote to J. S. Walker of the Vancouver Town Planning Commission in 1929 and to City Archivist J. S. Matthews in 1934 and 1936. Though written some fifty years after the events described, they are invaluable. See Matthews, *Early Vancouver,* 1:328; 3:207–8. See also Hamilton to Matthews, April 27, 1936 in Matthews, Uncatalogued Material, Vancouver City Archives.

27 Vancouver City Council Minutes, May 12, 1886. See also William C. McKee, "The History of the Vancouver Park System 1886–1929" (M.A. thesis, University of Victoria, 1976); and Eric Nicol, *Vancouver* (Toronto: Doubleday, 1970), pp. 78–83.

28 R. T. Williams, *British Columbia Directory,* 1892, pp. 788–90.

29 Ibid.; see also Williams, *British Columbia Directory,* 1889, pp. 254–71, for a valuable listing of all persons employed in the Pacific Division of the CPR.

30 Material on real estate activity in Vancouver is voluminous. Newspaper advertisements are an ever-present source, but for more precise insight, the Vancouver City Archives has an abundance of excellent material. The Vancouver Assessment Roll 1888, the David Oppenheimer MSS, and the F. C. Innes MSS are especially valuable. Robert A. J. McDonald, "City Building in the Canadian West: A Case Study of Economic Growth in Vancouver," *B.C. Studies* 43 (Autumn 1979): 3–28, provides a detailed look at the activities of a number of real estate entrepreneurs in Vancouver and the significant role they played in the city's economic growth.

31 Vancouver *News Advertiser,* June 1, 1886.

32 Quoted in Douglas Sladen, "Vancouver, a Great Seaport of the Twentieth Century," *Frank Leslie's Popular Monthly* 24 (May 1890): 513–22.

33 See Gunther Barth, *Instant Cities: Urbanization and the Rise of San Francisco and Denver* (New York: Oxford University Press, 1975); and Roger W. Lotchin, *San Francisco, 1846–56: From Hamlet to City* (New York: Oxford University Press, 1974).

34 Barth, *Instant Cities,* p. 155.

35 Seattle *Post Intelligencer,* January 1, 1891.

36 Between 1888 and 1892 the *Post Intelligencer* carried daily data on Seattle's receipt and shipment of merchandise by these three local lines. From month to month the data reveal a general use during the summer and fall months, and overall increase from year to year.

37 Nesbit, *"He Built Seattle,"* pp. 248–50.

38 For a richly detailed account of developments in Seattle see Leslie Blanchard, *The Street Railway Era in Seattle: A Chronicle of Six Decades* (Forty Fort, Pennsylvania: H. E. Cox, 1968), pp. 1–27. W. G. Ross, "Street Railways in Canada," *Canadian Magazine* (January 1902): 276–78, shows that between 1891 and 1897, Ottawa, Hamilton, Montreal, Winnipeg, St. John's, Halifax, and Quebec City all established electric railway concerns.

39 *Seattle City Directory,* 1892.

40 Bagley, *History of Seattle,* 2:545–52.

41 *Report of the Board of Park Commissioners, 1884–1904,* Special Collections Division, University of Washington Library.

42 For detailed treatment of the fire see Grant, *History of Seattle,* pp. 212–37; Bagley, *History of Seattle,* 1:419–28.

43   Thomas W. Prosch, *A Chronological History of Seattle from 1850 to 1897*, typescript, Seattle, 1891, p. 390. Available in Special Collections Division, University of Washington Library.

44   Grant, *History of Seattle*, p. 376.

45   Bagley, *History of Seattle*, 1:231–34.

46   Grant, *History of Seattle*, pp. 388–89.

47   The *U.S. Census, 1890*, does not provide a detailed occupational breakdown for Seattle nor does the *Census of Canada, 1891*, provide such a breakdown for Vancouver. This paragraph is based on the *U.S. Census, 1890, Population*, vol. VI, pt. 2, pp. 546–48, which breaks down the manufactures and skilled trades in Seattle. The occupational breakdown for 1900 in *U.S. Census, 1900, Population*, vol. II, pt. 2, pp. 591–93, is also helpful. For Vancouver see Williams, *British Columbia Directory, 1892*, pp. 788–90.

48   Jorgen Dahlie, "A Social History of Scandinavian Immigration, Washington State 1895–1910 (Ph.D. dissertation, Washington State University, 1967); Janice Reiff Webster, "Domestication and Americanization: Scandinavian Women in Seattle, 1888 to 1900," *Journal of Urban History* 4 (May 1978): 275–90; Sverre Arestad, "The Norwegians in the Pacific Coast Fisheries," *Pacific Northwest Quarterly* 24 (January 1943): 3–17.

49   *U.S. Census, 1890, Population*, vol. I, Pt. I, pp. 441–49, and Pt. II, p. 130.

50   Grant, *History of Seattle*, pp. 379–80.

51   Voters lists were a helpful but inexact source for determining property ownership. Voters with property in more than one ward were listed in each of these wards and as such inflated the number of owners in the city. In addition, nonresident owners could not be identified. Yet a random sampling of names from the voters list, evidence from the *Vancouver Assessment Roll of 1888*, and Vancouver City Directories all reinforced the general conclusions drawn from the voters lists. A random sample of 31 names from the 1888 voters list (approximately 2 percent of the 1,536 listed) showed 19 owners and 12 tenants. Of the 19 owners, in turn, the *Vancouver Assessment Roll of 1888* showed that 7 owned one lot each, and 12 owned two or more lots each. Two of the 19 owners had property in all five wards. Williams's *British Columbia Directory*, 1889, listed 11 of the 19 owners and 6 of the 12 tenants. Similarly, a random sample of 100 names from the 1892 voters list (approximately 2 percent of the 5,306 listed) showed 77 owners and 23 tenants. Of the 77 owners, 38 had property in one ward, 22 had property in two wards, 11 in three wards, 3 in four wards, and 3 in all five wards of the city. The *British Columbia Directory*, 1892, listed 40 of the 77 owners, and 10 of the 23 tenants.

52   See L. A. Hamilton to F. C. Innes, September 14, 1886, in F. C. Innes MSS, Vancouver City Archives. For a valuable sketch of Vancouver's sporting clubs, see Vancouver *News Advertiser*, August 7, 1889, p. 6. See also D. W. Holdsworth, "House and Home in Vancouver: Images of West Coast Urbanism, 1886–1929," in Gilbert A. Stelter and Alan F. S. Artibise, eds., *The Canadian City* (Toronto: McClelland and Stewart, 1977), pp. 186–211.

53   "CPR Aldermen" with their railway position and years on council were L. A. Hamilton, land commissioner 1886, 1887; W. F. Salsbury, treasurer 1889, 1893, 1894; Dr. J. M. Lefevre, physician 1887, 1888, 1889; J. M. Browning, land commissioner 1890; H. E. Connor, freight agent 1892; J. J. Gavin, conductor 1892; H. G. Painter, accountant 1896, 1897, 1898; H. B. Gilmour, machine shop foreman 1899. Identification was obtained primarily from Williams, *British Columbia Directory*. The 1889 issue, pp. 254–71, was especially valuable.

54 Abbott to City Clerk, *Vancouver City Clerk Incoming Correspondence* (hereafter cited as *Van CCl in Corr*), IV: 3364–69. Available in Vancouver City Archives.

55 Vancouver's action had clearly shocked and pained CPR officials. Five years later in separate visits to Vancouver, both President Van Horne and Vice President Shaughnessy referred to this incident. See Vancouver *News Advertiser,* September 8, 1897, p. 6, and October 27, 1897, p. 6.

56 Portland *West Shore,* September 1882, pp. 161–66.

57 Seattle *Post Intelligencer,* September 15, 16, 1883.

58 John W. Pratt, "The City of Seattle," *New England Magazine* 8 (May 1893): 292–303.

59 Kirk Munroe, "The Cities of the Sound," *Harpers Weekly* (January 1894): 35–36.

60 Erastus Brainerd, "Seattle," *Harper's Weekly* (November 1894): 1127–30.

61 See for example "T. H." in Seattle *Post Intelligencer,* September 15, 1883.

62 Seattle *Post Intelligencer,* quoted by Vancouver *News Advertiser,* October 2, 1887.

63 Portland *West Shore,* May 1889, p. 231.

64 H. Heywood, in *Boston Transcript,* as given in Vancouver *News Advertiser,* August 12, 1893, p. 2.

65 Vancouver *News Advertiser,* June 6, 1894, pp. 2 and 7, quoting a London *Times* correspondent.

66 Ibid.

67 D. B. W. Sladen, *On the Cars and Off* (London: Ward, Lock & Bowden), p. 368.

68 Vancouver *News Advertiser,* May 24, 1887.

69 Report of the Finance Committee for 1887, as given in Vancouver *News Advertiser,* December 29, 1887, p. 4.

70 Vancouver *News Advertiser,* January 1, 1888.

71 See *Victoria Colonist,* esp. 1886–88.

3 The Klondike Gold Rush

1 *Report of the Mayor of Seattle, 1899,* Comptroller File 7256, City Clerk's Office, Seattle (Cited hereafter as C.F.)

2 Seattle *Post Intelligencer,* July 25, 1897.

3 Seattle *Argus,* March 26, 1898. See also *Report of the Washington Bureau of Labor 1897–98.* Special Collections Division, University of Washington Library.

4 Vancouver *News Advertiser,* August 23, 1893.

5 *Report of the Mayor of Seattle, 1895–96,* C.F. 1289 and 2834.

6 *Report of the Board of Public Works, 1895,* C.F. 1289.

7 *Report of the Mayor of Seattle, 1899,* C.F. 7214; *Minutes of the Board of Health, 1891,* C.F. 181692.

8 *Report of the Law Department for 1895,* C.F. 1289.

9 Neil R. Knight, "History of Banking in Washington" (Ph.D. thesis, University of Washington, 1935), pp. 173–77.

10 *Van CCl in Corr,* VIII: 6966.

11 Vancouver *News Advertiser,* October 3, 10, 1894. For the earlier development of street railways, water, sewer, and lighting systems in the city see Patricia E. Roy, *Vancouver: An Illustrated History* (Toronto: James Lorimer, 1980), pp. 30–38.

12 *Van CCl in Corr,* XI: 8809–11.

13 See for example Vancouver *News Advertiser*, October 25, 1894; February 20, 1895; August 24, 1898.

14 *Annual Report, City of Vancouver*, 1925, Vancouver City Archives, provides a convenient summary of property assessment and tax data from 1886 to 1925.

15 *Report of the Vancouver Board of Trade, 1895–96*, p. 22, Vancouver City Archives.

16 Vancouver *News Advertiser*, February 4, 1896; December 16, 1896; May 10, 1897.

17 The letter of May 1, 1896, read, "I find advertised in a paper that at your city they are scarce of wimin and will pay a pretty good thing for some of our wimen. . . . If that may be true, I will tell you what I will do for you in that line. I am a young man and a rustler. I just come in this country last Dec. 14/95. I came here from Nebraska and Iowa and I am going back to Nebraska this coming fall, but I would like to get a car load of young ladies and widows to ship to your city and country. . . . I will agree to get you wimen if you will agree to send me your money in advance and leave it in the Salt Lake City bank for the purpose of paying their fares out to your country and give me so much a head for gettin them. I will insure yaw that I will get yaw some wimen." *Van CCl in Corr*, X: 8299.

18 See Vancouver *News Advertiser*, January 2, September 6, 1895; January 8, 1896; February 17, 1897.

19 The Eugene Semple MSS Manuscripts Division, University of Washington Library, provides many details on this Seattle and Lake Washington Waterway Company.

20 Robert C. Nesbit, *"He Built Seattle,"* pp. 278–86, covers D. H. Gilman's attempts to get financial backing.

21 *West Coast Lumberman*, March 1893, January 1895, January 1896.

22 *Vancouver City Council Minutes,* July 17, 1893, Vancouver City Archives (cited hereafter as *Van CC M.*) Vancouver *News Advertiser*, October 27, 1897.

23 "The Corporation of Vancouver vs. the Canadian Pacific Railway," July 14, 1894, *Van CCl in Corr*, VI: 6630–56.

24 For detailed statistical data on the production and shipment of wheat from the Pacific Northwest, see "Pacific Northwest Wheat Problems and the Export Subsidy," *Wheat Studies* (Food Research Institute, Stanford University) 10, no. 10 (Aug. 1934): 415–22.

25 Seattle *Post Intelligencer* and Seattle *Times,* July 17, 1897.

26 Seattle *Post Intelligencer,* July 28, 1897.

27 See Norbert MacDonald, "Seattle, Vancouver and the Klondike," *Canadian Historical Review* 49 (Sept. 1968): 234–46.

28 Hutchison, Kohl & Company of San Francisco bought out the Russian-American Company in 1868. By 1871, the new firm was known as the Alaska Commercial Company. See William Ogilvie, *Early Days in the Yukon* (London and New York: John Lane Company, 1913), pp. 64–70, 75–83.

29 *Abstract of the 11th U.S. Census (1890)* (Washington, D.C., 1894), gives Alaska a white population of 4,298. The total population was 32,052.

30 See *Report of the Governor of Alaska, 1889* (Washington, D.C., 1889).

31 Jonas A. Jonassen, "Portland and the Alaska Trade," *Pacific Northwest Quarterly* 30 (April 1939): 132–33; Ogilvie, *Early Days in the Yukon,* p. 68. The distribution of the Alaska salmon pack of 1889 showed San Francisco's dominance. Of a total pack of 702,993 cases, over 90 percent went to San Francisco; Portland got about 2 percent; the rest were lost in shipwrecks. *Report of the Governor of Alaska, 1890* (Washington, D.C., 1890), p. 20.

32   See Seattle *Post Intelligencer,* October 18, 1891.

33   Ibid., April 14, 1893.

34   See W. A. Mears, "History of the Alaska Trade," *Bulletin of the Portland Chamber of Commerce* (April 1905): 11; Seattle *Post Intelligencer,* July 2, 1892; January 3, 1897. Jonassen, "Portland and the Alaska Trade," p. 132.

35   Mears, "History of the Alaska Trade," p. 11. Seattle *Times,* August 15, 18, 20, 1896.

36   Seattle *Post Intelligencer,* January 3, 1897.

37   Ogilvie, *Early Days in the Yukon,* pp. 22–26, 34–40.

38   Report of Commissioner L. W. Herchmer of the North West Mounted Police, 1895, in Canada, Sessional Papers, 1896, no. 15, p. 21, University of British Columbia Library. See also Canada, Sessional Papers, 1898, paper no. 15, pp. 308, 309.

39   Report of Commissioner C. Constantine of the Yukon detachment, North West Mounted Police in Canada, Sessional Papers, 1897, paper no. 15, pp. 233, 237. Thomas Fawcett, Canada's first gold commissioner in the Yukon, noted the reliance on American facilities. See his report in Canada, Sessional Papers, 1898, paper no. 13, p. 74.

40   The *Excelsior* belonged to the Alaska Commercial Company, the *Portland* to the North American Transportation and Trading Company. Seattle *Post Intelligencer,* August 1–10, 1897.

41   Vancouver *News Advertiser,* July 29, August 2, 8, 1897. In the early summer of 1897, Vancouver had two locally owned steamship lines capable of providing service to Alaska; the Union Steamship Company ran the *Capilano* and the *Coquitlam,* each carrying about 100 tons. Evans, Coleman and Evans had a number of small vessels serving coastal logging camps and canneries. By making a trip to Victoria, tie-ups could be made with the Victoria-based Canadian Pacific Steamship Company and the Pacific Coast Steamship Company from San Francisco and Seattle. See *Report of Vancouver Board of Trade, 1897–98* (Vancouver, 1898), p. 32; Patricia Roy, "Railways, Politicians, and the Development of the City of Vancouver as a Metropolitan Centre, 1886–1929," (M.A. thesis, University of Toronto, 1963), p. 78; G. M. Schuthe, "Canadian Shipping in the British Columbia Coastal Trade," (M.A. thesis, University of British Columbia, 1950), pp. 22–30.

42   Jeanette Nichols, "Advertising and the Klondike," *Washington Historical Quarterly* 13 (Jan. 1922): 20–26. The Seattle *Times* (August 15, 1899) carried a detailed account of the activities of this Bureau of Information of the Seattle Chamber of Commerce.

43   In September, 1897, for example, approximately $980 was contributed, ranging from $75, given by Schwabacher Brothers, a wholesale firm, to the $5 given by an anonymous donor. See Seattle *Post Intelligencer,* September 30, 1897; March 11, 1898.

44   Nichols, "Advertising and the Klondike," pp. 23–26.

45   *Report of Vancouver Board of Trade, 1897–98,* pp. 11, 12; ibid., 1898–99.

46   The *Victoria Colonist* of September 30 and October 3, 1897, provides a number of examples.

47   Senators W. Templeman and W. J. MacDonald were very active on behalf of British Columbia's cities. Congressman J. H. Lewis and Senator J. L. Wilson frequently spoke for Seattle. By 1901, Brainerd was a paid lobbyist for Seattle, making $1,000 a month while serving in Washington, D.C.

48   Vancouver *News Advertiser,* July 21, 1897.

49   *Report of Vancouver Board of Trade, 1897–98,* pp. 21–22; Vancouver *News Advertiser,* November 5, 1897.

50 A miner's blankets, personal clothing, cooking utensils, and 100 pounds of food were exempt. Duty was charged only on the excess. See letter of J. McDougall, Commissioner of Customs, to Collector of Customs, Vancouver, as printed in *Victoria Colonist*, August 20, 1897. For discussion of the rush and the customs controversy, see F. W. Howay, W. N. Sage, and H. F. Angus, *British Columbia and the United States* (Toronto: Ryerson Press, 1942), esp. pp. 354–59; Innis, *Settlement and the Mining Frontier*, pp. 178–212.

51 See, for example, Seattle *Post Intelligencer*, July 25, October 25, November 7, 1897. In July, a Vancouver newspaper had predicted possible difficulties: "Americans are imbued with the idea that it is rather patriotic . . . to evade the payment of taxes of any kind to the British authorities." Vancouver *News Advertiser*, July 29, 1897.

52 An advertisement of the Vancouver Board of Trade pointed out, "All goods purchased in Vancouver will be certified by the Customs Officers there, and be admitted free of duty, thus saving time, trouble and money to the miner." *Vancouver Province*, September 25, 1897. See also Vancouver *News Advertiser*, January 19, 1898. For similar Victoria advertisements, see *Victoria Colonist*, September 15, 1897. See letter by group of Australians in Vancouver *News Advertiser*, December 18, 1897; also editorials of December 27, January 4, January 8, 1898.

53 Report of Inspector F. L. Cartwright of the North West Mounted Police, 1898, in Canada, Sessional Papers, 1899, paper no. 15, p. 112.

54 Virtually every issue of the Vancouver *News Advertiser* and *Victoria Colonist* of December 1897, January and February 1898, discussed this or some similar controversy: see esp. Vancouver *News Advertiser*, January 26, 1898. Report of Commissioner C. T. Wood of the North West Mounted Police, 1898, in Canada, Sessional Papers, 1899, paper no. 15, p. 47.

55 See Robert Craig Brown, *Canada's National Policy, 1883–1900: A Study in Canadian-American Relations* (Princeton: Princeton University Press, 1964), pp. 299–314; John W. Dafoe, *Clifford Sifton in Relation to His Times* (Toronto: Macmillan, 1931), pp. 157–72.

56 Frank Leeds, special correspondent of the *Cincinnati Post*, visited Vancouver and judged prices there to be lower than on Puget Sound; see Vancouver *News Advertiser*, February 26, 1898. After a visit to Seattle, George Duncan, passenger agent of the Canadian Pacific Railway, found some prices lower there than in Vancouver; see *News Advertiser*, October 24, 1897.

57 See for example, *Victoria Colonist*, July 21, 30, 1897; *Vancouver Province*, December 25, 1897; Seattle *Post Intelligencer*, July 29, October 26, November 10, 1897; *Report of the Seattle Chamber of Commerce, 1897*, pp. 66–67.

58 Times Printing Co. to Colonist Printing & Publishing Co., as printed in *Vancouver Province*, August 7, 1897; Seattle *Post Intelligencer*, February 2, 1898; Vancouver *News Advertiser*, February 23, 24, 1898.

59 Seattle *Post Intelligencer*, July 19, 1897; *Victoria Colonist*, July 20, 1897; Vancouver *Province*, July 24, 1897.

60 Vancouver *News Advertiser*, February 3, 13, 1898, discusses customs regulations in detail. *Report of Vancouver Board of Trade, 1897–98*, p. 32, lists the main shipping lines from Vancouver. The Union Steamship Company added *Cutch* to *Coquitlam* and *Capilano*. Evans, Coleman and Evans chartered the 2,708-ton *Ningchow*.

61 Vancouver *News Advertiser*, April 2, 1898.

62 Ibid., October 5, 25, November 3, 1898. Victoria businessmen were also disappointed. See *Victoria Colonist*, October 21, 28, 1898.

63   Margaret C. Rodman, "The Trend of Alaskan Commerce through the Port of Seattle" (M.A. thesis, University of Washington, 1955), shows that in 1955 Seattle was still the commercial and financial capital for Alaska. The Pacific and Arctic Railway and Navigation Company (incorporated in West Virginia) operated in American territory to the summit, the British Columbia Railway Company in British Columbia (May 8, 1897), and the British Yukon Mining Trading and Transportation Company (June 29, 1897) in the Yukon. Innis, *Settlement and Mining Frontier*, p. 213.

64   Report of Superintendent Z. T. Wood of the North West Mounted Police, 1900, in Canada, Sessional Papers, 1901, paper no. 289, p. 5.

65   The population of the Yukon in 1901 was 27,219, by 1911 it had declined to 8,512, and by 1921 to 4,157. *Census of Canada 1921*, vol. I, p. 3.

66   In addition, there were 645 from Canada, 208 from England, 69 from Scotland, 65 from France, 48 from Ireland, 46 from Germany, 39 from Sweden, and 120 others. Report of Superintendent P. C. H. Primrose of the North West Mounted Police, 1899, in Canada, Sessional Papers, 1900, paper no. 15, p. 54.

67   Of fourteen volumes of personal reminiscences investigated, in every case but two, Americans bought their supplies in the United States, British and Canadians in Canada. For a listing of those volumes, see MacDonald, "Seattle, Vancouver and the Klondike," p. 245, n. 56.

4   Critical Growth Cycles

1   *U.S. Census, 1910*, vol. I, pp. 80–83; *Census of Canada, 1911*, vol. I, pp. 535–37. David M. Darling, "Patterns of Population Mobility in Vancouver, 1891–1931" (M.A. thesis, Simon Fraser University, 1978), shows that social mobility patterns and persistence rates in Vancouver were very similar to those in American cities. For the years studied, about one in five of Vancouver's blue-collar workers climbed to white-collar status within ten years, whereas one in twenty of its white-collar workers slipped to the blue-collar status. Similarly, an average of 43 percent of Vancouver's residents left the city within any ten-year period. For a detailed summary of patterns in American cities, see Stephan Thernstrom, *The Other Bostonians: Poverty and Progress in the American Metropolis 1880–1970* (Cambridge: Harvard University Press, 1973), esp. pp. 220–61.

2   Jean Barman, *Growing Up British in British Columbia: Boys in Private Schools* (Vancouver: University of British Columbia Press, 1984), provides an incisive analysis of one aspect of this phenomenon.

3   The Boston-based firm owned and managed railway and lighting properties, not only in Boston itself, but in Minneapolis, Savannah, Houston, and El Paso, as well as Sydney, Nova Scotia, and San Juan, Puerto Rico. The franchise arrangement in Seattle as discussed in Seattle city council on January 18, 1900, and in the *Post Intelligencer* on January 22, 1900.

4   H. Bartholomew and Associates, *A Plan for the City of Vancouver* (Vancouver: Wrigley Printing, 1930), pp. 87–90; *Annual Report, Department of Public Utilities, City of Seattle*, 1911–12, pp. 44–47, City Clerk's Office, Seattle.

5   Blanchard, *The Street Railway Era in Seattle*, pp. 42–56; Bartholomew, *A Plan for the City of Vancouver*, pp. 131–34.

6   S. D. Reid of Kerrisdale claimed that C. M. Woodworth had purchased a parcel of land in

Point Grey for about $2,000, but had promptly disposed of it for $25,000 to $30,000 shortly after the completion of the B.C. Railway line in that region. Vancouver *News Advertiser,* January 10, 1912, p. 18.

7   *Census of Canada, 1911,* vol. I, p. 249; J. A. Paton, "The Inside Story of Point Grey," *B.C. Magazine* (July 1911): 735–37.

8   *Vancouver Province,* January 19, 1907, pp. 25–27, provides a detailed street-by-street breakdown of all building permits issued in the city to 1906. Vancouver *News Advertiser,* January 5, 1913, p. 29, gives data on 1912. For a detailed analysis of the changing patterns in Kitsilano housing design over the years see Deryck W. Holdsworth, "Vernacular Form in the Urban Context" (M.A. thesis, University of British Columbia, 1971).

9   Vancouver *News Advertiser,* January 3, 1905.

10 Ibid., January 26, 1913, p. 21, has an excellent composite photograph of the major buildings that had recently been completed.

11 *Report of City Engineer (Seattle) 1905,* C.F. 29185.

12 For a detailed account see A. H. Dimock, "Preparing the Groundwork for a City: The Regrading of Seattle Washington," *Transactions of the American Society of Civil Engineers* 92 (1928): 717–34.

13 See *Report of City Engineer 1905,* C.F. 29185, and "Mayor Cotterill to City Council March 17, 1913," in C.F. 54815, for detailed statistics.

14 R. J. McDougall, "Vancouver Real Estate," *B.C. Magazine* (June 1911): 607.

15 This was estimated from a sampling of representative house prices listed in Vancouver newspapers.

16 Vancouver *News Advertiser,* January 2, 1910.

17 Ibid., January 22, 1905.

18 McDougall, "Vancouver Real Estate," p. 603.

19 U.S. Department of State, Dispatches of U.S. Consuls in Vancouver, B.C., 1890–1906. See L. E. Dudley to F. R. Loomis, August 22, 1905, and Dudley to R. Baron, January 13, 1906. Available on microfilm, University of British Columbia.

20 J. P. Nicolls, "Real Estate Values in Vancouver," April 1954, Vancouver City Archives, p. 26.

21 Vancouver *News Advertiser,* January 1, 1911, p. 17, provides a detailed description of the changes during the previous decade. An excellent print entitled "Panoramic View of the City of Vancouver, British Columbia, 1898," is available in Dennis M. Churchill, "False Creek Development" (M.A. thesis, University of British Columbia, 1953), p. 47.

22 Churchill, "False Creek Development," pp. 48–77.

23 Jeremey Barford, "Vancouver's Inter-urban Settlements" (B.A. essay, University of British Columbia, 1966), p. 18.

24 Mansel G. Blackford, "Reform Politics in Seattle During the Progressive Era 1902–16," *Pacific Northwest Quarterly* 59 (Oct. 1968): 177–86, argues that there was no consistent class alignment on reform issues in Seattle. Rather the position of upper, middle, and working class, voters depended on the specific reform issue and how it affected their needs and aspirations. Samuel P. Hays, "The Politics of Reform in Municipal Government During the Progressive Era," *Pacific Northwest Quarterly* 55 (Oct. 1964): pp. 157–69, stresses that municipal reform in Seattle and other American cities was primarily the result of upper-class leaders pursuing their own self-interests.

25 The following paragraphs on the activities and beliefs of municipal officials are based primarily on an examination of Vancouver City Council Minutes, 1899–1915.

26 B.C. Electric Railway Company Ltd., *29 Years of Public Service,* (Vancouver, 1926), p. 39.

27 See Vancouver *News Advertiser,* January 19, 1906, and letter to editor by C. M. Woodward in *News Advertiser,* January 9, 1914, p. 4. Whether the British Columbia Electric Railway contributed to the defeat of those plebiscites is unknown. For an analysis of the diverse lobbying efforts of that company see Patricia E. Roy, "The Fine Arts of Lobbying and Persuading: The Case of the B.C. Electric Railway," in David S. MacMillan, ed., *Canadian Business History* (Toronto: McClelland and Stewart, 1972), pp. 239–54.

28 In this respect, Vancouver closely followed the patterns revealed in a number of U.S. cities between 1900 and 1917. Vancouver City Council Minutes, December 28, 1907; January 6, 1908; January 13, 1908; January 19, 1911; May 30, 1911; January 24, 1912; 1913 passim.

29 Brian Bullen, "Vancouver's Flirtation with Municipal Reform 1907–12" (unpublished essay, University of British Columbia, 1980), provides a detailed analysis.

30 Vancouver City Council Minutes, November 4, 1902; December 8, 1902; May 4, 1903; February 29, 1904; April 24, 1904; February 27, 1905.

31 The city had approached the federal government in 1895 for title to the foreshore on English Bay, but abandoned its efforts when informed that it first had to gain authorization from foreshore property owners. Vancouver City Clerk's Correspondence, 1895, passim.

32 McKee, "The History of Vancouver Park System, 1886–1929," pp. 146–49.

33 Both Stanley Park of 1,000 acres and Hastings Park of 160 acres had been granted to the city without cost in the 1880s. Between 1902 and 1912 Vancouver spent approximately a million dollars for sixteen parcels of parkland, which together amounted to about 60 acres. Bartholomew, *A Plan for the City of Vancouver,* pp. 177–78. For an example of public concern about Stanley Park see Letters to the Editor in Vancouver *News Advertiser,* January 21, 1903; and January 22, 1903. See also Robert A. J. McDonald, "Holy Retreat or 'Practical Breathing Spot'?: Class Perceptions of Vancouver's Stanley Park, 1910–13," *Canadian Historical Review* 45 (June 1984): 127–53.

34 Olmstead Bros. MSS, Box 1, Folder I, Manuscripts Division, University of Washington. Frederick Law Olmstead, Sr., the founder of the organization, had first achieved national attention in the 1850s as the author of the pre–Civil War classic *A Journey Through the Southern States.* He later moved into landscape architecture, and as the designer of New York City's Central Park in the 1860s, soon established himself as the nation's foremost practitioner of a previously unknown field.

35 See Frederick Law Olmstead, Jr., and Theodora Kimball, eds., *Forty Years of Landscape Architecture* (Cambridge: MIT Press, 1973).

36 The Olmstead Plan is available in *Report of the Board of Park Commissioners, 1884–1904,* pp. 44–85.

37 Ibid.

38 *Annual Report of the Park Board for 1922* (Seattle) is especially valuable, City Clerk's Office, Seattle, C.F. 88803. It provides a detailed breakdown of annual income and expenditure from 1891 to 1922. In addition see *Report of the Superintendent of Parks 1909 & 1913.*

39 McKee, "History of the Vancouver Park System," pp. 146–49.

40 James A. Barnes, "Comprehensive Planning in Seattle," Seattle City Planning Commis-

sion, typescript, November 1954. Available in Government Research Assistance Library, Seattle City Hall.

41 Virgil R. Bogue, *Plan of Seattle* (1911).

42 Mansel G. Blackford, "Civic Groups, Political Action and City Planning in Seattle 1892–1915," *Pacific Historical Review* 49 (Nov. 1980): 574–76.

43 Barnes, "Comprehensive Planning in Seattle," p. 13.

44 Sale, *Seattle: Past to Present,* pp. 103–4.

45 William H. Wilson, "How Seattle Lost the Bogue Plan: Politics versus Design," *Pacific Northwest Quarterly* 75 (Oct. 1984): 171–80.

46 Precise comparisons of the occupational breakdown in Seattle and Vancouver are difficult, for not only do occupational categories differ slightly from nation to nation, but also from census to census within each nation. Yet the categories that are directly comparable show striking similarities and leave no doubt about the overall similarity of the occupational breakdown in the two cities. In 1910–11, for example, of Seattle's work force of 122,285 "manufacturing and mechanical industries" accounted for 33 percent. In Vancouver, "manufacturers and mechanical industries," plus "building trades," accounted for 36 percent of the 50,628-person work force. Similarly, "trade and transportation" accounted for 31 percent in Seattle and 32 percent in Vancouver; "domestic service" 14 percent in Seattle, 13 percent in Vancouver; and "professional service" was 7 percent in Seattle and 8 percent in Vancouver. See *U.S. Census, 1910, Population,* vol. IV, pp. 195–207, and *Census of Canada, 1911,* vol. VI, pp. 286–96.

47 Vancouver *News Advertiser,* March 11, 1901, p. 4.

5 A Generation of Business Leaders

1 Biographical details are from the following sources: Bagley, *History of Seattle,* 3:152–55; C. B. Bagley, *History of King County Washington* (Chicago: S. J. Clarke, 1929), 2:274–80; C. H. Hanford, *Seattle and Environs 1852–1924* (Chicago: Pioneer Historical Publishing, 1924), 2:290–96; C. A. Snowden, *History of Washington* (New York: Century History Company, 1909), 5:202–4; *Successful American* (Seattle), (New York Writer's Press Association, Nov. 1906), p. 248. For Baker's obituary, see Seattle *Times,* March 13, 1919, and Seattle *Post-Intelligencer,* March 14, 1919. The principal details of Baker's will are from Probate no. 25036, Washington State Court House. See Polk's *Seattle City Directory,* 1890 to 1918, for Baker's business affiliations and changes of address.

2 Biographical details are from J. B. Kerr, *Biographical Dictionary of Well Known British Columbians* (Vancouver: Kerr & Begg, 1870); F. W. Howay and E. O. S. Scholefield, *British Columbia from Earliest Times to the Present* (Vancouver: S. J. Clarke, 1913), vols. 3, 4, 5; Additional MSS no. 54, Vancouver City Archives, has information on McLennan and a host of other prominent Vancouverites.

3 *General Historical and Descriptive Review of the City of Seattle, Washington* (San Francisco: San Francisco Journal of Commerce, 1890); Grant, *History of Seattle; Volume of Memoirs and Genealogy of Representative Citizens of the City of Seattle and County of King, Washington* (New York: Lewis Publishing, 1903); Seattle *Republican,* Greater Seattle Edition, December 25, 1903; *Sketches of Washingtonians* (Seattle: W. C. Wolfe, 1906); *Successful American,* Nov. 1906; *Cartoons and Caricatures of Seattle Citizens*

(Seattle: Associated Cartoon Service, 1906); H. A. Chadwick, *Men Behind the Seattle Spirit: The Argus Cartoons* (Seattle: H. A. Chadwick, 1906); Snowden, *History of Washington,* vols. 2 and 3; F. Calvert, ed., *The Cartoon: A Reference Book of Seattle's Successful Men* (Seattle: Metropolitan Press, 1911); F. Harper, ed., *Who's Who on the Pacific Coast* (Los Angeles: Harper, 1913); Bagley, *History of Seattle,* vols. 2 and 3; *Who's Who in the Northwest* (Portland, Ore.: Writers' Press Association, 1917), vol. 2; E. M. Desmond, ed., *Seattle Leaders* (Seattle: Pioneer Printing, 1923); C. T. Conover, *Mirrors of Seattle* (Seattle: Lowman and Hanford, 1923); Hanford, *Seattle and Environs 1852–1924,* vols. 2 and 3; *Who's Who in Washington State* (Seattle: A. H. Allen, 1927); Bagley, *History of King County Washington.* These sources varied widely in scope, content, and value. The most useful and informative were the biographical volumes in the histories by Grant, Bagley, Hanford, and Snowden, along with the *Volume of Memoirs and Genealogy.* The biographical sketches in these volumes averaged about three pages. For a full presentation of the sampling technique, and of the data obtained, see Norbert MacDonald, "The Business Leaders of Seattle 1880–1910," *Pacific Northwest Quarterly* 50 (Jan. 1959): 1–13.

4 For a vivid "behind the scenes" insight into how subscription volumes were prepared and edited, see John W. Caughey, *Hubert Howe Bancroft* (Berkeley: University of California Press, 1946), pp. 313–29.

5 Besides the items listed in note 2, *Who's Who in Western Canada* (1911) was helpful as were numerous accounts in *Vancouver Province* and *Vancouver Sun.* Of all the sources, the biographical volumes in Howay and Scholefield, *British Columbia from Earliest Times to the Present,* were most valuable.

6 Robert A. J. McDonald, "Business leadership in Vancouver 1890–1914" (Ph.D. dissertation, University of British Columbia, 1977).

7 The final sample consisted of thirty-one "presidents," four "managers," and one "general superintendent."

8 U.S. Bureau of the Census, *Historical Statistics of the United States 1789–1945,* p. 63.

9 Prior to 1940 the U.S. Census gave only the number of persons attending school and not the highest level of schooling attained.

10 From data by J. P. Shaw, "Statistics of College Graduates," *Quarterly Publications of the American Statistical Association* 17 (1920): 337.

11 The absence of information on education could of course be the result of the general paucity of information on many Vancouver leaders, rather than on deliberate secrecy.

12 It is significant that Seattle's business leaders were quite similar in background to the type that Mowry showed became Progressive leaders in California. Both groups tended to be from the Midwest and East, North European in origin, from old American stock, and well educated. Financially both groups were comfortable and often joined the Masons and Chamber of Commerce. As a group, the business leaders were less well educated than the Progressive leaders. Whereas almost 30 percent of the Seattle leaders were foreign-born, none of the Progressive leaders for whom data were available were foreign-born. If we reject all foreign-born business leaders from our group, strong similarities between Seattle's native-born business leaders and California's Progressive leaders are evident. Though Seattle's business leaders might have voted for Progressive candidates, there is no mention in the biographical sources that any of them became Progressive leaders in Washington. We might conclude that, although Progressive leaders usually came from a prosperous, well-educated, Protestant, old American back-

ground, many with such a background did not become Progressive leaders. See George E. Mowry, *The California Progressives* (Berkeley: University of California Press, 1951), chap. 4, esp. pp. 87, 88. See also Alfred D. Chandler, Jr., "The Origins of Progressive Leadership," in E. E. Morison, ed., *Letters of Theodore Roosevelt* (Cambridge: Harvard University Press, 1954), 8 : 1462–65.

13 *Seattle City Directory,* 1909.

14 *Census of Canada, 1911,* vol. II, *Religions and Origins,* Table VI, p. 158.

15 Even this is far from exhaustive. Seattle business leaders also belonged to the Seattle Tennis Club, Press Club, Canadian Club, Civic Club, Deutscher, Lumbermen's Club, Olympic Golf Club, Swedish Club, United Workmen, Nile, Eagles, Knights of Pythias, Y.M.C.A., Moose, Woodmen of the World, and Redmen. None of these, however, were joined by five or more business leaders. Approximately the same percentage of native-born and foreign-born business leaders joined the Rainier Club.

16 The U.S. studies include F. W. Taussig and C. S. Joslyn, *American Business Leaders* (New York: Macmillan, 1932); W. Lloyd Warner and James C. Abegglen, *Occupational Mobility in American Business and Industry, 1928–1952* (Minneapolis: University of Minnesota Press, 1955); William Miller, "American Historians and the Business Elite," *Journal of Economic History* 9 (May, 1949): 184–208; Mabel Newcomer, *The Big Business Executive: The Factors That Made Him 1900–1950* (New York: Columbia University Press, 1955); C. Wright Mills, "The American Business Elite: A Collective Portrait," *Journal of Economic History,* 5 (Dec. 1945): 20–44. For the Canadian elite, see John Porter, *The Vertical Mosaic: An Analysis of Social Class and Power in Canada* (Toronto: University of Toronto Press, 1965), which focuses primarily on the mid-twentieth century. Chapter 9, "The Economic Elite and Social Structure," pp. 264–309, is especially valuable.

17 The Seattle material is located in the Probate Section, Washington State Court House, the Vancouver material in Probate Office, Supreme Court of British Columbia.

18 R. A. J. McDonald points out that of the ninety men who constituted Vancouver's business elite in the 1910–13 period, only seven had also been members of the 1890–93 elite. See "Business Leadership in Vancouver 1890–1914," pp. 148–52.

19 The Nathan quote is from William E. Leuchtenburg, *The Perils of Prosperity 1914–32* (Chicago: University of Chicago Press, 1958), p. 150.

6 World War I and the 1920s

1 Details are from *Vancouver Sun* and *Vancouver Province,* August 1914.

2 See *Annual Report, City of Vancouver,* 1941, p. 63, for year-by-year population data from 1886–1941. The original federal census of 1921 gave Vancouver's population as 117,218. This was later changed to 163,220 to include some 46,000 persons who lived in South Vancouver and Point Grey. These two municipalities did not officially amalgamate with Vancouver until 1929.

3 *Vancouver Sun,* September 25, 1915, p. 8. I am indebted to Sharon Slutsky for her unpublished research on Vancouver during WWI.

4 Sydney F. Wise, *The Official History of the Royal Canadian Air Force,* vol. 1, *Canadian Airmen and the First World War* (Toronto: University of Toronto Press, 1980), pp. 633–39.

5 Ibid.

6 *Vancouver Sun,* August 4, 1919, p. 8.

7 Michael Bliss, *A Canadian Millionaire: The Life and Times of Sir Joseph Flavelle* (Toronto: Macmillan, 1978), pp. 365–70. During World War I Flavelle served as chairman of Canada's Ottawa-based Imperial Munitions Board.

8 J. S. Marshal, "History of the Burrard Dry Dock Company," typescript, Special Collections Division, University of British Columbia Library (see chap. 4).

9 Precise statistical data are sparse on wartime shipbuilding and employment in Vancouver. The data for 1916 and 1920 are estimates. For 1917, 1918, and 1919 see *Annual Report, Vancouver Board of Trade, 1917–19,* and *Port Industries Annual of British Columbia, 1919.*

10 Seattle *Argus,* August 8, 1914. For a similar viewpoint see E. Selwin's article in the Seattle *Post Intelligencer,* July 29, 1914, "What Effect Will a General European War Have on the United States?"

11 P. Baxter, "Shipbuilding on Puget Sound," Seattle *Argus* December 15, 1917, pp. 12–32, provides a detailed survey. Specific production figures for 1918 yard by yard, are available in Seattle *Post Intelligencer,* January 1, 1919, p. 13.

12 Seattle *Post Intelligencer,* January 1, 1919.

13 "Washington's Men Who died in the Great War," ibid., January 5, 1919, magazine section, pp. 2, 3, shows that the State of Washington had 58,000 men in the armed services, of whom 910 died. A count of these with Seattle addresses showed 237 deaths. Of these, 107 were killed in action, 34 died of wounds, 82 died of disease, 15 other deaths. It is noteworthy that of the 58,000 service men from Washington State, 4,700 were in either the Canadian or British forces.

14 Estimated on the basis of data in G. W. L. Nicholson's *Canadian Expeditionary Force 1914–19* (Ottawa: Queen's Printer, 1962), pp. 546–48; and Wise, *Canadian Airmen and the First World War,* p. 636.

15 The best work on the topic is Robert L. Friedheim, *The Seattle General Strike* (Seattle: University of Washington Press, 1964); I am indebted to it for my basic coverage. For a brief version see R. L. Friedheim, "The Seattle General Strike of 1919," *Pacific Northwest Quarterly* 52 (July 1961): 81–98. Other major works include Anna Louise Strong, *Seattle General Strike* (Seattle: Seattle Union Record, 1919); and Harvey O'Connor, *Revolution in Seattle: A Memoir* (New York: Monthly Review Press, 1964).

16 Robert L. Friedheim and Robin Friedheim, "The Seattle Labor Movement 1919–20," *Pacific Northwest Quarterly* 55 (Oct. 1964): 146–56.

17 Ibid., pp. 155–56.

18 *New York Times,* February 9, 1919, quoted in Friedheim, *Seattle General Strike,* p. 182.

19 Seattle *Argus,* October 4, 1919; January 24, 1920.

20 For the national implications of the strike see R. K. Murray, *Red Scare: A Study in National Hysteria 1919–20* (Minneapolis: University of Minnesota Press, 1955); and William E. Leuchtenburg, *Perils of Prosperity 1919–32* (Chicago: University of Chicago Press, 1958).

21 Paul A. Phillips, *No Power Greater: A Century of Labour in British Columbia* (Vancouver: B.C. Federation of Labour, 1967), pp. 72–74, 80–81; Stuart M. Jamieson, *Times of Trouble: Labour Unrest and Industrial Conflict in Canada 1900–66,* Task Force on Labour Relations, Study no. 22 (Ottawa, 1968), pp. 164–67, 182–85; Roy, *Vancouver,* pp. 93–94.

22 This paragraph is based primarily on the *Report of the Royal Commission on Dominion Provincial Relations* (Rowell-Sirois Report, Ottawa, 1940), vol. 1, esp. pp. 122–23. See

also L. D. Claine, D. Patterson, and J. Rae, "The Regional Impact of Economic Fluctuations," *Canadian Journal of Economics* 7 (August 1974): 381–401; Ron Shearer, J. Young, and G. Monroe, *Trade Liberalization and a Regional Economy* (Toronto: University of Toronto Press, 1973).

23 See Figure 7 for a comparison of the earlier construction boom with that of the 1920s.

24 These estimates are based on statistical data compiled by the *Vancouver Sun* for 1920–27, available in *British Columbia Today* (1928). See also "Millions for New Building," *Vancouver Province,* March 23, 1926, special Real Estate Edition, and *Industrial Survey of Vancouver* (1929) published by the Vancouver Board of Trade.

25 *Harbour and Shipping* (Vancouver), January 1930.

26 *Vancouver Province,* May 23, 1926.

27 For a classic analysis of life in one American city during the 1920s see Robert S. Lynd and Helen M. Lynd, *Middletown: A Study in American Culture* (New York: Harcourt Brace, 1929). Leuchtenberg, *Perils of Prosperity, 1919–32,* is also valuable.

28 *Report of the Mayor of Seattle* for 1922, 1928, C.F. 90804, 100236.

29 J. W. A. Bolling, "Vancouver Traffic Survey, 1929," City Clerk's Correspondence, Series 9, File 4.

30 Blanchard, *The Street Railway Era in Seattle,* is an extensively illustrated, well-researched, and valuable monograph that covers the entire history of street railways in the city. For developments from 1919 to 1941 see pp. 98–133.

31 For the view of some "insiders," see the exchange between Mayor H. Caldwell, Corporation Counsel Meier, and the Superintendent of Public Utilities in April and May of 1920. All are included in C.F. 77815.

32 For the grand jury's report of January 31, 1921, see C.F. 80218. See George Cotterill's report to city council in C.F. 71684 for an especially penetrating critique of the original purchase.

33 See Harry L. Purdy, "The Cost of Municipal Operations of the Seattle Street Railway," University of Washington, *Publications in the Social Sciences* 8 (August 1929): 1–28; Anna Bell Lechner, "Seattle Municipal Street Railway" (M.A. thesis, University of Washington, 1936).

34 Blanchard, *The Street Railway Era in Seattle,* pp. 111, 129.

35 The literature on the rise and decline of the street railway in the United States is very extensive. For a focus on developments in specific cities see, for example, Clay McShane, *Technology and Reform: Street Railways and the Growth of Milwaukee 1887–1900* (Madison: University of Wisconsin Press, 1974); Charles W. Cheape, *Moving the Masses: Urban Public Transit in New York, Boston and Philadelphia 1880–1912* (Cambridge: Harvard University Press, 1980); Paul Barrett, *The Automobile and Urban Transit: The Formation of Public Policy in Chicago, 1900–30* (Philadelphia: Temple University Press, 1983); Howard Preston, *Automobile Age Atlanta: The Making of a Southern Metropolis 1900–35* (Athens: University of Georgia Press, 1979). For a crisp analysis showing that the automobile was but one of many factors contributing to decline see Donald L. Dewees, "The Decline of American Street Railways," *Traffic Quarterly* 24 (October 1970): 563–81. Mark S. Foster has done extensive work on urban transportation developments. See *From Streetcar to Superhighway: American City Planners and Urban Transportation 1900–40* (Philadelphia: Temple University Press, 1981); "The Model-T, the Hard Sell, and Los Angeles's Urban Growth: The Decentralization of Los Angeles during the 1920's," *Pacific Historical Review* 44 (Nov. 1975): 459–84; "The Western

Response to Urban Transportation: A Tale of Three Cities 1900–45," *Journal of the West* 18 (July 1979): 31–39.

Comparable literature on developments in Canada is more limited. Among items of interest are Richard M. Binns, *Montreal's Electric Streetcars: An Illustrated History of the Tramway Era 1892–1959* (Montreal: Railfare Enterprises, 1973); Michael J. Doucet, "Mass Transit and the Failure of Private Ownership: The Case of Toronto in the Early Twentieth Century," *Urban History Review* 3–77 (Feb. 1978): 3–33; Donald F. Davis, "Mass Transit and Private Ownership: An Alternative Perspective in the Case of Toronto," *Urban History Review* 3–78 (Feb. 1979): 60–98; H. W. Blake, *The Era of Streetcars in Winnipeg, 1881–1955* (Winnipeg: Hignell Printing, 1971).

36 Most emphasize that the automobile did not act alone and that a variety of other factors were also significant. On this Dewees, "The Decline of American Street Railways," is especially pertinent. Similarly, Paul Barrett, *The Automobile and Urban Transit,* writes, "The automobile by itself did not determine the fate of urban transportation in Chicago . . . misguided city policy . . . made private transportation the rational practical alternative for those who could afford it" (p. 210). For a comprehensive, sympathetic treatment of the role and impact of the automobile, see John B. Rae, *The Road and the Car in American Life* (Cambridge: MIT Press, 1971). James J. Flint, *The Car Culture* (Cambridge: MIT Press, 1975), is a much more critical appraisal. Blaine Brownell, "A Symbol of Modernity: Attitudes Toward the Automobile in Southern Cities in the 1920's," *American Quarterly* (March 1972): 20–44, captures the change during the decade from one of enthusiastic approval to one of rising concern and doubt.

37 In Seattle's case, weekday passengers and daytime traffic declined by 5 percent between 1921 and 1926, whereas Sunday passengers and evening traffic declined 25 percent. *Report of Superintendent of Public Utilities,* C.F. 107439.

38 For a representative sampling from the 1920s see Report of City Engineer to City Council, December 16, 1920, C.F. 79695; Peter Witt on Municipal Street Railways, December 10, 1921, C.F. 83267; Superintendent of Railways to City Council, November 30, 1921, C.F. 82984; Proposals for Monorail System, 1927, C.F. 108601; Karl Kay and Associates to City Council, November 3, 1928, C.F. 119975; Seattle Division of Railwaymen's Republican Club to City Council, January 26, 1929, C.F. 120022.

39 Report, Seattle Municipal Railway, 1934, C.F. 147297.

40 Report of Street Railway Committee to City Council, November 5, 1931, C.F. 133504.

41 W. M. Brown, Manager of Municipal Railways to City Council, November 15, 1932, C.F. 134613.

42 *Report to the City of Seattle on its Municipal Street Railway System,* the Beeler Organization, New York, 1935, C.F. 138985.

43 The Beeler Report of 1937 is in C.F. 153931; a further Beeler Report was issued in 1939.

44 Blanchard, *The Street Railway Era in Seattle,* p. 129.

45 *Report of the Seattle Transit System 1940,* C.F. 169799, gives a detailed account of the changeover.

46 Blanchard, *The Street Railway Era in Seattle,* p. 132.

47 *Report of the Seattle Transit System 1942,* C.F. 176743, shows a profit of $54,439 in 1940, $84,984 in 1941, and $1,053,861 in 1942.

48 Patricia E. Roy, "The British Columbia Electric Railway Company 1897–1928: A British Company in British Columbia" (Ph.D. dissertation, University of British Columbia, 1970).

49 Ibid., pp. 191–266.

50 Ibid., pp. 294–352.

51 The *Vancouver News Herald,* March 1, 2, 10, 11; April 12, 18, 19; July 4, 6, 29, 1932.

52 Smith's report and Adam's reply are covered at length in *Vancouver News Herald,* August 7, 1935.

53 See *Vancouver Sun,* April 4, 1938, and July 18, 1939.

54 Walter Van Nus, "The Fate of City Beautiful Thought in Canada 1893–1930," in Gilbert A. Stelter and Alan F. J. Artibise, eds., *The Canadian City: Essays in Urban History* (Toronto: McClelland and Stewart, 1977).

55 Brahm Wiesman, "Provincial Planning Legislation in Canada 1912–75," paper presented to Canadian Urban History Conference, University of Guelph, May 1977. See also Van Nus, "The Fate of City Beautiful Thought in Canada," pp. 172–76.

56 John Bottomley, "Experience, Ideology and the Landscape: The Business Community, Urban Reform, and the Establishment of Town Planning in Vancouver 1900–40" (Ph.D. dissertation, University of British Columbia, 1977), pp. 154–73.

57 Norman J. Johnston, "Harland Bartholomew: His Comprehensive Plans and the Science of Planning" (Ph.D. dissertation, University of Pennsylvania, 1964), pp. 13, 14. See also Norman J. Johnston, "Harland Bartholomew: Precedent for the Profession," *Journal of the American Institute of Planners* (March 1973): 115–24.

58 Bartholomew, *A Plan for the City of Vancouver.*

59 Ibid., pp. 86–140.

60 Ibid., pp. 141–68.

61 Ibid., pp. 168–210, esp. 173–75, 183–84, 205–7, 210.

62 Ibid., pp. 238–45.

63 A Preliminary Report upon Economic Background and Population, prepared as a revision of the Commission's 1930 Report, Harland Bartholomew and Associates, 1944, Vancouver City Archives.

64 City Comptroller F. Jones and Corporation Counsel D. E. McTaggart to Mayor and Council, December 21, 1945, in "Town Planning Commission," RG 9, Series A-1, 1946, in Vancouver City Archives. Bartholomew's basic fee was $20,000. Later printing costs came to about $6,000.

65 The nine reports were entitled *Economic Background and Population Growth, Transit Planning, Civic Centre, Downtown Business District, Metropolitan Airport, Parks Recreation Schools, Decentralization and Regional Planning, The Major Street Plan, The Appearance of the City.* These reports averaged about 40 pages each.

66 See Barnes, "Comprehensive Planning in Seattle." For an analysis of the limited planning achievements during World War II see Carl Abbott, "Planning for the Home Front in Seattle and Portland, 1940–45," in Roger W. Lotchin, ed., *The Martial Metropolis: U.S. Cities in War and Peace* (New York: Praeger, 1984), pp. 163–89.

7 The Response to the Depression

1 Robert S. Lynd and Helen M. Lynd, *Middletown in Transition* (New York: Harcourt Brace, 1937); Studs Terkel, *Hard Times: An Oral History of the Great Depression* (New York: Pantheon Books, 1970); Barry Broadfoot, *Ten Lost Years 1929–39: Memories of Canadians Who Survived the Depression* (Toronto: Doubleday, 1973), provide invalu-

able insights into the experiences of a host of Americans and Canadians during the Depression.

2   Robert E. Graves, "Business Government: Party Politics and the B.C. Business Community 1928–33" (M.A. thesis, University of British Columbia, 1976).

3   Mayor Frank Edwards to City Council, June 3, 1929, C.F. 122036.

4   Mayor Edwards to City Council, November 10, 1930, C.F. 128840. Over the years local unemployment was intensified by the arrival of unemployed transients. For the pattern in the Canadian city see Patricia E. Roy, "Vancouver: 'The Mecca of the Unemployed' 1907–29" in Alan F. J. Artibise, ed., *Town and City: Aspects of Western Canadian Urban Development* (Regina: Canadian Plains Research Center, University of Regina, 1981), pp. 393–413.

5   L. M. Grayson and Michael Bliss, eds., *The Wretched of Canada: Letters to R. B. Bennett 1930–35* (Toronto: University of Toronto Press, 1971).

6   Report of Mayor's Commission for Improved Employment, August 11, 1931, in Seattle Municipal Reference Library (cited hereafter as SMRL).

7   *Vancouver Province,* July 16, 1938.

8   "Government Employment and Payrolls 1929–38, City of Seattle," U.S. Department of Labor, Bureau of Labor Statistics, Division of Construction and Public Employment, June 1942, in C.F. 174931.

9   F. Waters to Vancouver Harbour Commission, July 20, July 27, September 9, 1931, in "Unemployment and Relief," Additional MSS no. 43, vol. VIII, no. 1, Vancouver City Archives.

10   Relief and Employment Committee, February 8, 1932 (cited hereafter as *R. & E. Comm.*). Available in Vancouver City Archives.

11   Ibid.

12   Ibid., November 7, 1932.

13   Ibid., June 23, 1932.

14   Ibid., December 14, 1931.

15   *Van CC M,* February 6, 1894.

16   *R. & E. Comm.,* April 5, 1921, November 28, 1921.

17   Ibid., February 16, 1920; February 20, 1928; February 12, 1930; February 9, 1931.

18   *Vancouver Province,* October 5, 20, 1931.

19   The *Seattle Municipal News* provides many examples. See December 29, 1929; May 17, 1930; May 31, 1930. The November 7, 1931, issue pointed out, "A recent study . . . shows that Seattleites think less favourably of their municipal employees than do the citizens of any of the other thirty-nine largest cities in the country."

20   See Arthur Hillman, "The Unemployed Citizens' League of Seattle," University of Washington, *Publications in the Social Sciences* 5 (Feb. 1934): 181–270. William H. Mullins, "Self-Help in Seattle, 1931–32: Herbert Hoover's Concept of Cooperative Individualism and the Unemployed Citizens' League," *Pacific Northwest Quarterly* 72 (Jan. 1981): 11–19.

21   Report of Mayor's Commission on Improved Employment, December 19, 1931, C.F. 133991. See also William H. Mullins, "San Francisco and Seattle During the Hoover Years of the Depression 1929–33" (Ph.D. dissertation, University of Washington, 1975), pp. 69–71, 71–74, 91.

22   Hillman, "Unemployed Citizens' League," pp. 198–99.

23   Mayor Harlin to City Council, January 20, 1932, C.F. 134328.

24 *Vancouver Province,* August 8, 1933.
25 See Joseph P. Harris, "Seattle Gaily Elects a Mayor," *National Municipal Review* 21 (1932), for a detailed treatment.
26 Don Duncan, "We're for Meyers," Seattle *Times,* November 5, 1967.
27 Seattle *Times,* July 30, 1932.
28 Ibid., July 17, 1932.
29 Dore to H. C. Carroll, June 6, 1932, C.F. 136100.
30 See C.F. 136108, 136317 for details.
31 Dore to City Council, June 13, 1932, C.F. 136236.
32 *Seattle Municipal News,* October 15, 1932.
33 This discussion of the UCL during 1932, 1933, is taken from Hillman, "Unemployed Citizens' League," pp. 210–33; Mullins, "San Francisco and Seattle During the Hoover Years," pp. 91–6, 124–25; Mullins, "Self-Help in Seattle 1931–32," pp. 13–18. The UCL received considerable attention from national publications. See, for example, *Business Week,* May 4, 1932; *Atlantic,* October 1932; *Collier's,* December 31, 1932.
34 For a convenient summary of the response of Philadelphia; Milwaukee, Wisc.; Rochester, N.Y.; Ann Arbor, Mich.; and Muncie, Ind., see Mullins, "San Francisco and Seattle During the Hoover Years," esp. chap. 5.
35 Seattle *Times,* April 26, July 10, 1933.
36 State Treasurer to City Council, May 26, 1933, C.F. 130144.
37 *Seattle Municipal News,* April 28, 1934.
38 Mayor Charles Smith to City Council, June 4, 1934, C.F. 143794.
39 Mayor's message for 1934, C.F. 137204.
40 C.F. 137593.
41 *Report of Department of Buildings,* 1936–37, C.F. 158998.
42 *Vancouver Province,* January 3, 1935.
43 Ibid., January 2, 1935.
44 Ibid., March 9, 1935, for Bradshaw Report.
45 See *Vancouver Province,* January 26, 1935, for Pattulo statement. *Financial Post,* as quoted in *Vancouver Province,* February 1, 1935, also shows that spokesmen in Saskatoon and Edmonton supported McGeer's ideas.
46 *Vancouver Province,* February 11, 22, 1935.
47 Ibid., March 8, 1935.
48 *Vancouver Province,* March 11, 1936.
49 See for example *Vancouver Sun,* esp. December 4, 5, 1935.
50 Nomination Book and Record of Elections 1924–1949, City of Vancouver, Vancouver City Archives.
51 *N.P.A. Minutes,* November 12, 1937, Vancouver City Archives. Those at the original organization meeting included J. MacPherson, B. S. Brown, S. S. McKeen, E. W. Rhodes, General Odlum, R. Holland, D. Pratt, and W. L. Craig. See also Andrea B. Smith, "The Origins of the NPA: A Study in Vancouver Politics 1930–40" (M.A. thesis, University of British Columbia, 1981). John Taylor, "How the N.P.A. Was Started and Why," *Vancouver Sun,* June 6, 1967; and Fern Miller, "Vancouver Civic Political Parties: Developing a Model of Party System Change and Stabilization" (Research paper prepared as part of Ph.D. comprehensive examination, Department of Political Science, Yale University, 1972).
52 See Phelps, *Public Works in Seattle.*
53 For the range and diversity of New Deal involvement in the cities see Mark Gelfand, *A*

Nation of Cities: The Federal Government and Urban America, 1933–65 (New York: Oxford University Press, 1975), chaps. 2, 3, 4.

54 Ibid., pp. 27–28, 34–39, 384–85.

55 William E. Leuchtenburg, *Franklin D. Roosevelt and the New Deal* (New York: Harper and Row, 1963).

56 See "Terms and Conditions on P.W.A Projects," in C.F. 156725.

57 See Carl W. Smith, State Administrator WPA to Frank J. Laube, City Councillor, August 19, 1940, for a detailed inventory on WPA projects carried out in King County between July 1935 and January 1940.

58 C.F. 147543, 147562.

59 In a letter to City Council, July 30, 1940 (C.F. 167031), J. H. Griffith wrote, "what self-respecting family wants to live in a tenement built by a maternal government for the underprivileged."

60 See E. R. Hoffman, Regional Director PWA to City Engineer N. A. Carle, May 4, 1937, in C.F. 155246.

61 By 1938 the regional director of the PWA was actively encouraging applications for grants. C.F. 159381.

62 Gordon C. McKibben, "Non Partisan Politics: A Case Study of Seattle 1928–53" (M.A. thesis, University of Washington, 1954).

63 *Vancouver Province,* August 15–25, 1937.

64 For a detailed look at the WUL, written by a member, see Ronald Liversedge, *Recollections of the On to Ontario Trek* (Toronto: Mclelland and Stewart, 1973), esp. chaps. 2, 3, 4. This section on the WUL and its activities in British Columbia is based on Paul Phillips, *No Greater Power: A Century of Labour in British Columbia,* esp. pp. 101–21; and Stuart M. Jamieson, *Times of Trouble: Labour Unrest and Industrial Conflict in Canada,* esp. pp. 230–45, 267–70, 487–500, 507–10. See also M. Lane, "Unemployment During the Depression: The Problem of the Single Unemployed Transient in British Columbia 1930–38" (B.A. thesis, University of British Columbia, 1966).

65 *Vancouver Province,* December 15, 1938.

66 Ibid., July 12, 1939. By this time the federal government paid 40 percent of direct relief costs, provincial government paid 40 percent, and municipal government 20 percent. Aid to transients was divided on a 50/50 basis between federal and provincial governments. See ibid., January 24, 1939.

67 Quoted in William E. Leuchtenberg, "The Great Depression," in C. Vann Woodward, *The Comparative Approach to American History* (New York: Basic Books, 1968), p. 308.

68 *Vancouver Province,* December 6, 1939.

8 World War II and the Postwar Decades

1 Two of the most valuable and comprehensive studies are Richard Polenberg, *War and Society: The United States, 1941–45* (Philadelphia: Lippincott, 1972), which focuses primarily on the activities of diverse public agencies, and John Morton Blum, *V Was for Victory: Politics and American Culture during World War II* (New York: Harcourt Brace Jovanovich, 1976), devotes more attention to the experiences and adaptations of the "little man." For a thorough coverage of developments in a single state see Alan Clive, *State of War: Michigan in World War II* (Ann Arbor: University of Michigan Press, 1979). See also Gerald Nash, *The American West Transformed: The Impact of the Second*

World War (Bloomington: University of Indiana Press, 1985); Eliot Janeway, *The Struggle for Survival: A Chronicle of Economic Mobilization in World War II* (New Haven: Yale University Press, 1951); Richard S. Kirkendall, *The United States, 1929–45: Years of Crisis and Change* (New York: McGraw-Hill, 1974).

2   Polenberg, *War and Society,* pp. 131–32.

3   Kirkendall, *The United States, 1929–45,* sees the development of the American military establishment during World War II as a "radical departure." Similarly, Polenberg in *War and Society,* p. 237, writes, "If the military-industrial complex reached maturity in the era of the Cold War, it just as surely was born and nurtured in World War II."

4   For those who maintain that the military-industrial complex developed much earlier, see Lotchin, ed. *The Martial Metropolis: U.S. Cities in War and Peace.* In the Introduction he writes, "The military industrial complex did not simply grow out of the industrial necessities of the United States during and after World War II. It originated from the urban imperatives of the country and well before World War II." See also Paul A. C. Koistinen, "The Military Industrial Complex in Historical Perspective: The Interwar Years," *Journal of American History* 56 (March 1970): 819–39; R. W. Lotchin, "The City and the Sword: San Francisco and the Rise of the Metropolitan-Military Complex, 1919–41," *Journal of American History* 65 (March 1979): 996–1020; R. W. Lotchin, "The Metropolitan-Military Complex in Comparative Perspective: San Francisco, Los Angeles, and San Diego 1919–41," *Journal of the West* 18 (July 1979): 19–30.

5   There is no major study of the impact of World War II on Canadian society. For general treatment of the war, with emphasis on decision making, see J. L. Granatstein, *Canada's War: The Politics of the Mackenzie King Government 1939–45* (Toronto: Oxford University Press, 1975); Donald Creighton, *Dominion of the North: A History of Canada* (Toronto: Macmillan, 1957); R. D. Cuff and J. L. Granatstein, *Canadian-American Relations in Wartime* (Toronto: Haakkert, 1975).

6   Rolf Knight, *Along the No. 20 Line: Reminiscences of the Vancouver Waterfront* (Vancouver: New Star Books, 1980), vividly recaptures the working world of Vancouver's Depression-World War II generation. For the Bill White quote, see p. 114. Also see J. S. Marshall, "History of Burrard Dry Dock Company," 1963. This valuable but unpaged typewritten manuscript is available in the University of British Columbia Library, Special Collections.

7   "Down Our Ways," December 21, 1944, published by West Coast Shipbuilders, July 1942 to February 1946, in Vancouver City Archives.

8   *Vancouver Province,* March 7, 1942. See also "Shipyard Rises from Mudflats," ibid., January 6, 1942.

9   K. Munson and G. Swanborough, *Boeing: An Aircraft Album* (New York: Arco, 1971), p. 9.

10 *The Boeing Beam,* May 26, 1944, published by the Public Relations Department, Boeing Aircraft Company of Canada.

11 *Vancouver Province,* July 27, 1944.

12 See "Boeing Aircraft Company of Canada," a newspaper clipping file in Vancouver City Archives.

13 *Vancouver Province,* September 10, 1945. See also Peter M. Bowers, *Boeing Aircraft Since 1916* (London: Putnam, 1966), p. 215.

14 The manufacturing plant on Sea Island was later acquired by Canadian Pacific Airlines as a repair depot. *Vancouver Province,* March 2, 1949.

15 Phillip J. Funigiello, *The Challenge to Urban Liberalism: Federal-City Relations during World War II* (Knoxville: University of Tennessee Press, 1978). See pp. 3–38 for an analysis of nationwide migratory patterns.

16 U.S. House of Representatives, *National Defense Migration Hearings,* 77th Congress, 22d Sess., Pt. 30, 10603–06 (cited hereafter as *National Defense Migration Hearings*).

17 Ibid.

18 Seattle *Argus,* September 23, 1939.

19 Ibid., September 14, 1940.

20 According to a statement by Chairman C. T. Egtvedt in 1945, Boeing had 1,585 employees at the end of 1937, 2,569 at the end of 1938, and 5,821 at the end of 1939. Ibid., August 25, 1945.

21 Ibid., September 7, 1940.

22 U.S. Department of Labor, Bureau of Labor Statistics, Industrial Area Study no. 19 (January 1945), "Impact of the War on the Seattle-Tacoma Area," pp. 1–10.

23 Seattle *Argus,* March 22, 1941.

24 Ibid., April 5, 1941.

25 Ibid., May 24, June 7, 1941.

26 Ibid., Christmas issue, December 1941.

27 By 1944, 57 percent of the women employed by Boeing were in "direct factory work," Seattle *Argus,* November 11, 1944.

28 Munson and Swanborough, *Boeing,* p. 69.

29 Seattle *Argus,* November 6, 1943.

30 Karen Anderson, *Wartime Women: Sex Roles, Family Relations and the Status of Women During World War II* (Westport, Conn.: Greenwood Press, 1981), focuses on developments in Baltimore, Detroit, and Seattle. See esp. pp. 13–15, 31, 158–63.

31 Of the total employment of 385,000, 195,000 were in manufacturing employment. By September 1944, total employment had declined to 368,000 and manufacturing employment to 183,000. "Impact of the War on the Seattle-Tacoma Area," pp. 41–42.

32 Munson and Swanborough, *Boeing,* p. 214.

33 U.S. House of Representatives, *Investigation of Congested Areas,* Hearings, 78th Congress, 1st Sess., no. 164, "A Report on the Puget Sound Area," p. 1212 (cited hereafter as *Congested Areas Hearings*); "Impact of the War on the Seattle-Tacoma Area," p. 43.

34 "Impact of the War on the Seattle-Tacoma Area," p. 42.

35 Anderson, *Wartime Women,* p. 15.

36 Nash, *The American West Transformed,* p. 79.

37 "Impact of the War on the Seattle-Tacoma Area," pp. 1–2.

38 In 1890, for example, 286 blacks accounted for 0.7 percent of the city's population, whereas in 1940, 3,789 blacks made up 1.0 percent of the population. In 1950, Seattle had 15,666 blacks or 3.4 percent of the population. See *U.S. Census, 1890,* vol. I, Pt. I, pp. 557, 583; *U.S. Census, 1940,* vol. II, Pt. 7, p. 401; *U.S. Census, 1950,* vol. II, Pt. 47, pp. 67, 100.

39 Seattle *Argus,* October 9, December 18, 1943.

40 Black-white relations in Seattle shared much in common with Detroit, for example, but with a virtual absence of outright violence. For a thorough analysis of developments in Detroit see Clive, *State of War: Michigan in World War II,* esp. pp. 130–69.

41 See Howard A. Droker, "Seattle Race Relations During the Second World War," *Pacific Northwest Quarterly* 67 (Oct. 1976): 163–74, for a detailed, penetrating treatment.

42 The dispute extended for some eight months from the fall of 1940 to the spring of 1941, and was covered by the local papers. See Seattle *Argus,* esp. March 29, April 5, 26, May 31, 1941.

43 The FEPC had been established by executive order of President Roosevelt in June 1941. It aimed to prevent racial discrimination in all defense projects.

44 Droker, "Seattle Race Relations," p. 164.

45 Ibid.

46 Ibid., p. 165.

47 Sale, *Seattle: Past to Present,* pp. 163–67.

48 Sam Bass Warner, *Urban Wilderness: A History of the American City* (New York: Harper and Row, 1972), pp. 230–46, provides a thoughtful discussion of this phenomenon. See also Abbott, "Planning for the Home Front in Seattle and Portland 1940–45." He shows that such wartime planning was fragmented and temporary, with limited impact on postwar development in either city.

49 Catherine Jill Wade, "Wartime Housing Limited, 1941–47: Canadian Housing Policy at the Crossroads" (M.A. thesis, University of British Columbia, 1984).

50 There is a very extensive body of literature on this grim episode. Among the major works that treat developments in Canada are Forrest E. LaViolette, *The Canadian Japanese and World War II: A Sociological and Psychological Account* (Toronto: University of Toronto Press, 1948); Ken Adachi, *The Enemy That Never Was: A History of the Japanese-Canadians* (Toronto: McClelland and Stewart, 1976); Barry Broadfoot, *Years of Sorrow, Years of Shame. The Story of Japanese Canadians in World War II* (Toronto: Doubleday, 1977); W. P. Ward, *White Canada Forever: Popular Attitudes and Public Policy Toward Orientals in British Columbia;* Ann Gomer Sunahara, *The Politics of Racism: The Uprooting of Japanese Canadians During the Second World War* (Toronto: James Lorimer, 1981). See also Patricia E. Roy, "The Evacuation of the Japanese, 1942," in J. M. Bumstead, ed., *Documentary Problems in Canadian History* (Georgetown, Ont.: Irwin Dorsey, 1969), vol. 2; and Robert W. O'Brien, "Evacuation of Japanese from the Pacific Coast: Canadian and American Contrasts," *Washington State College Research Studies* 14 (March 1946): 113–20. For valuable bibliographical essays on the topic, see M. A. Sunahara and G. T. Wright, "The Japanese Canadian Experience in World War II: An Essay on Archival Resources," and Patricia E. Roy, "White Canada Forever: Two Generations of Studies," both in *Canadian Ethnic Studies* 2, no. 2 (1979): 78–87, and 97–109.

The literature on developments in the United States is voluminous. A good starting point is Howard Sugimoto, "A Bibliographical Essay on the Wartime Evacuation of Japanese from the West Coast Areas," in H. Conroy and T. S. Miyakawa, eds., *East Across the Pacific: Historical and Sociological Studies of Japanese Immigration and Assimilation* (Santa Barbara, Calif.: American Bibliographical Center, Clio Press, 1972), pp. 140–50. Among some of the major works are Carey McWilliams, *Prejudice: Japanese-Americans: Symbols of Racial Intolerance* (Boston: Little, Brown, 1944); Morton Grodzins, *Americans Betrayed: Politics and the Japanese Evacuation* (Chicago: University of Chicago, 1949); Monica Sone, *Nisei Daughter* (Boston: Little Brown, 1953); Stetson Conn, "Japanese Evacuation from the West Coast," in S. Conn et al., eds., *The United States Army in World War II: The Western Hemisphere* (Washington, D.C.: Office of the Chief of Military History, Department of the Army, 1960, 1964), pp. 115–49; Bill Hosokawa, *Nisei: The Quiet Americans* (New York: W. Morrow, 1969); Audrie Girdner and Anne Loftis, *The Great Betrayal* (New York: Macmillan, 1969); Roger Daniels, *Concentration Camps,*

U.S.A.: Japanese Americans and World War II (New York: Holt, Rinehart & Winston, 1971); Roger Daniels, *The Decision to Relocate the Japanese-Americans* (Philadelphia: Lippincott, 1975).

51 Ward, *White Canada Forever,* pp. 144–47.

52 Ibid., p. 149.

53 Broadfoot, *Years of Sorrow,* p. 198.

54 Sunahara, *The Politics of Racism,* pp. 35–37, 42–48.

55 Daniels, *Decision to Relocate the Japanese Americans,* chap. 2, esp. pp. 14–21.

56 Ibid., p. 15.

57 *National Defense Migration Hearings,* pp. 11404–11409.

58 Ibid., pp. 11468–11469.

59 Calvin F. Schmidt, "Pre-war and Wartime Migration to Seattle," *Washington State College Research Studies* 13 (March 1945): 10–16.

60 Millikin MSS, April 6, 1942, University of Washington Library, Box 12, Folder 18.

61 Seattle *Argus,* August 22, 1942.

62 Daniels, *Decision to Relocate the Japanese-Americans,* pp. 27–28.

63 For a detailed discussion of *Hirabayashi* v. *U.S., Korematsu* v. *U.S.,* and Ex. parte Endo, see Daniels, *Concentration Camps, U.S.A.,* chap. 7.

64 Patricia E. Roy, "The Soldiers Canada Didn't Want: The Chinese and Japanese Citizens," *Canadian Historical Review* 59 (Sept. 1978): 44–59.

65 Adachi, *The Enemy That Never Was,* pp. 293–95.

66 Sunahara, *The Politics of Racism,* pp. 131–45. A public opinion poll showed that 80 percent of Canadian respondents favored the return of issei (first-generation, Japanese-born immigrant) to Japan. A comparable poll in the U.S. showed that only 29 percent of Americans favored such a policy. O'Brien, "Evacuation of Japanese from the Pacific Coast."

67 This estimate is based on casualty statistics for the State of Washington.

68 Seattle *Argus,* August 10, 1946.

69 Ibid.

70 Ibid., March 27, 1948; June 13, 1953.

71 Murray C. Morgan, *Century 21: The Story of the Seattle World's Fair* (Seattle: Acme Press, 1963), is the standard work on the topic.

72 Tim Hill, *Citizens Handbook on Transportation Planning in Seattle* (Seattle: Councilman T. Hill, Seattle City Council, 1972), pp. 13–15.

73 Kenneth R. Geiser, Jr., *Urban Transportation Decision Making: Political Processes of Urban Freeway Controversies* (Cambridge: MIT, 1971), pp. 10–21.

74 *Planning for Thoroughfares: Central Freeway,* City of Seattle Planning Commission, January 3, 1957, esp. pp. 3–16.

75 *Planning for Thoroughfares: Empire Expressway,* City of Seattle Planning Commission, December 12, 1957. *Planning for Thoroughfares: Northwest Expressway,* City of Seattle Planning Commission, September 18, 1958.

76 For a detailed analysis of developments in Seattle, see Geiser, *Urban Transportation Decision Making,* pp. 47–126. See also Ruth Wolf, "Block That Freeway," *Seattle Magazine,* February 1969. Both the *Post Intelligencer* and the *Times* carried numerous articles on freeway issues throughout the 1960s.

77 For election results, see Seattle *Post Intelligencer,* February 13, 1968.

78 V. Setty Pendakur, *Cities, Citizens and Freeways* (Vancouver: V. S. Pendakur, 1972),

pp. 105–70. This study, by a specialist in urban transportation, a professor in the School of Community and Regional Planning, University of British Columbia, and a former Vancouver City Alderman, provides a comprehensive coverage of planning and transportation developments in Vancouver between 1953 and 1972. I am indebted to it both for its ideas and evidence.

79 Ibid., pp. 4–6, 15, 52.

80 Ibid., pp. 11–13, 53; 50–54; 15–57.

81 Ibid., pp. 59–73. See *Vancouver Sun* and *Vancouver Province,* October, November, and December 1967, for day-by-day developments.

9 Thirty Years of Municipal Politics

1 For a brief, compact analysis of Seattle see Edward C. Banfield, *Big City Politics: A Comparative Guide to the Political Systems of Atlanta, Boston, Detroit, El Paso, Los Angeles, Miami, Philadelphia, St. Louis, Seattle* (New York: Random House, 1965), pp. 133–47. The Seattle section of that book is based on Charles W. Bender's "A Report on Politics in Seattle" (1961), available in the University of Washington Library. The best single study on Vancouver is Paul Tennant's thoughtful, incisive "Vancouver Civic Policies, 1929–80," *B.C. Studies* 46 (Summer 1980): 3–27. See also Fern Miller, "Vancouver Civic Political Parties: Developing a Model of Party-System Change and Stabilization," *B.C. Studies* 25 (Spring 1975): 3–27; Thomas J. Plunkett, *Urban Canada and its Government: A Study of Municipal Organization* (Toronto: Macmillan, 1968), pp. 143–48.

2 McKibben, "Non Partisan Politics: A Case Study of Seattle, 1928–53, pp. 155–56.

3 *City of Vancouver, Municipal Year Book* is published annually and provides a convenient summary.

4 *Vancouver Province,* December 9, 1937; December 15, 1938.

5 Smith, "The Origins of the NPA: A Study in Vancouver Politics, 1930–40."

6 Miller, "Vancouver Civic Political Parties," esp. pp. 7–13.

7 Ibid., pp. 8, 9.

8 The Citizens' League of Winnipeg, Manitoba, shared much in common with Vancouver's Non-Partisan Association. But unlike the NPA's virtually unopposed domination of Vancouver, the Citizens' League faced sustained opposition from "Labour." For a detailed and rigorous analysis see J. E. Rae, "The Politics of Class: Winnipeg City Council 1919–45," in Carl Berker and Ramsay Cook, eds., *The West and the National* (Toronto: McClelland and Stewart, 1976), pp. 232–49.

9 McKibben, "Non Partisan Politics: A Case Study of Seattle," p. 33.

10 Blackford, "Reform Politics in Seattle During the Progressive Era 1902–16."

11 See George W. Scott, "The New Order of Cincinnatus: Municipal Politics in Seattle During the 1930's," *Pacific Northwest Quarterly* 64 (Oct. 1973): 137–46.

12 Although both the Seattle Municipal League and the Non-Partisan Association in Vancouver shared an interest in "good government" and drew their membership and support from the more prosperous, established members of the community, they evolved along different lines. The Seattle organization, founded in 1910, was interested in a whole series of urban issues and problems. It operated on a year-round basis, published a variety of analyses and reports, and became a kind of local government research organization. Its assessments and recommendations on various local candidates guided Seattle's voters in a host of elections. As it emphasized municipal experience as well as efficiency

and economy, it tended to favor incumbents. The Vancouver Non-Partisan Association, on the other hand, only appeared in 1937. Like Seattle's Municipal League it followed two years after the establishment of a nonpartisan, at-large electoral system in the city. It operated primarily at election times and was essentially a slate-making organization. Membership was smaller and more closely identified with the business community, and its activities were narrower and less publicized. Over the years the NPA developed some of the attributes of a civil political party. See Lee Pendergrass, "Urban Reform and Voluntary Association: A Case Study of the Seattle Municipal League 1910–29" (Ph.D. dissertation, University of Washington, 1972). A briefer version by the same author entitled "The Formation of a Municipal Reform Movement: The Municipal League of Seattle" is in *The Pacific Northwest Quarterly* 66 (Jan. 1975): 13–25. On the NPA see Miller, "Vancouver's Civic Political Parties."

13 See for example Mayor Devin's message to Council, June 17, 1946, C.F. 189507.

14 *Vancouver Province,* December 6, 1958.

15 *Vancouver Sun,* December 10, 1966.

16 Seattle *Argus,* May 31, 1952.

17 Tennant, "Vancouver Politics and the Civic Party System," p. 8.

18 For a detailed statement of the duties and responsibilities of Vancouver's Board of Administration, see Plunkett, *Urban Canada and its Government,* esp. pp. 145–48.

19 For a detailed examination and expose see Donald Gutstein, *Vancouver Ltd.* (Toronto: J. Lorimer, 1975), esp. pp. 98–110, 151–68. Alderman Harry Rankin provides a more generalized critique in his *A Socialist Perspective for Vancouver* (Toronto: Progress Books, 1974), esp. pp. 7–21.

20 Banfield, *Big City Politics,* pp. 133–46.

21 Ibid., p. 145.

22 James Malpin, "Our Musty, Crusty City Council," *Seattle Magazine* (May 1965): 12–16, 46–48.

23 Mayor Gordon Clinton argued in a speech to the Metropolitan Democratic Club on January 21, 1964, that "Seattle's urgent need" was for a "strong-mayor system."

24 Banfield, *Big City Politics,* p. 144.

25 Ibid., p. 141.

26 The literature on the activity of such organizations is extensive. Among the valuable items are Banfield; *Big City Politics,* Mark H. Sidran, "Middle Class Urban Political Conflict: The Case of Seattle" (B.A. thesis, Harvard, 1973), which treats the Pike Place Market Controversy; and Morgan, *Century 21: The Story of Seattle's World Fair.* Geiser, *Urban Transportation Decision Making,* discusses the R. H. Thomson Freeway issue on pp. 46–124. John Fisher, "Seattle's Modern Day Vigilantes," *Harper's Magazine* (May 1969): 14–26, is a lively, provocative discussion of Forward Thrust and James Ellis. Wolf, "Block that Freeway," and Patrick Douglas, "So Long Ed," *Seattle Magazine* (January 1970), are also instructive. Items that focus more specifically on the business community include Delbert B. Miller, *International Community Power Structure: Comparative Studies of Four World Cities* (Bloomington: Indiana University Press, 1970); chap. 5 treats "the Seattle Business Leader." The April 1968 issue of *Seattle Magazine* discusses "The Establishment," with various listings of who they were, and how they rated.

27 Edward C. Banfield and James Q. Wilson's *City Politics* (Cambridge: Harvard University Press, 1963) provides a systematic analysis of nonpartisanship on pp. 155–67.

Eugene C. Lee, *The Politics of Nonpartisanship* (Berkeley: University of California Press, 1960), treats the impact of nonpartisanship on six medium-sized cities in California.

28 In the 1970s, however, this movement had become much more common. Thus Mayor Wes Uhlman (1970–78) served ten years as a Democrat in the Washington state legislature, and Councilmen Sam Smith, Paul Krobell, Tim Hill, Floyd Miller, and others also served as state legislators.

29 In the late 1970s Aldermen Harcourt and Kennedy sought unsuccessfully to win provincial seats, and former Mayor Arthur Phillips became Liberal MP.

30 Banfield, *Big City Politics*, p. 139.

31 The *Vancouver Municipal Year Book*, 1938 to 1968.

32 Between 1938 and 1968, for example, H. Wilson served twenty-four years, C. Miller seventeen years, E. Adams sixteen years, and J. W. Cornett ten years.

33 These persons with their time on council between 1938 and 1968 were M. Mitchell—twenty-six years, Levine—twenty-four years, R. Jones—nineteen years, F. F. Powell—sixteen years, C. Massart—seventeen years, F. Laube—sixteen years, G. M. Carroll—thirteen years, J. Scavotto—twelve years, W. L. Norton—twelve years, F. Miller—twelve years, H. Edwards—twelve years, P. Alexander—twelve years. See "City Officials" in Seattle Municipal Reference Library.

34 There are a number of recent exceptions, however, including F. Bowers, S. Pendakur, G. Puil, H. Rankin, H. Boyce.

35 The *Vancouver Municipal Year Book* provides both the business and residential addresses of all city aldermen.

36 See note 33 for a listing of those councilmen and women. Addresses were obtained from the *Seattle City Directory*.

37 Douglas, "So Long Ed."

38 The combined tenures of Mayors Arthur Langlie, 1938–41; William Devin, 1942–51; Gordon Clinton, 1956–63; and Dorm Braman, 1964–68; were seen by C. A. Crosser, former executive secretary of the Seattle Municipal League as a "Golden Era of City Government in Seattle," in which the city had "lived within its income" and avoided "cronyism," "bumbling operations," and "graft." See his article in *Seattle Municipal News*, March 10, 1969.

39 For an understanding of the 1960s in Seattle one would be hard-pressed to better the insight gained from the thoughtful, incisive articles in *Seattle Magazine* (1964–70). Vietnam, student unrest, freeway construction, urban planning, the drug culture, Boeing, city politics, "the Establishment," women's liberation, white racism, and black militancy—all are treated.

40 Seattle *Times*, July 30, 1968.

41 Mayor Dorm Braman to University Rotary Club, October 18, 1968.

42 "Seattle's Racial Gap," a Special Report by the Seattle Urban League, July, 1968.

43 Similar evidence and conclusions were provided by a State of Washington Commission. See "Race and Violence in Washington State," Report of the Commission on the Causes and Consequences of Civil Disorder, A. Ludlow Kramer, Chairman (February 1969). The June 1968 issue of *Seattle Magazine* entitled "White Racism in Seattle," focuses on the difficulties faced by blacks in jobs, housing, police relations, and school integration.

44 A study by the Rand Corporation pointed out that the high level of savings in Seattle, coupled with extensive unemployment insurance payments, enabled the city to get

through this recession. It added "aerospace employees had a marked tendency to adjust downward but remain employed. . . . Seattle's aerospace recession was not a new phenomenon of a middle class crash; it started in aerospace, but as always it was lower income and status groups who were hit the hardest." "Seattle's Adaptation to Recession," R. B. Rainey, Jr., et al., Rand Corporation, R–1352–NSF, pp. 1–4, 27. The earlier data are from Washington State Employment Security Department as quoted in *Report on Conditions in Seattle's Model Neighborhood 1968–74*," p. 25, in Government and Research Assistance Library, City Hall, Seattle.

45 *Seattle Business,* October 10, 1977.

46 Seattle Human Rights Department as quoted in *Report on Conditions in Seattle's Model Neighborhood 1968–74.*

47 The "official" history of the Uhlman administration is provided in Michael Eagan, *Seattle: Renaissance of America's Most Liveable City* (Seattle: Medium Rare, 1978). For a brief, laudatory but persuasive analysis of Uhlman's role see Walt Crowley, "So Long Wes," *The Weekly,* April 22–May 3, 1977. See also Ed Sullivan, "Seattle After Wes: We've Come a Long Way, Mister," *Seattle Business,* October 10, 1977. The introductory paragraph reads, "A city that was once described as the 'cultural dustbin' of the nation is today viewed as one of the country's most 'liveable' cities. If both extremes are true, that's quite a turn-around—and a large chunk of the credit has to go to Wesley Carl Uhlman." Four experienced observers provide their assessment in "So Long Wes," *The Weekly,* January 4, 1978.

48 Miller, "Vancouver Civic Political Parties," p. 14.

49 According to a TEAM founder, "The old NPA has traditionally been the corporate downtown group. . . . The group of people backing NPA and the City Hall bureaucrats all had a vision for Vancouver in the 1950's—post war materialist, development at any cost, emphasis on more buildings and physical facilities. In the early 1960's a change in values began to take place. An expanding professional middle class began to express concerns for other things—environmental and social. Their lack of representation to city government led to the founding of T.E.A.M." Quoted in Miller, "Vancouver Civic Political Parties," p. 21.

50 *Vancouver Sun,* December 12, 1968.

51 Tennant, "Vancouver Civic Politics," p. 13.

52 Ibid.

53 The actual breakdown on city council was NPA—five, TEAM—one, COPE—one, Independents—three. On the School Board it was NPA—seven, TEAM—two, and on the Parks Board NPA—five, TEAM—two.

54 This paragraph relies on Tennant, "Vancouver Civic Politics," pp. 16–19.

55 No attempt was made to give the number of families living in poverty in the two cities, for like "middle-class income," "poverty" is not easily or precisely defined. If one applied the contemporary standard that any family that receives less than one half the median family income is in poverty, this would mean that over 10 percent of the families in both cities were still living in poverty in 1970.

56 See Banfield and Wilson, *City Politics,* pp. 40–44, 123, 329–30, Banfield, *Big City Politics,* pp. 144–46, Tennant, "Vancouver Civic Politics," pp. 3–8.

57 Over the years city electoral systems in the United States and Canada have evolved in a way that is contradictory to what one might expect. In the U.S. congressional system, for example, the representative has traditionally been seen as a delegate who spoke for the

specific needs and wishes of the district that elected him or her. Under the British parliamentary system, on the other hand, the MP was expected to exercise personal judgment, so as to act in the best interest of the nation as a whole, rather than for the specific interests of his or her constituency. On this basis one might assume that U.S. cities would tend to have ward systems, where council members spoke for the interests of a specific district, and that Canadian cities would have at-large systems. Paradoxically, however, more U.S. cities now follow the "British" model, in that seven out of eight cities in the United States with populations over 100,000 have an at-large system. All of Canada's larger cities, with the single exception of Vancouver, follow the "American" model, that is they have a ward system.

10   The 1970s, 1980s, and a Look Backward

1   The best account of this prolonged and significant conflict is Patrick Douglas, "Up Against the System in Seattle," *Harper's* (April 1972): 91–94.

2   Paul Goldberger, "Centerpiece of Vancouver: Gimmick-free Courthouse," *New York Times,* November 25, 1979. See also *Time,* October 1, 1979, pp. 50–51.

3   For "Quality of Life" articles or essays see *Harper's,* January 1975; *Christian Science Monitor,* May 21, 1975; *Atlantic Monthly,* April 1976; *Puget Soundings,* June 1976; *Saturday Review,* August 21, 1976; *Town and Country,* October 1977; *Family Circle,* November 1977; *New West,* December 5, 1977; *Time,* December 1977. The most detailed and comprehensive of all such studies is Ben-Chieh Liu, *Quality of Life Indicators in U.S. Metropolitan Areas 1970,* prepared for the U.S. Environmental Protection Agency, May 7, 1975. For each of sixty-five large Standard Metropolitan Statistical Areas (SMSA), data were collected on 123 separate factors, which in turn were organized into five basic components—economic, political, environmental, health and education, social. No final rating of all sixty-five metropolitan areas was provided, but charts in a summary volume of the same name suggested that Portland, Oregon, ranked first, closely followed by three cities, Seattle, Minneapolis, and Sacramento.

4   Toronto *Saturday Night,* January/February 1979.

5   London *Sunday Times Magazine,* November 1978.

6   Seattle *Post Intelligencer,* August 27, 1972.

7   Between January 25, 1976, and February 11, 1976, the *Post Intelligencer* carried a very valuable series entitled "Seattle in Transition." Done by twelve different reporters who focused on issues such as the economy, population trends, the downtown, manners and morals, the arts, sports, education, crime and transportation, the series treated the changes that had occurred in Seattle from 1966 to 1976. The quotation is by Bill Sieverling and is from ibid., January 25, 1976.

8   Ibid., June 2, 1979. Though colorful the statement was inaccurate. In a three-game series played in 1917, the Seattle Metropolitans defeated the Montreal Canadiens for the Stanley Cup, then the unquestioned symbol of hockey supremacy.

9   Mayor C. Royer, *Budget Message to Seattle City Council,* October 3, 1978, City Clerk's Office, Seattle.

10   Some of the difficulties entailed by a rise in demand for city services at a time when population is falling are treated in *Understanding Vancouver* (December 1977), Vancouver City Planning Department, esp. pp. 3.15 to 3.18.

11   For regional comparisons of an earlier era see Carlos A. Schwantes, *Radical Heritage:*

Labor Socialism and Reform in Washington and British Columbia 1885–1917 (Seattle: University of Washington Press, 1970).

12   In a witty, tongue-in-cheek article Emmett Watson "agreed" with Tuai about the need to "keep intellectuals in their place." Later letter writers showed that about half of them had taken the spoof seriously, and considered his proposition a good one. See Seattle *Post Intelligencer,* September 25, and October 4, 1972.

13   This pattern was especially true prior to World War II. In 1930 for example, of 292 active policemen, 170 were born in the United Kingdom, and of 14 senior officials, 11 were from the United Kingdom. At that time British immigrants made up about 30 percent of Vancouver's population. *Van CCl in Corr,* vol. 140, "Police Department 1930."

14   The annual reports of the Seattle Police Department (1926–78) and the Vancouver Police Department provide an abundance of statistical data on criminal activity. But changes and differences in definition and classification, as well as periodic intensification or slackening of police effort, lead to aberrations, inconsistencies, and ambiguities. Consequently, all such comparative data must be used cautiously. One might assume that there could be little ambiguity about murder. But the number of murders "committed" or "reported" differ from the numbers of persons "arrested" or "charged." Yet these distinctions are sometimes not made explicit. As a general rule the number of murders committed exceed the number of persons arrested by about 1.5 to 2 times. Unsolved murders, family violence, and suicide account for much of the difference.

15   This section on comparative house prices is based on Michael A. Goldberg, "Housing and Land Prices in Canada and the U.S.," *Urban Land Economics Publications,* Faculty of Commerce and Business Administration, University of British Columbia, Reprint no. 46 (1977): 207–53. Section III, "Seattle and Vancouver Under the Microscope," 221–40, has been especially helpful.

16   For a strong case against the proposal see Edward R. Waxman, "Politics and Transportation Planning in the Seattle Metropolitan Area" (Master of Urban Planning thesis, University of Washington, 1968).

17   In 1979, for example, Seattle Metro Transit had an operating deficit of $44 million, based on operating expenses of $65 million and operating revenue of $21 million. Subsidies from sales taxes amounted to $29 million, from motor vehicle excise taxes, $22 million, and from U.S. federal grants and "other," $5 million. The system's total revenue for 1979 amounted to $77 million. It is also noteworthy that from 1974 to 1980 total federal grants to Seattle Metro Transit from the Urban Mass Transportation Administration amounted to over $100 million. See Doyle Schigeo Saito, "Seattle's Metro Transit: A Case Study of Operating Efficiency 1973–80" (M.Sc. thesis, University of Washington, 1981), esp. pp. 14–38.

18   Material on Vancouver's ALRT is very extensive. Articles in *Quarterly Review* published by the Vancouver City Planning Department since 1974 were especially helpful, as were diverse reports by the GVRD; see especially "Rapid Transit Project: Final Report Summaries and Staff Committee Recommendations," December 1979. Michael C. Poulton, "Vancouver's Advanced Light Rail Transit: The Last Hurrah," paper given at the Transportation Conference, University of Warwick, Warwick, England, July 13–16, 1981, provided a penetrating critique. Newspaper coverage was also helpful. For summaries see *Vancouver Sun,* December 11, 1985, and January 3, 1986.

19   *Vancouver Sun,* Oct. 4, 1986, provides the specific statements.

20   Roger E. Bolton, *Defense Purchases and Regional Growth* (Washington, D.C.: Brookings

Institution, 1966). See Table A-1, "Estimated Annual Defense Purchases by Station and Region 1951–62," pp. 152–53. U.S. Department of Defense, "Military Prime Contract Awards by State, 1962–82."

21   See *Community Readjustment to Reduced Defense Spending: Case Studies of Potential Impact on Seattle-Tacoma, Baltimore, and New London-Groton, Norwich,* by U.S. Arms Control and Disarmament Agency, Washington, D.C., 1965. See esp. pp. 76–80.

22   Ibid., Appendix no. 1, Pt. II, p. 45. See pp. 40–43 for a discussion of the approach, and the way in which it differs from that followed by C. M. Tiebout.

23   Charles M. Tiebout, "The Regional Impact of Defense Expenditures: Its Measurement and Problems of Adjustment," in Roger E. Bolton, ed., *Defense and Disarmament: The Economics of Transition* (Englewood Cliffs, N.J.: Prentice Hall, 1966), pp. 125–39, esp. pp. 132–34.

24   See *Annual Report of the Boeing Company, 1960–80.* The "10-K Forms" submitted to the Securities and Exchange Commission are especially helpful.

25   See Doris H. Pieroth, "Desegregating the Public Schools in Seattle, Washington 1954– 68" (Ph.D. dissertation, University of Washington, 1979); Howard Droker, "The Seattle Civic Unity Committee and the Civil Rights Movement 1944–64" (Ph.D. dissertation, University of Washington, 1974); Nand Hart-Nibbrig, "School Desegregation Politics: Seattle, Washington," *Washington Public Policy Notes,* no. 1 (Winter 1979); Seattle *Post Intelligencer,* December 15, 1977.

26   Edgar Wickberg et al., *From China to Canada,* provides a comprehensive, authoritative treatment of the Chinese community in Vancouver.

27   See Daniel William Shannon, "A Cross National Comparison of Public Participation in Urban Shoreline Policy Development" (Ph.D. dissertation, University of Washington, 1979). He argues that Seattle followed a model of "democratic participation" in its handling of the Lake Union issue. This involved active and direct public participation in policymaking, with the original impetus coming from the community itself, and with frequent reliance on the courts for settlement of disputes. Vancouver's approach to False Creek, on the other hand, followed a "democratic leadership" model. In this case policy initiatives came from higher levels, established authorities remained in control, public participation was more limited and indirect, and court challenges absent. See also Frederick J. Elligott, "The Planning Decision-Making Process of Vancouver's False Creek: A Case Study 1968–1974" (M.A. thesis, University of British Columbia, 1977); Robert K. Burkinshaw, *False Creek: History, Images and Research Sources* (Vancouver: Vancouver City Archives, 1984), pp. 45–64.

28   Because of drowning accidents at city beaches the Vancouver city clerk was instructed in 1908 to write officials in other Canadian and American cities and ask what precautions were taken to prevent such accidents. The reply from Seattle read, "This city has no such precautionary measures in effect, nor as far as I am informed are there any in effect by private corporations or offices. For your further information [I] would say that there are no bathing beaches within the limits of the city." H. M. Carroll to W. McQueen, September 2, 1908, in *Van CCl in Corr,* vol. 25 (1908).

Bibliography

The 1986 publication of *Vancouver Centennial Bibliography,* 4 vols., compiled by Linda L. Hale under the auspices of the Vancouver Historical Society, has made all existing bibliographies on that city obsolete. With over 15,000 citations, it is an exhaustive coverage of all aspects of the city's life and history. Whether one is looking for material on Vancouver's Sikhs or Ukrainians, its politicians, architectural developments, public finances, or drug trade, everything is presented in a logical, systematic manner.

Many of the sources for Vancouver are available in the Special Collections of the University of British Columbia Library, the Vancouver Public Library, the Provincial Archives of British Columbia, Victoria, and in the Vancouver City Archives. The latter contains complete city council minutes, council committees' minutes, the mayors' papers, city clerks' correspondence, and the records of a host of civic departments. Diverse semipublic records, as well as manuscripts and privately donated material from business firms, labor unions, clubs, and churches make for an immensely rich, well-organized, useable collection.

No comparable bibliography or archives exists for Seattle, and though material is abundant it tends to be more dispersed. The University of Washington Library has the most significant collection. Its Special Collections Division and Manuscripts and Archives Division are especially valuable. Both divisions have a statewide orientation, but with extensive materials on Seattle itself. The City Clerk's Office, the Seattle Municipal Reference Library, the Seattle Public Library, and the Seattle Museum of History and Industry all have worthwhile collections. But Seattle's official records are limited; most of the early records were lost in the 1889 Fire. Though one can locate subsequent department reports to city council, as well as decisions made and ordinances passed, the city council minutes and the mayors' correspondence are unavailable.

The bibliography that follows is a highly selective one. I have listed only those items which helped shape my ideas, or provided significant evidence for my account.

I. Primary Sources

A. NEWSPAPERS AND DIRECTORIES

Henderson's *British Columbia Gazetteer and Directory*, 1899–1910.
Henderson's *Vancouver Directory*, 1910–20.
Seattle *Argus*.
Seattle *Daily Call*.
Seattle *Daily Chronicle*.
Seattle Municipal News.
Seattle *Post Intelligencer*.
Seattle *Times*, 1896.
Seattle *Weekly Intelligencer*, 1873–74.
Seattle *West Coast Lumberman*.
Vancouver *News Advertiser*, 1887–1917.
Vancouver *News Herald*, 1932–35.
Vancouver Province, 1894–.
Vancouver Sun, 1912–.
Vancouver World, 1888–1924.
Victoria Colonist, 1859–1900.
Williams, R. T., ed. *British Columbia Directory 1882/83, 1884/85–1899*.

B. FEDERAL CENSUS DOCUMENTS

United States

Census of the United States: 1870
    Vol. 1 *Population and Social Statistics*
Census of the United States: 1880
    Vol. 1 *Population*
Census of the United States: 1890
    Vol. 1 Part I *Population*
    Vol. 6 Part II *Manufactures*
Census of the United States: 1900
    Vol. 1 Part 1 *Population*
    Vol. 2 Part 2 *Population*
Census of the United States: 1910
    Vol. 1 *Population: General Report and Analysis*
    Vol. 4 *Population: Occupation Statistics*
    Vol. 9 *Manufactures*
Census of the United States: 1920
    Vol. 3 *Population: Composition and Characteristics*
    Vol. 4 *Population: Occupations*
Census of the United States: 1930
    Population, Vol. 1: *Number and Distribution of Inhabitants*
    Population, Vol. 3, Part 2: *Reports by States*
    Population, Vol. 4: *Occupations by State*

Census of the United States: 1940
> *Population,* Vol. 1: *Number of Inhabitants*
> *Population,* Vol. 2, Part 7: *Reports by States*
> *Population,* Vol. 3: *The Labor Force,* Part 5

Census of the United States: 1950
> *Census of Population,* Vol. 1: *Number of Inhabitants*
> *Census of Population,* Vol. 2: *Characteristics of the Population, Part 47, Washington*
> *Census of Population,* Vol. 3: *Census Tract Statistics: Seattle and Adjacent Area*

Census of the United States: 1960
> *Census of Population,* Vol. 1, Part 49, *Washington*
> *Census of Population and Housing, Census Tracts: Seattle-Everett*

Census of the United States: 1970
> *Census of Population,* Vol. 1, Part 49: *Washington*
> *Census of Population and Housing, Census Tracts: Seattle-Everett*

Census of the United States: 1980
> *Census of Population,* Vol. 1, Part 49, *Washington*

Canada

Census of Canada: 1890/91
> Vol. 1: *Population*

Census of Canada: 1901
> Vol. 1: *Population*
> Vol. 3: *Manufactures*

Census of Canada: 1911
> Vol. 1: *Areas and Population*
> Vol. 2: *Religious Origins and Birthplace*
> Vol. 3: *Manufactures*

Census of Canada: 1921
> Vol. 1: *Population, Number, Sex and Distribution*
> Vol. 2: *Population, Age, Conjugal Condition, Birthplace*
> Vol. 4: *Occupations*

Census of Canada: 1931
> Vol. 1: *Population*
> Vol. 4: *Population—Cross Classifications*
> Vol. 7: *Population—Occupations and Industries*

Census of Canada: 1941
> Vol. 2: *Population*
> Vol. 4: *Population—Cross Classifications*
> Vol. 7: *Gainfully Employed by Occupation and Industry*

Census of Canada: 1951
> Vol. 1: *Population General Characteristics*
> Vol. 3: *Housing and Families*
> Vol. 7: *Labor Force Occupations and Industry*

Census of Canada: 1961
> Vol. 1: *Population*
> Vol. 2: *Households and Families*
> Vol. 3: *Labour Force*

Census of Canada: 1971

    Vol. 1: *Population*

    Vol. 2: *Households*

    Vol. 3: *Economic Characteristics*

Census of Canada: 1981

    Vol. 2: *Provincial Series, British Columbia, Population*

C. OTHER GOVERNMENT DOCUMENTS

British Columbia *Sessional Papers 1885–1886*. Victoria: R. Wolfenden, Government Printer.

Canada *Sessional Papers 1897–1901*. Ottawa: S. E. Dawson, Queen's Printer.

U.S. Arms Control and Disarmament Agency. *Community Readjustment to Reduced Defense Spending: Case Studies of Potential Impact on Seattle-Tacoma, Baltimore, and New London-Groton, Norwich*. Washington, D.C., 1965.

U.S. Department of Defense. "Military Prime Contract Awards by State, 1962–82." Washington, D.C., 1983.

U.S. Department of Labor, Bureau of Labor Statistics, Division of Construction and Public Employment. "Government Employment and Payrolls 1929–38, City of Seattle." Washington, D.C., June 1942.

U.S. Department of Labor, Bureau of Labor Statistics, Industrial Area Study. "Impact of the War on the Seattle-Tacoma Area." no. 19 (January 1945).

U.S. House of Representatives. *Investigation of Congested Areas*. Hearings, 78th Congress, 1st sess. no. 164. "A Report on the Puget Sound Area."

U.S. House of Representatives. *National Defense Migration Hearings*. 77th Congress, 22d sess., Pt. 30, 10603–06.

D. CITY DOCUMENTS

Seattle City Clerk's Office

Annual Reports of the Mayor, 1890–.

Annual Reports of Departments, 1890–. Comptroller File, intermittent only.

Police Department, Annual Report, 1926–78.

Vancouver City Archives

Annual Report, City of Vancouver, 1886–.

Assessment Roll of 1888.

City Clerks' Correspondence, 1886–.

City Council Minutes, 1886–.

Mayors' Papers, 1886–.

Nomination Book and Record of Elections, 1924–49.

Police Department, Annual Report, 1886–.

E. OTHER PRIMARY SOURCES

Barnes, James A. "Comprehensive Planning in Seattle." Seattle City Planning Commission. Typescript. Seattle, November 1954.

Bartholomew, Harland, and Associates. *A Plan for the City of Vancouver.* Vancouver: Wrigley Printing, 1930.

Bell-Irving, Henry O. MSS. Vancouver City Archives.

Boeing Airplane Company. *Annual Report, 1960–80.*

Bogue, Virgil R. *Plan of Seattle.* Seattle, 1911. Special Collection Division, University of Washington Library.

Denny, Arthur A. *Pioneer Days on Puget Sound.* Seattle: C. B. Bagley, Printer, 1888.

Matthews, J. S. *Early Vancouver: Narratives of Pioneers of Vancouver, B.C.* Typescript. 7 vols. Vancouver, 1932–33. Vancouver City Archives.

Nicolls, J. P. "Real Estate Values in Vancouver." April 1954. Vancouver City Archives.

Olmstead Bros. MSS. University of Washington Library, Manuscripts Division.

Oppenheimer, David. MSS. Vancouver City Archives.

Plats, King County, I. University of Washington Library, Special Collections Division.

Probates. Probate Office, Supreme Court of British Columbia, Vancouver.

Probates. Probate Section, Washington State Court House, Seattle.

Prosch, Thomas W. *A Chronological History of Seattle from 1850 to 1897.* Typescript. Seattle, 1891. Special Collections Division, University of Washington Library.

Semple, Eugene. MSS. University of Washington Library, Manuscripts Division.

Townley, Thomas O. MSS. Vancouver City Archives.

II. Secondary Sources

A. BOOKS AND ARTICLES

Abbott, Carl. "Planning for the Home Front in Seattle and Portland 1940–45." In Roger W. Lotchin, ed., *The Martial Metropolis,* pp. 163–89.

Adachi, Ken. *The Enemy That Never Was: A History of the Japanese-Canadians.* Toronto: McClelland and Stewart, 1976.

Anderson, Karen. *Wartime Women: Sex Roles, Family Relations and the Status of Women during World War II.* Westport, Conn.: Greenwood Press, 1981.

Artibise, Alan F. J. "The Urban West: The Evolution of Prairie Towns and Cities to 1930." *Prairie Forum* 4 (1979): 237–62.

Bagley, Clarence B. *History of Seattle.* 3 vols. Chicago: S. J. Clarke, 1916.

Bancroft, Hubert Howe. *History of Washington, Idaho and Montana 1845–89.* San Francisco: A. L. Bancroft, 1890.

Banfield, Edward C. *Big City Politics: A Comparative Guide to the Political Systems of Atlanta, Boston, Detroit, El Paso, Los Angeles, Miami, Philadelphia, St. Louis, Seattle.* New York: Random House, 1965.

Barman, Jean. *Growing Up British in British Columbia: Boys in Private Schools.* Vancouver: University of British Columbia Press, 1984.

Barrett, Paul. *The Automobile and Urban Transit: The Formation of Public Policy in Chicago, 1900–30.* Philadelphia: Temple University Press, 1983.

Barth, Gunther. *Instant Cities: Urbanization and Rise of San Francisco and Denver.* New York: Oxford University Press, 1975.

Baxter, P. "Shipbuilding on Puget Sound." Seattle *Argus,* December 15, 1917, pp. 12–32.

Bender, Charles W. "A Report on Politics in Seattle." In Edward C. Banfield, *Big City Politics,* pp. 133–47.

Berton, Pierre. *The National Dream: The Great Railway 1871–81*. Toronto: McClelland and Stewart, 1970.

Blackford, Mansel G. "Civic Groups, Political Action and City Planning in Seattle 1892–1915." *Pacific Historical Review* 49 (Nov. 1980): 557–80.

———. "Reform Politics in Seattle During the Progressive Era 1902–16." *Pacific Northwest Quarterly* 59 (Oct. 1968): 177–86.

Blanchard, Leslie. *The Street Railway Era in Seattle: A Chronicle of Six Decades*. Forty Fort, Penn.: H. E. Cox, 1968.

Blum, John Morton. *V Was for Victory: Politics and American Culture During World War II*. New York: Harcourt Brace Jovanovich, 1976.

Bolton, Roger E. *Defense Purchases and Regional Growth*. Washington, D.C.: Brookings Institution, 1966.

Broadfoot, Barry. *Ten Lost Years 1929–39: Memories of Canadians Who Survived the Depression*. Toronto: Doubleday, 1973.

———. *Years of Sorrow, Years of Shame. The Story of the Japanese Canadians in World War II*. Toronto: Doubleday, 1977.

Brownell, Blaine. "A Symbol of Modernity: Attitudes Toward the Automobile in Southern Cities in the 1920's." *American Quarterly* (March 1972): 20–44.

Burkinshaw, Robert K. *False Creek: History, Images and Research Sources*. Vancouver: Vancouver City Archives, 1984.

Cail, Robert E. *Land, Man and the Law: The Disposal of Crown Lands in British Columbia 1871–1913*. Vancouver: University of British Columbia Press, 1974.

Cheape, Charles W. *Moving the Masses: Urban Public Transit in New York, Boston and Philadelphia 1880–1912*. Cambridge: Harvard University Press, 1980.

Clive, Alan. *State of War: Michigan in World War II*. Ann Arbor: University of Michigan Press, 1979.

Conant, Roger. *Mercer's Belles: The Journal of a Reporter*. Ed. Lenna A. Deutsch. Seattle: University of Washington Press, 1960.

Cuff, R. D., and Granatstein, J. L. *Canadian-American Relations in Wartime*. Toronto: Haakkert, 1975.

Daniels, Roger. *Concentration Camps, U.S.A.: Japanese Americans and World War II*. New York: Holt, Rinehart & Winston, 1971.

———. *The Decision to Relocate the Japanese-Americans*. Philadelphia: Lippincott, 1975.

Davis, Donald. "Mass Transit and Private Ownership: An Alternative Perspective in the Case of Toronto." *Urban History Review* 3–78 (Feb. 1979): 60–98.

Dewees, Donald L. "The Decline of American Street Railways." *Traffic Quarterly* 24 (October 1970): 563–81.

Dimock, A. H. "Preparing the Groundwork for a City: The Regrading of Seattle Washington." *Transactions of the American Society of Civil Engineers* 92 (1928): 717–34.

Doucet, Michael J. "Mass Transit and the Failure of Private Ownership: The Case of Toronto in the Early Twentieth Century." *Urban History Review* 3–77 (Feb. 1978): 3–33.

Droker, Howard A. "Seattle Race Relations During the Second World War." *Pacific Northwest Quarterly* 67 (Oct. 1976): 163–74.

Flint, James J. *The Car Culture*. Cambridge: MIT Press, 1975.

Fogelson, Robert M. *The Fragmented Metropolis: Los Angeles, 1850–1930*. Cambridge: Harvard University Press, 1967.

Foster, Mark S. *From Streetcar to Superhighway: American City Planners and Urban Transportation 1900–40*. Philadelphia: Temple University Press, 1981.

———. "The Model-T, the Hard Sell, and Los Angeles's Urban Growth: The Decentralization of Los Angeles during the 1920's." *Pacific Historical Review* 44 (Nov. 1975): 459–84.

———. "The Western Response to Urban Transportation: A Tale of Three Cities 1900–45." *Journal of the West* 18 (July 1979): 31–39.

Friedheim, Robert L. *The Seattle General Strike*. Seattle: University of Washington Press, 1964.

Friedheim, Robert L., and Friedheim, Robin. "The Seattle Labor Movement 1919–20." *Pacific Northwest Quarterly* 55 (Oct. 1964): 146–56.

Funigiello, Phillip J. *The Challenge to Urban Liberalism: Federal-City Relations During World War II*. Knoxville: University of Tennessee Press, 1978.

Geiser, Kenneth R., Jr. *Urban Transportation Decision Making: Political Processes of Urban Freeway Controversies*. Cambridge: MIT, 1971.

Gelfand, Mark. *A Nation of Cities: The Federal Government and Urban America, 1933–65*. New York: Oxford University Press, 1975.

Goldberg, Michael A. "Housing and Land Prices in Canada and the U.S." *Urban Land Economics Publications*. Faculty of Commerce and Business Administration, University of British Columbia. Reprint no. 46 (1977): 207–53.

Goldberg, Michael A., and Mercer, John. *The Myth of the North American City*. Vancouver: University of British Columbia Press, 1986.

Granatstein, J. L. *Canada's War: The Politics of the Mackenzie King Government 1939–45*. Toronto: Oxford University Press, 1975.

Grant, Frederick J. *History of Seattle*. New York: American Publishing and Engraving, 1891.

Grayson, L. M., and Bliss, Michael, eds. *The Wretched of Canada: Letters to R. B. Bennett 1930–35*. Toronto: University of Toronto Press, 1971.

Gutstein, Donald. *Vancouver Ltd*. Toronto: J. Lorimer, 1975.

Hanford, C. H. *Seattle and Environs 1852–1924*. Chicago: Pioneer Historical Publishing, 1924.

Hart-Nibbrig, Nand. "School Desegregation Politics: Seattle, Washington." *Washington Public Policy Notes* 7, no. 1 (Winter 1970).

Hays, Samuel P. "The Politics of Reform in Municipal Government During the Progressive Era." *Pacific Northwest Quarterly* 55 (Oct. 1964): 157–69.

Hill, Tim. *Citizens' Handbook on Transportation Planning in Seattle*. Seattle: Councilman T. Hill, Seattle City Council, 1972.

Hillman, Arthur. "The Unemployed Citizens' League of Seattle." University of Washington. *Publications in the Social Sciences* 5 (Feb. 1934): 181–270.

Holdsworth, D. W. "House and Home in Vancouver: Images of West Coast Urbanism, 1886–1929." In Gilbert A. Stelter, and Alan F. J. Artibise, eds., *The Canadian City*.

Hosokawa, Bill. *Nisei: The Quiet Americans*. New York: W. Morrow, 1969.

Howay, F. W. "Early Settlement on Burrard Inlet." *British Columbia Historical Quarterly* 1 (April 1937): 101–14.

Howay, F. W., Sage, W. N., and Angus, H. F. *British Columbia and the United States*. Toronto: Ryerson Press, 1942.

Howay, F. W., and Scholefield, E. O. S. *British Columbia from Earliest Times to the Present*. 4 vols. Vancouver: S. J. Clarke, 1913.

Innis, Harold A. *Settlement and the Mining Frontier*. Toronto: Macmillan, 1936.

Jamieson, Stuart M. *Times of Trouble: Labour Unrest and Industrial Conflict in Canada 1900–66*. Task Force on Labour Relations, study no. 22. Ottawa, 1968.

Karlin, Jules. "The Anti-Chinese Outbreaks in Seattle 1885–86." *Pacific Northwest Quarterly* 39 (April 1948): 103–30.

Kellet, John R. *Railways and Victorian Cities*. Toronto: University of Toronto Press, 1979.

Kirkendall, Richard S. *The United States, 1929–45: Years of Crisis and Change*. New York: McGraw-Hill, 1974.

Knight, Rolf. *Along the No. 20 Line: Reminiscences of the Vancouver Waterfront*. Vancouver: New Star Books, 1980.

Koistinen, Paul A. D. "The Military Industrial Complex in Historical Perspective: The Interwar Years." *Journal of American History* 56 (March 1970): 819–39.

Lamb, W. Kaye. "The Pioneer Days of the Trans-Pacific Service." *British Columbia Historical Quarterly* 1 (July 1937): 149–60.

LaViolette, Forrest E. *The Canadian Japanese and World War II: A Sociological and Psychological Account*. Toronto: University of Toronto Press, 1948.

Leuchtenburg, William E. "The Great Depression." In C. Vann Woodward, *The Comparative Approach to American History*. New York: Basic Books, 1968, pp. 296–314.

———. *Franklin D. Roosevelt and the New Deal*. New York: Harper and Row, 1963.

Liu, Ben-Chieh. *Quality of Life Indicators in U.S. Metropolitan Areas 1970*. Washington, D.C.: U.S. Environmental Protection Agency, 1975.

Liversedge, Ronald. *Recollections of the On to Ontario Trek*. Toronto: McClelland and Stewart, 1973.

Lotchin, Roger W. "The City and the Sword: San Francisco and the Rise of the Metropolitan-Military Complex, 1919–41." *Journal of American History* 65 (March 1979): 996–1020.

———, ed. *The Martial Metropolis: U.S. Cities in War and Peace*. New York: Praeger, 1984.

Lynd, Robert S., and Lynd, Helen M. *Middletown: A Study in American Culture*. New York: Harcourt Brace, 1929.

———. *Middletown in Transition*. New York: Harcourt Brace, 1937.

McCormack, A. R., and MacPherson, Ian, eds. *Cities in the West: Papers of the Western Canada Urban History Conference*. Ottawa: National Museum of Canada, 1975.

MacDonald, Norbert, "The Business Leaders of Seattle 1880–1910." *Pacific Northwest Quarterly* 50 (Jan. 1959): 1–13.

———. "The Canadian Pacific Railway and Vancouver's Development to 1900." *B.C. Studies* 35 (Autumn 1977): 3–35.

———. "Population Growth and Change in Seattle and Vancouver 1880–1960." *Pacific Historical Review* 39 (Aug. 1970): 297–321.

———. "Seattle, Vancouver and the Klondike." *Canadian Historical Review* 49 (Sept. 1968): 234–46.

McDonald, Robert A. J. "Holy Retreat or 'Practical Breathing Spot'?: Class Perceptions of Vancouver's Stanley Park, 1910–13." *Canadian Historical Review* 45 (June 1984): 127–53.

———. "City Building in the Canadian West: A Case Study of Economic Growth in Vancouver." *B.C. Studies* 43 (Autumn 1979): 3–28.

McDougall, R. J. "Vancouver Real Estate." *B.C. Magazine* (June 1911): 597–607.

McShane, Clay. *Technology and Reform: Street Railways and the Growth of Milwaukee 1887–1900*. Madison: University of Wisconsin Press, 1974.

Malpin, James. "Our Musty, Crusty City Council." *Seattle Magazine* (May 1965).

Melder, F. E. "History of the Discovery and Physical Development of the Coal Industry in the State of Washington." *Pacific Northwest Quarterly* 29 (April 1938): 151–65.

Miller, Delbert B. *International Community Power Structure: Comparative Studies of Four World Cities*. Bloomington: Indiana University Press, 1970.

Miller, Fern. "Vancouver Civic Political Parties: Developing a Model of Party-System Change and Stabilization." *B.C. Studies* 25 (Spring 1975): 3–27.

Miller, William. "American Historians and the Business Elite." *Journal of Economic History* 9 (May 1949): 184–208.

Mills, C. Wright. "The American Business Elite: A Collective Portrait." *Journal of Economic History*, 5 (Dec. 1945): 20–44.

Morgan, Murray. *Century 21: The Story of Seattle's World Fair*. Seattle: Acme Press, 1963.

———. *Skid Road: An Informal Portrait of Seattle*. New York: Viking Press, 1951.

Morley, Alan. *Vancouver: From Milltown to Metropolis*. Vancouver: Mitchell Press, 1961.

Morton, James W. *The Enterprising Mr. Moody, the Bumptious Captain Stamp*. North Vancouver: J. J. Douglas, 1977.

Mullins, William H. "Self-Help in Seattle, 1931–32: Herbert Hoover's Concept of Cooperative Individualism and the Unemployed Citizens' League." *Pacific Northwest Quarterly* 72 (Jan. 1981): 11–19.

Munson, K., and Swanborough, G. *Boeing: An Aircraft Album*. New York: Arco, 1971.

Murray, R. K. *Red Scare: A Study in National Hysteria 1919–20*. Minneapolis: University of Minnesota Press, 1955.

Nash, Gerald. *The American West Transformed: The Impact of the Second World War*. Bloomington: University of Indiana Press, 1985.

Nesbit, Robert. *"He Built Seattle": A Biography of Judge Thomas Burke*. Seattle: University of Washington Press, 1961.

Nicol, Eric. *Vancouver*. Toronto: Doubleday, 1970.

O'Brien, Robert W. "Evacuation of Japanese from the Pacific Coast: Canadian and American Contrasts." *Washington State College Research Studies* 14 (1946): 113–20.

Ormsby, M. A. *British Columbia: A History*. Toronto: Macmillan, 1958.

Pendakur, V. Setty. *Cities, Citizens and Freeways*. Vancouver: V. S. Pendakur, 1972.

Pendergrass, Lee. "The Formation of a Municipal Reform Movement: The Municipal League of Seattle." *Pacific Northwest Quarterly* 66 (Jan. 1975): 13–25.

Phelps, Myra L. *Public Works in Seattle: A Narrative History, the Seattle Engineering Department 1875–1975*. Seattle: Kingsport Press, 1978.

Phillips, Paul A. *No Power Greater: A Century of Labour in British Columbia*. Vancouver: B.C. Federation of Labour, 1967.

Plunkett, Thomas J. *Urban Canada and its Government: A Study of Municipal Organization*. Toronto: Macmillan, 1968.

Polenberg, Richard. *War and Society: The United States, 1941–45*. Philadelphia: Lippincott, 1972.

Porter, John. *The Vertical Mosaic: An Analysis of Social Class and Power in Canada*. Toronto: University of Toronto Press, 1965.

Purdy, Harry L. "The Cost of Municipal Operations of the Seattle Street Railway." University of Washington. *Publications in the Social Sciences* 8 (Aug. 1929): 1–28.

Rae, John B. *The Road and the Car in American Life*. Cambridge: MIT Press, 1971.

Rankin, Harry. *A Socialist Perspective for Vancouver.* Toronto: Progress Books, 1974.

Reps, John W. *Cities of the American West: A History of Frontier Urban Planning.* Princeton, N.J.: Princeton University Press, 1979.

Roy, Patricia E. *Vancouver: An Illustrated History.* Toronto: James Lorimer, 1980.

———. "The Soldiers Canada Didn't Want: The Chinese and Japanese Citizens." *Canadian Historical Review* 59 (Sept. 1978): 44–59.

———. "Vancouver: 'The Mecca of the Unemployed' 1907–29." In Alan F. J. Artibise, ed., *Town and City: Aspects of Western Canadian Urban Development.* Regina: Canadian Plains Research Center, University of Regina, 1981, pp. 393–413.

Sale, Roger. *Seattle: Past to Present.* Seattle: University of Washington Press, 1976.

Schwantes, Carlos A. *Radical Heritage: Labor Socialism and Reform in Washington and British Columbia 1885–1917.* Seattle: University of Washington Press, 1970.

Scott, George W. "The New Order of Cincinnatus: Municipal Politics in Seattle During the 1930's." *Pacific Northwest Quarterly* 64 (Oct. 1973): 137–46.

Sladen, Douglas. "Vancouver, a Great Seaport of the Twentieth Century." *Frank Leslie's Popular Monthly* 24 (May 1890): 513–22.

Smith, Duane A. *Rocky Mountain Mining Camps: The Urban Frontier.* Bloomington: Indiana University Press, 1967.

Snowden, C. A. *History of Washington: The Rise and Progress of an American State.* New York: Century History Company, 1909.

Sone, Monica. *Nisei Daughter.* Boston: Little Brown, 1953.

Stelter, Gilbert A. "The Urban Frontier in Canadian History." *Canadian Issues* 1 (Spring 1975): 99–114.

Stelter, Gilbert A., and Artibise, Alan F. J., eds. *The Canadian City: Essays in Urban History.* Toronto: McClelland and Stewart, 1977.

———. *Shaping the Urban Landscape: Aspects of the City-Building Process.* Ottawa: Carleton University Press, 1982.

Strong, Anna Louise. *Seattle General Strike.* Seattle: Seattle Union Record, 1919.

Sunahara, Ann Gomer. *The Politics of Racism: The Uprooting of Japanese Canadians During the Second World War.* Toronto: James Lorimer, 1981.

Tennant, Paul. "Vancouver Civic Policies, 1929–80." *B.C. Studies* 46 (Summer 1980): 3–27.

Terkel, Studs. *Hard Times: An Oral History of the Great Depression.* New York: Pantheon Books, 1970.

Thernstrom, Stephan. *The Other Bostonians: Poverty and Progress in the American Metropolis 1880–1970.* Cambridge: Harvard University Press, 1973.

Tiebout, Charles M. "The Regional Impact of Defense Expenditures: Its Measurement and Problems of Adjustment." In Roger E. Bolton, ed., *Defense and Disarmament: The Economics of Transition.* Englewood Cliffs, N.J.: Prentice Hall, 1966.

Van Nus, Walter. "The Fate of City Beautiful Thought in Canada 1893–1930." In Gilbert A. Stelter, and Alan F. J. Artibise, eds., *The Canadian City: Essays in Urban History,* pp. 162–85.

Voisey, Paul. "The Urbanization of the Canadian Prairies 1871–1916." *Histoire Sociale-Social History* 8 (May 1975): 77–101.

Wade, Richard C. *The Urban Frontier: The Rise of Western Cities 1790–1830.* Cambridge: Harvard University Press, 1959.

Ward, W. Peter. *White Canada Forever: Popular Attitudes and Public Policy Toward Orientals in British Columbia.* Montreal: McGill-Queens University Press, 1978.

Warner, Sam Bass. *Urban Wilderness: A History of the American City.* New York: Harper and Row, 1972.

Watt, Roberta Frye. *Four Wagons West: The Story of Seattle.* Portland, Ore.: Binsford Mort, 1931.

Webster, Janice Reiff. "Domestication and Americanization: Scandinavian Women in Seattle, 1888 to 1900." *Journal of Urban History* 4 (May 1978): 275–90.

Wickberg, Edgar, et al. *From China to Canada: A History of the Chinese Communities in Canada.* Toronto: McClelland and Stewart, 1982.

Wilson, William H. "How Seattle Lost the Bogue Plan: Politics versus Design." *Pacific Northwest Quarterly* 75 (Oct. 1984): 171–80.

Wolf, Ruth. "Block That Freeway." *Seattle Magazine,* February 1969.

B. THESES AND DISSERTATIONS

Bottomley, John. "Experience, Ideology and the Landscape: The Business Community, Urban Reform, and the Establishment of Town Planning in Vancouver 1900–40." Ph.D. Dissertation, University of British Columbia, 1977.

Brooks, G. W. S. "Edgard Crowe Baker: An Entrepreneur in Early British Columbia." M.A. Thesis, University of British Columbia, 1976.

Dahlie, Jorgen. "A Social History of Scandinavian Immigration, Washington State 1895–1910." Ph.D. Dissertation, Washington State University, 1967.

Darling, David M. "Patterns of Population Mobility in Vancouver, 1891–1931." M.A. Thesis, Simon Fraser University, 1978.

Droker, Howard. "The Seattle Civic Unity Committee and the Civil Rights Movement 1944–64." Ph.D. Dissertation, University of Washington, 1974.

Elligott, Frederick J. "The Planning Decision Making Process in Vancouver's False Creek: A Case Study 1968–1974." M.A. Thesis, University of British Columbia, 1977.

Graves, Robert E. "Business Government: Party Politics and the B.C. Business Community 1928–33." M.A. Thesis, University of British Columbia, 1976.

Holdsworth, Deryck W. "Vernacular Form in the Urban Context." M.A. Thesis, University of British Columbia, 1971.

Lane, M. "Unemployment During the Depression: The Problem of the Single Unemployed Transient in British Columbia 1930–38." B.A. Thesis, University of British Columbia, 1966.

Lechner, Anna Bell. "Seattle Municipal Street Railway." M.A. Thesis, University of Washington, 1936.

McDonald, Robert A. J. "Business Leadership in Vancouver 1890–1914." Ph.D. Dissertation, University of British Columbia, 1977.

McKee, William C. "The History of the Vancouver Park System, 1886–1929." M.A. Thesis, University of Victoria, 1976.

McKibben, Gordon C. "Non Partisan Politics: A Case Study of Seattle 1928–53." M.A. Thesis, University of Washington, 1954.

Mullins, William H. "San Francisco and Seattle During the Hoover Years of the Depression 1929–33." Ph.D. Dissertation, University of Washington, 1975.

Pendergrass, Lee. "Urban Reform and Voluntary Association: A Case Study of the Seattle Municipal League 1910–29." Ph.D. Dissertation, University of Washington, 1972.

Pieroth, Doris H. "Desegregating the Public Schools in Seattle, Washington 1954–68." Ph.D. Dissertation, University of Washington, 1979.

Rodman, Margaret C. "The Trend of Alaskan Commerce through the Port of Seattle." M.A. Thesis, University of Washington, 1955.

Roy, Patricia E. "The British Columbia Electric Railway Company 1897–1928: A British Company in British Columbia." Ph.D. Dissertation, University of British Columbia, 1970.

———. "Railways, Politicians, and the Development of the City of Vancouver as a Metropolitan Centre, 1886–1929." M.A. Thesis, University of Toronto, 1963.

Saito, Doyle Schigeo. "Seattle's Metro Transit: A Case Study of Operating Efficiency 1973–80." M.Sc. Thesis, University of Washington, 1981.

Schuthe, G. M. "Canadian Shipping in the British Columbia Coastal Trade." M.A. Thesis, University of British Columbia, 1950.

Shannon, Daniel William. "A Cross National Comparison of Public Participation in Urban Shoreline Policy Development." Ph.D. Dissertation, University of Washington, 1979.

Smith, Andrea B. "The Origins of the NPA: A Study in Vancouver Politics, 1930–40." M.A. Thesis, University of British Columbia, 1981.

Wade, Catherine Jill. "Wartime Housing Limited, 1941–47: Canadian Housing Policy at the Crossroads." M.A. Thesis, University of British Columbia, 1984.

Waxman, Edward R. "Politics and Transportation Planning in the Seattle Metropolitan Area." Master of Urban Planning Thesis, University of Washington, 1968.

Wynne, Robert. "Reaction to the Chinese in the Pacific Northwest and British Columbia." Ph.D. Dissertation, University of Washington, 1964.

Index